ISBN 0-87666-590-3

Tartini
HIS LIFE
and
TIMES

Prof. Dr. Lev Ginsburg

Edited by Dr. Herbert R. Axelrod.
Translated from the Russian by I. Levin.

PAGANINIANA PUBLICATIONS, INC.
211 West Sylvania Avenue, Neptune City, New Jersey 07753

Front endpaper: An Engraving of the interior of S. Antonio, Padua

Table of Contents

David Oistrakh

Preface

Giuseppe Tartini is one of the leading figures of the Italian school of violin-playing in the 18th century, a school whose art is as meaningful today as it ever has been. Tartini's music is expressive, sincere, warm and melodious, and it is in these qualities that lies its appeal. The music of that period is declamatory and recitative in character, so it seems that words alone are lacking to give full expression to the thoughts and feelings embodied in it.

One can find in Tartini's works the main types of violin technique, something fairly complex for the violinist to this day. His truly exceptional familiarity with the instrument and his exceptionally imaginative use of the technical possibilities of the violin as a means of expression are remarkable. His inquiring mind led this fine composer and violinist to assert principles and modes of execution that were to become classical. Sufficient evidence for this conclusion can be found in his *The Art of Bowing (L'Arte del Arco)*, where in fifty variations on a Gavotte by Corelli he uses the most varied technical devices, each in accord with a specific aim.

Such marvelous compositions of Tartini's as his Sonatas in E minor and G minor (*The Devil's Trill*) or his Concerto in D minor have been with me since my youth, throughout my life as a musician; these and other works by Tartini are now played by my pupils, but his music never loses its freshness for me, its color and its emotional impact.

Tartini's extraordinary originality of thought, the richness of the melodic, harmonic and rhythmic idiom in his Sonata in E minor; the noble passion, the deep lyricism and temperament of *The Devil's Trill*; and the softly expressive quality, the purity and directness of his Concerto in D minor always move and appeal to me. I consider his *Devil's Trill* sonata to be of such importance that I not infrequently conclude my solo concert (recital) programs by performing it.

Many other works by this Italian composer retain their interest for the modern violinist (from the point of view of their execution); in addition to the concertos and solo sonatas there are also his marvelous sonatas for two violins and bass and other works. I hail the appearance of this book wholeheartedly, for it draws attention to the life and work of an outstanding musician of the past whose best works are capable of moving and inspiring performers and listeners even now.

1968

D. OISTRAKH

Giuseppe Tartini

Introduction

In the history of 18th century music for the violin, Giuseppe Tartini comes directly after Arcangelo Corelli, who won his way to fame by his magnificent attainments in the spheres of the violin sonata and the concerto grosso, and Antonio Vivaldi, who made an immense contribution to the development of the violin concerto. Tartini completes this glorious trio, a veritable constellation in the Italian school of violin-playing. The importance of his work extends far beyond the borders of his country and the era in which he lived.

This eminent musician, performer and composer, who followed the school of Corelli and developed it further, raised the art of violin-playing to new heights. He was also a splendid teacher and for half a century headed the Paduan school of violin-playing. With his great learning and command of method, Giuseppe Tartini made history in the field of music by his superb talent as a performer, the artistry of his compositions and his advanced views on teaching and methodology. The latter still largely retain their importance for us today.

Only a small part of Tartini's works has been published, and he did not publish a consistent exposition of the principles of his school of violin-playing. However, if we recall his famous *Devil's Trill* and *The Art of Bowing (50 Variations on a Gavotte by Corelli)* or his well known *Letter to a Pupil,*[1] in which he sets forth laconically the main methodological principles of the system and gives advice on teaching, in conjunction with his *Treatise on Ornaments,* which reflects his progressive views on the esthetic aspects of musical performance, this body of work is sufficient to give us a clear conception of Tartini's importance as a composer, violinist and teacher.

The combination of such different aspects of Tartini's manifold activities was not so very unusual in an epoch when a composer was himself the chief performer of his works and would often teach music, too. What is amazing is the clarity and originality with which the gifted musician displayed his abilities in each of these fields—and to these fields we must add the field of musical science as well.

Tartini stands as the last great representative of the classical Italian school of violin-playing and at the same time as a herald of the early romantic trends in composition and performance.

There can hardly be a violinist in the world who has ignored Tartini's sonatas. It is noteworthy that the *Devil's Trill* Sonata has appeared in over twenty editions, each of which, supplied with the cadenza of the performer, reflects one stage or another in the development of the art of violin-playing. A large number of Tartini's splendid sonatas and concertos, equally interesting artistically and technically, still await performers.

Although *50 Variations on a Gavotte by Corelli* has become a bibliographical rarity, this work of Tartini's would be extremely useful to the teacher. Combining as it does both musical and technical merits, it is of exceptional interest not only in the bowing technique but also in the technique of the violinist's use of his left hand as well.

Lastly, though the tracts of this Italian musician, artist and thinker have lost neither their esthetic nor their methodological value, they are known to few, as is his *Letter to a Pupil*, the essay on method already referred to. The main principles of that essay have been used and developed further in the practice and theory of violin-playing.

Giuseppe Tartini had considerable influence on his contemporaries and on subsequent generations of musicians. The influence of his music and of his principles in performing and teaching was felt in many countries. It can be traced in the compositions of a number of his contemporaries. Tartini's influence had even been discovered by an older contemporary of his, Antonio Vivaldi. It is likewise to be found in the music of Niccolo Laurenti and Luigi Boccherini. Historians have even found traces of Tartini's violin style in the works of the young Mozart. Citations from Tartini, "one of the most splendid violinists of our times," appear frequently in the pages of Leopold Mozart's *School for the Violin* (1756). Johann Christian Bach composed a concerto for the clavecine in the Tartini manner *(alla maniera di Tartini)*, and Charles Henri Blainville, a French musician of the 18th century, rearranged six of Tartini's sonatas as concerti grossi, just as Francesco Geminiani, Corelli's pupil, had done with his master's sonatas.

At the turn of the century variations for violin and orchestra on a theme of Tartini's *(Introduccion, Andante y Variaciones sobre un tema de Tartini)* were written by Joan Manén, and even in the middle of the 20th century Luigi Dallapiccola, an Italian composer, wrote two suites (divertissements) for violin and orchestra, calling them *Tartiniani* (1951, 1955).

Tartini's rich, expressive music, with its elements of democracy and early realism, may well arouse the interest and enthusiasm of both performers and audiences today.

This book, written in commemoration of the 275th anniversary of Tartini's birth, is for the purpose of drawing the attention of musical performers and teachers of music to the heritage he left and to his progressive views on esthetics and teaching, which are of interest to us today. The author has made use of old, partly forgotten or previously unknown material, documents and manuscripts from archives and also new sources, which have helped him in his attempt to re-create the living image of Tartini the musician.

THE AUTHOR

Chapter 1

Italian Violin-Playing in the 17th and 18th Centuries

 In Italy it was not only the human voice that began to *sing*. The principle that singing is breathing took a firm hold on all the music. It is well known how the *violin began to sing*. Soon there came into being style, and forms, and a special kind of music-making, in which the chief figure was the soloist.

Boris Asafyev

Giuseppe Tartini enters the history of violin-playing at a time when this type of music had reached a high point of development in several countries besides Italy. One must perforce recall the performance and compositions of such 17th century violinists as Heinrich Ignaz Franz von Biber (1644-1704) in Czechoslovakia or Johann Jacob Walther (1650-17??) and Johann Paul Westhof (1656-1705) in Germany during the first half of the 18th century; also the Czech violinists Frantisek Benda (1709-1786) and Jan Vaclav Antonin Stamic (1717-1757) and the French violinists Jean-Baptiste Senaillé (1687-1730) and Jean-Marie Leclair (1697-1764) and many others—all contemporaries of Giuseppe Tartini—rose to fame.

The development of violin-playing in Europe in the 17th and 18th centuries one way or another reflected the beneficial impact of the Italian violin school, which had early reached its prime.

Owing to historical conditions, feudalism in Italy was ousted by bourgeois relationships earlier than in many other countries. These relationships were more progressive at that time and helped to create a new, democratic culture in a country that Friedrich Engels called the first capitalist nation.

It was, as we know, on Italian soil that the Renaissance blossomed most profusely. After creations of genius in the spheres of painting, sculpture, architecture and literature came attainments in music. From the 16th to 18th centuries worldwide recognition was accorded to Italian opera and musical theory and to the Italian schools for bow instruments and clavier.

The progress of Italian bow instruments, in which an echo of the ideas of the Renaissance was felt, was strikingly manifest in the early

Johann Christian Bach

Jean Marie Le Clair

maturing of the violin and cello schools, in the appearance of the sonata and concerto forms and in the exceptional achievements of the violin-makers who created unexcelled models of bow instruments (Amati, Guarneri, Stradivari and others).

With the beginning of the economic depression of the 18th century, Italy exported not only her opera singers but also her instrumentalists, mainly violinists and cellists. They appeared in all the countries of Europe. There was hardly a court or a chapel without its splendid Italian musicians, who were highly valued everywhere.[1]

The fame of the Italian violinists spread so far that people began to call Italy the birthplace of the violin. Without wishing in the least to belittle either the importance of the country in the history of the violin or the achievements of Italian violinists and violin-makers at the dawn of the epoch of the violin, one must still refrain from a too literal understanding of this manner of speaking. Other countries besides Italy, among them Slavic countries,[2] played an important role in the appearance of the violin and the bow instruments related to it.

It would scarcely be right to attribute the credit for creating the violin to any one country or to make an attempt to trace the "inventor" of the violin.[3] Many had a hand in its creation and development: folk musicians and professionals, simple craftsmen and outstanding specialists in the making of bow instruments, talented inventors and scholars from many countries. The violin was brought into being by the musical life of generations, and its constant improvement was the result of the growing needs of various peoples and lands.

There can, however, be no question as to the outstanding importance of Italian music and Italian musicians and their leading role in the early development of the violin (and the cello) in the 17th and 18th centuries.

Giuseppe Tartini owed the immense achievements that determined his prominent role in the history of violin-playing chiefly to his own gifts and his dedicated work; however, the soil had been prepared by the whole preceding development of Italian violin-playing.

To get a better understanding of Tartini's historical importance, it is necessary to acquaint oneself, even if only briefly, with the evolution of violin-playing in Italy over the course of the 17th and 18th centuries, *i.e.*, the period when the names of Corelli, Vivaldi and Tartini shine like brilliant stars against the colorful background of the Italian culture of bow instruments.

The source of the art of violin-playing in Italy, as in many other countries, lies in the musical culture of its people, the development of which led, in the 15th and 16th centuries, to the appearance of the violin itself and of the entire violin family. Its dynamically color-

16

ful and warm yet carrying sound, the violin's ability to "sing" expressively on each string and the potentially unlimited scope it gives the virtuoso are all qualities that accord with the needs of folk music. It is these qualities that determined the democratic sphere in which the violin was first used in its early days as it was played mainly by folk musicians (fiddlers).

For almost two centuries the violin and kindred instruments had to vie with the viol group of instruments (viol da gamba), which were in the main bound up with the music of feudal lords and the aristocracy and were adapted perfectly to its needs. The expressive qualities of the viols (or gambas) and the matt, subdued, muted sound of the six strings tuned in fourths and thirds corresponded extremely well to the esthetic requirements of the music played in the castles of the feudal lords. The gamba combined well with the lute and frequently even took over its functions in the accompaniment of song or other instruments; this was facilitated not only by the fourth-third tuning of the viol, but also by the frets on the fingerboard and the slightly rounded shape of the bridge, which simplified the playing of chords.

Meanwhile, the viol did not in the least satisfy the needs of the simple folk, who wanted music for their boisterous folk festivals, at fairs and in inns. Any attempt to increase the pressure of the bow on the string inevitably led to having neighboring strings being brought into play, which precluded the possibility of producing a clear "singing" on a single string. The music the simple folk wanted at home had to be warm and heartfelt. Here again the viol was unacceptable, because the frets on it hindered vibration and the melting of one note into another, which are the very qualities that make the singing of a violin or a cello akin to the singing of the human voice.

If to all this we add the technical advantages of the violin and the other members of its family and consider also the outstanding motive qualities of these instruments, we will not have to go far to find an explanation for the victory they ultimately won over the viol family.

This victory, which gained a firm foothold only in the latter half of the 18th century, resulted from the democratization of musical culture, which had ousted the feudalistic forms of music-playing and given the music itself a new content. It was likewise a result of the replacement of the polyphonic by the homophonic style, (homophonic-harmonic), which required clear, expressive and singing that was warm, rich and full of feeling.

It was by no means at once that the viol ceded its position to the violin. There was a fierce struggle between the adherents of the two instrumental groups. The struggle took the form of a heated literary debate, reflecting a struggle between different esthetic outlooks; the supporters of the moribund culture of the aristocracy tried to defend their beloved "noble" viol against the relentless advance of the "sim-

Player on the viola da gamba

Giuseppe Tartini

ple folks' " violin, which was bound up with the new democratic trends.[4]

This struggle was clearly distinguishable in pre-revolutionary France, where a polemical treatise called *Defence of the Bass Viol against the Enterprises of the Violin and the Pretensions of the Violoncello* was written by Hubert le Blanc and published in 1740.

But life itself and the requirements of musical development were on the side of the violin and its greater wealth of expressive potentials. In the 18th century it won a final victory in France as well, as it had in England and in Germany, other places in which the viol had reached a high level of development.

The ousting of the viol by the violin was completed first in Italy, where the violin had been one of the predominant and favorite musical instruments since the 17th century.[5]

The first instances of Italian professional music for the violin appeared in the violin parts of ensemble compositions of the 16th century. At that period there were as yet only faint traces of the coming differentiation between bow and wind instruments. Among the bow instruments, the violin and viol groups were only just beginning to oppose each other; it was only slowly and gradually that the specific technical and expressive possibilities of the violin came to be recognized. We will not dwell further upon this early period; we will pass over instead to the beginning of the 17th century, *i.e.,* to the time of the appearance of those violin compositions that have in part survived to our time.[6]

Early instances of Italian music for the violin are the *Sonata con tre violini* by Giovanni Gabrieli, which was written at the turn of the 16th and 17th centuries and published in 1615, sonatas for the violin that were the first of the *Concerti Ecclesiastici* by Andrea and Giovanni Cima (1610) and several others.

At this period, too, the art of violin-playing took shape largely within the framework of orchestral and ensemble music. One of the earliest instances of the use of the violin in an ensemble with mixed instruments is the violin part from the *French Canzona* (1602) by Lodorico Viadana (Grossi)[7], containing elements of passage technique, though this is limited to the first position.

The participation of the violin in opera orchestras was of great importance to the cultivation of its cantilena and technical qualities; its development here was stimulated by both cantabile vocal parts and by imitative functions that were not infrequently assigned to the violins and required methods of execution and technique that were new for those times.

The violin parts in the compositions of Claudio Monteverdi (1567-1643), one of the founders of Italian opera, whose part in the development of the orchestra was considerable, can be cited as an example of this. Monteverdi possessed a conscious urge to create contrasts in tone-color related to the individualization of the

Claudio Montverdi

separate groups of instruments, particularly the violins. In a musical composition he wrote for the stage, called *The Combat of Tancred and Clorinda* (1624), he was one of the first to use violin techniques such as the pizzicato and the tremolo with full awareness of their expressive significance. The short, dry sounds of the pizzicato are used by him to depict the sound of weapons in the scene of the combat. It was only in Monteverdi's hands that the prototype of the tremolo, which had been used prior to this, ceased to bear a casual nature and signified, to use his own words, "an imitation of agitated speech."[8]

Earlier still, in *Orpheus* (1607), an opera by the same composer, the violin parts contain episodes that are of technical interest, since they require a fair amount of digital dexterity and well-developed coordination of the movements of the fingers and the bow.[9] It is of interest to note that, whereas in Giovanni Gabrieli's canzona for six voices (1615) the upper limit of the violin's compass is d^3, which requires the use of the third position (one of the early examples of change of position), in Monteverdi's *Magnificat* (1610) we find f^3, indicating the fifth position on the violin fingerboard.

The manner in which he used the violin confirms the fact that Monteverdi was an outstanding violinist. In the foreword to his third book of madrigals (1592) he speaks of himself as a violinist of the chapel of Vincenzo Gonzaga, Duke of Mantua; he worked there from 1590 to 1613, after which he led the chapel of St. Mark's in Venice. His fruitful activities for the best part of a quarter of a century as violinist and maestro di cappella in Mantua enable us to call him the head of the Mantuan violin school.

The talented violinist and composer Salomone Rossi might be called an adherent of this school. He worked in the chapel in Mantua from 1587 to 1628 and was the author of some early compositions for the violin and of ensemble sonatas for two and four concerted violins. The Mantuan school of the 17th century was also represented by wonderful violinists such as Dario Castello, composer of the *Sonate Concertate* (1621), something very daring for his time, and the no less well-known musician Carlo Farina, who wrote many instrumental works, including the *Capriccio Stravagante* (1627). In this composition, undoubtedly under the influence of the manner in which the violin was played by the simple folk, he used sound imitation methods, requiring great technical skill from the violinist.[10] Monteverdi and his pupils or followers made their own independent contribution to the development of the violin.

Monteverdi's greatest importance, however, lay in his considerable development of the expressive sphere of the violin, and this was connected with his desire to democratize and dramatize music. In his foreword to *The Combat of Tancred and Clorinda* he demands that musical instruments should be played to imitate the verbal expression of feelings. This should be done not only by an

21

agitated tremolo on the violin but also by dynamic inflections such as, for instance, the morendo effect in the final bar of Clorinda's scene "questa ultima nota va in arcata morenda."

The new technical expressive means introduced by Monteverdi into the violin parts reflected his principles in esthetics and execution and influenced the subsequent development of violin-playing.

The principal types of violin music in the 17th century were the suite, the trio sonata (more often than not a composition for two violins and bass) and the sonata for a solo violin and bass (connected with the trio sonata in origin).[11] Towards the end of the century the concerto grosso also took definite shape and became one of the paths along which the solo violin concerto developed. It is to the Italian violinists that we are largely indebted for the formation of all these types of composition.

One of the more prominent violinists of the first half and middle of the century was Biagio Marini (1597-1665). According to Andreas Moser, while still in Mantua, Marini was a pupil of Monteverdi's for several years, which gives us the right to consider him as belonging to the Mantuan school. The gifted musician received the beginnings of his musical education as a violinist in his native town, Brescia, apparently under the well-known violinist and composer Giovanni Battista Fontana (who died in 1631), who later (in Venice) was connected with Monteverdi as well.

However that may be, when Marini arrived in Venice in 1615, he became a violinist in St. Mark's chapel, which was led by Monteverdi, and for three years he continued as Monteverdi's pupil.[12] Then, after several years at Brescia and Parma, he spent the period between 1623 and 1645 in Germany, where, like Farina, he absorbed some of the features of the "Spielmanns" (fiddlers). One of these features was the polyphonic use of the violin, and he himself exerted a beneficial influence on the development of the violin in Germany. On his return to his native land, Marini worked in Milan and Ferrara; he spent the remainder of his life in Venice, where he published a number of his compositions.

Marini was famed as an outstanding and original violinist who put a high degree of expression into his playing and displayed great technical skill. One can judge this to a certain extent not only from what his contemporaries said but also from his own numerous compositions, in which his inventive powers on the technical side are manifest.

His first opus, which appeared in 1617 under the name of *Affetti musicali*, contains one of the first violin sonatas. True, it is designed for "the violin or the cornett," but in the instrumental compositions following this one Marini no longer gave any alternative, and the technical expressive capabilities that are specific to the violin are brought out in an increasingly clearly defined manner.

The *Aria di Romanesca* (1620) from Marini's third opus may serve as an example of an early composition for the violin. This piece, written for the violin and bass, is in the form of variations. In style it is close to the suite; after the principal part comes an expressive contrast in the form of a galliard and a courante, in both of which the bass of part one is retained. In addition to the cantilena elements in this piece, he uses such technical devices as a dotted bowing, skips across a string, passages of guavers and the so-called Lombard rhythm; the upper limit of the compass is c³.

In Marini's works, too, there are early examples of the violin tremolo and the designation of the legato bowing.

The search for the specific style of the violin (at the same time as the search for musical form) is carried on in Marini's subsequent work. In his *Capriccio* with only two violins playing double notes he creates the impression of a violin quartet. In his *Capriccio for Three Strings* he requires that the two lower strings should be brought closer together to achieve the effect of "the style of playing on a lyre."[13] In one of his sonatas of 1626 (the *Sonata per Violino d'Inventione*[14]) Marini gives the solo instrument a pause of eight bars to retune the E-string into a C-string (scordatura) to make it possible to use the technique of doublestops in the cantilena and passages. Marini's melodic compass (just as Corelli's after him) seems nowhere to go beyond the third position, whereas his compatriot and younger contemporary Marco Uccellini goes as far as the sixth position in one of his sonatas (1649).

All these and similar pieces by Marini characterize him at a period when he was moved by the desire to discover new possibilities in the technique of playing. Later he was drawn more and more to the idea of improving the form of his compositions. The melodic language of his music grew more expressive, and his skill in counterpoint increased.

His most mature compositions are his *Sonate da chiesa e da camera* (1655), in which the specific features of the style of each of these types are clearly outlined: the "sacred" sonatas are usually more severely polyphonic, while the "secular" sonatas (mainly suites) make wide use of the style of dance music.

Of the predecessors of the renowned Corelli that came after Marini, one might name a number of fine violinist-composers who were united in the Bologna school of violin-playing in the 17th century. At that time the Italian city of Bologna was a great center of the arts. Carlo Goldoni called it "the Italian Athens." So-called academies played a prominent role in the city's musical life. These societies brought together outstanding composers, instrumentalists and singers and arranged meetings with music and discussion. Especially worthy of note was the Academia di Filarmonici, founded in 1666; for admission to it one had to take a very stiff test. In his early youth Arcangelo Corelli, who was later to head the violin school of Rome, was a member of this academy.

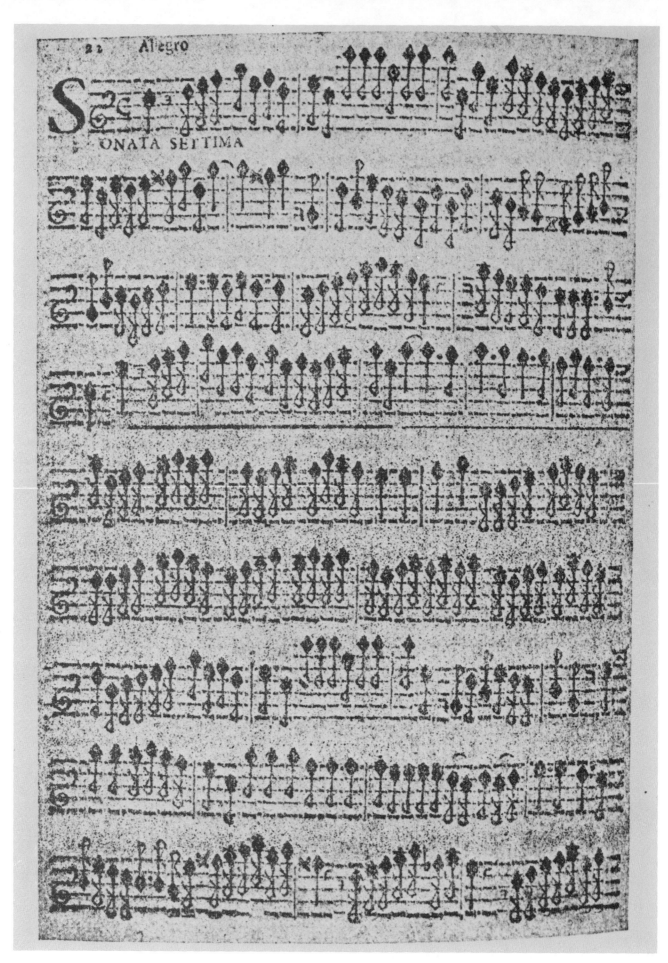

Manuscript page from Corelli's seventh sonata

Arcangelo Corelli

San Petronio had an excellent chapel which was of no less importance in the history of Italian music than those of St. Mark's in Venice and St. Peter's in Rome.

Well-known violinists such as Giovanni Battista Vitali, Giacomo Benvenuti, Leonardo Brugnoli and Giuseppe Torelli played in the Bologna chapel, which was led in the latter half of the 17th century by the violinist Maurizio Cazzati and later by Giovanni Paolo Colonna and Giacomo Antonio Perti. Among the great musicians of the Bologna violin school, which, according to Marc Pincherle,[15] was founded by Ercole Gaibara "detto il violino" (*i.e.*, "dubbed the violin"), we find violinists and composers such as Pietro degli Antonii, Giovanni Battista Bassani, Giuseppe Aldrovandini, Bartolomeo Bernardi and Arcangelo Corelli.[16]

All these and many other Bolognese musicians of the latter half of the 17th century were no longer drawn by the desire to pursue the technical possibilities discovered in the violin; their path lay the formation of a new expressive style.

The development of the art of violin-playing in Italy in the first half of the century was largely characterized by a search for new technical expressive means and at times by a certain abuse of such technical sonic devices as the col legno, pizzicato, ponticello and scordatura. The second half of the century, however, witnessed an increasing desire to create a deeper emotional and expressive content, to typify forms, to develop a mutual enrichment between chamber and sacred music in the sonata and concerto forms and to make a judicious selection of the instrumental means of expression. All this was especially true of both the best musicians in the Bologna school and of Arcangelo Corelli, who was connected with this school and had attained classical perfection in his art.

There were features that the most eminent of the violinist composers of the Bologna school had in common: increased emotionality, lyricism, simplicity and clarity in expression and form. The school has to its credit the creation of a large number of instrumental pieces (mainly for the violin) — symphonies (sinfonie), concertos, sonatas — that have partially retained their artistic significance and have paved the way for the appearance of the renowned Corelli.

It is in the sonatas of the Bolognese musicians that the first mutual interpenetration of the elements of chamber and sacred music is to be found. Little by little there developed a crystallization of the expressive functions of the separate parts of a cycle often made up of four movements having a tempo sequence of slow, fast, slow, fast. The concert style of concerto grosso continued to develop alongside.

In this process a considerable role was played by a contemporary of Corelli's, Giuseppe Torelli (1658-1709), an outstanding adherent of the school. In addition to his solo violin sonatas Torelli composed a number of concerti grossi, some with two concerted violins (1709). Some of these sonatas came close in form to the solo violin concerto, with the distinction between soli and tutti clearly marked. The artistic merits of these works extend to an improvement of the form, which included a three-movement structure of fast, slow, fast; the technical expressive texture of the violin part was noticeably developing.

In the violin music by the Bologna composers there is a combination of elements of homophony and polyphony; sometimes so-called hidden polyphony is used, as for instance by Antonii. While preserving a relatively limited range (mainly d^3) a passage technique is developed, connected with legato and détaché strokes and also with dotted strokes. In the slow movements recitative features are frequently retained, and a realization of the cantabile potentials of the violin gradually grows stronger (Antonii, Bassani, Vitali). From time to time (but much less often than with Marini) double notes and arpeggios appear (Torelli).

In this brief review of pre-Tartini Italian violin-playing, special attention must be given to two of his older contemporaries, Corelli and Vivaldi.

The ties between Arcangelo Corelli (1653-1713) and the Bologna school are confirmed by Corelli himself: on the title pages of three of his first opera (opuses)—trio sonatas written in 1681, 1685 and 1689—he calls himself "Arcangelo Corelli from Fusignano, called the Bolognese." He went to Bologna at the age of thirteen, and his masters were the violinist Ercole Gaibara and his pupil Leonardo Brugnoli.[17] Within four years Corelli had already become a member of the Academia de Filarmonici.

He settled in Rome in the 1670's (according to some, in 1675) and remained there to the end of his life. He performed as a violinist, led the best chapels, composed music for the violin and gave lessons in violin playing. He followed the artistic and pedagogical principles of the Bologna school and developed them further; he also founded and headed the Roman violin school. Among his numerous pupils were Francesco Geminiani and Pietro Locatelli, outstanding violinists who composed a great deal of music for their instrument.

Corelli wrote forty-eight trio sonatas that were made up into four volumes (Op.1-4, the last of which appeared in 1694), twelve sonatas for violin and bass (Op.5, published in 1700) and twelve concerti grossi (Op.6, published posthumously in 1714, although they were known five years earlier). The development and perfection of the concerti grossi proceeded along the lines of selection and generalization of the artistic rules that had taken shape in the works of Corelli's predecessors and contemporaries (mainly in the Bologna school) and, naturally, were a direct result of the immense creativity of Corelli himself. This was manifested in the richness and profundity of his music and his constant search for new forms at a time when there were as yet no fixed canons in this field.

In speaking of Corelli's music and its stylistic characteristics, one must bear in mind their connection with his style of execution. Corelli the composer is inseparable from Corelli the performer. According to Corelli's pupils and other contemporaries, his style of execution was distinguished by exceptional expressiveness and dignity. He could be lyrical, thoughtful and absorbed and at the same time animated, emotional, headlong.

By limiting the compass of the violin to three positions (*i.e.,* two and a half octaves), roughly the equivalent of the compass of the human voice, and by limiting his bowing technique to the détaché and legato strokes, Corelli strove to obtain a greater effect from the expressive means he used so sparingly. His use of polyphonic devices (two voices) and arpeggio bowing and bariolé were rather daring for his time.

In his music he developed a cantilena specifically for the violin—a broad breathing of the bow. According to Geminiani, the sound produced by Corelli was like that of a "sweet trumpet,"[18] and a French contemporary said that a bow stroke by Corelli's pupil Giambattista Somis lasted so long that it took your breath away.[19] Corelli's virtuosity is chiefly manifested in the fast "fugued" parts of his works, requiring accurate coordination of the fingering and bow movements and the technique of skipping across the strings as well.

Corelli's trio sonatas, his solo sonatas with bass and his concerti grossi are divided according to the custom of the time into "church" and "chamber," though in the actual music this division has to a large extent lost its original significance.

We know that the marks of the church style in instrumental music at that time[20] were austerity, frequent utilization of polyphonic devices, fugued fast movements, appellation of the movements according to the tempo and an organ bass part (usually figured). The chamber style was distinguished by clearer manifestation of folk influences, appellation of the movements according to dance forms (which brought out their dance character) and having bass parts assigned not to the organ but to the clavecine (cembalo).[21] An important role in the formation of the sonata and the concerto was played by the interpenetration and the mutual enrichment of both these styles, accompanied by a rejection of the elements of the abstract nature of the church style and a democratization of instrumental music, a deepening of its substance.

Corelli's searching led to the fact that grave or adagio trio sonatas, so characteristic of the church style, occasionally appear even in his chamber music. In his fifth "church" sonata for violin and bass he uses a jig, a dance of folk origin, and in his "church" concerto grosso No. 8 we find a "Pastorale" (the allegro final) permeated with the spirit of folk music. In Corelli's music, the very form of the trio sonata evokes its secular, democratic source in the music-making of the people.

This is also true of his famed *Folia,* twenty-three variations on a theme emanating from the people. This piece concludes Corelli's fifth opus of solo violin sonatas. As Marc Pincherle remarks, the very form of these variations allowed the composer, in the final part of his opus, to summarize all the technicalities that had been used in the sonatas prior to it.[22] But the significance of this work lies not in the variety of violin technicalities alone but in the combination, so peculiar to Corelli, of both artistic and technical principles. The expressiveness of the theme and the piece as a whole accounts for the endurance of the *Folia* (in numerous revisions as well as in the original form) as a concert piece as well as for teaching purposes. The theme of Corelli's *Folia* (an already existing theme that he modified) was to be used later by many composers, including Alexander Alabiev in his ballet *The Magic Drum*, Ferenz Liszt in his *Spanish Rhapsody* and Sergei Rachmaninov in his *Variations on a Theme of Corelli*, Op.42.

An outstanding role in the development of the solo violin concerto, which is at its source closely bound up with the concerto grosso style, was played by Corelli's compatriot and younger contemporary Antonio Vivaldi (1678-1741) who was born in Venice and died in Vienna.

Vivaldi learned to play the violin from his father, who was a violinist in St. Mark's; Giovanni Legrenzi taught him to play the organ and also the theory of music. At one time Antonio Vivaldi was first violin in the Cathedral chapel, and he taught for over thirty years (1703-1740).[23] From 1714 he led the orchestra and choir in the Music Seminary of the girls' conservatory (Ospedale della Pietà) in Venice.[24] The time spent with the conservatory orchestra proved extremely useful in his creative work on the concerto form.

Vivaldi wrote over five hundred works, most of which are concertos;[25] there are among his compositions many "symphonies," trio sonatas, sonatas for violin and bass and for cello and bass and about forty operas, cantatas, motets and other pieces.[26]

It is of interest to note that the last of the trio sonatas in his first opus, which came out in Venice in 1705, contains variations on *La Folia*, which stresses the composer's familiarity with Corelli. It is not difficult to perceive related features in the melody and texture of other compositions by the two violinists.

Vivaldi's violin sonatas (Op.2 and 5), for all their merits, did not have any real influence on the development of the art of the violin. The main and far from minor importance of Vivaldi as a composer lies in his concertos, which in part contain elements of the concerto grosso, but in part display marks of the early classical violin concerto. The violin is used in them as a solo concerto instrument and is masterfully employed by the violinist-composer both in the expressive cantilena and in virtuoso ("motor") movements that were usually written in rondo-like form.

Portrait sketch of Antonio Vivaldi, the only known authentic likeness

An Italian concert party

Florentine court musicians

There are already four solo violin concertos[27] as well as eight concerti grossi[28] in Vivaldi's first collection of concertos (Op.3), which came out in 1712 under the title of *Estro Armonico* ("Harmonic Inspiration"). Further collections of Vivaldi's works also contain numerous violin concertos.

Vivaldi's concertos are characterized by greater expressiveness; his contemporaries stressed the fact that they contained emotion, passion, the lively so-called "Lombard style."

The three-movement cycle (fast, slow, fast) became firmly established in Vivaldi's concertos. The composer made subtle use of the principle of artistic contrast not only between the movements, but often by introducing it into the development of the first movement of the concerto, which, with Vivaldi, generally consists of five tutti and four soli. He combines this contrast between the energetic fast movements and the slow "singing" movement that divides them, with their unity. These and other features of his concepts (for instance, tonality sequence) allow us to place Vivaldi very high in estimating his influence on the development of the sonata form and on the creation of the classical concerto of the 18th century. It must be said that the form established by Vivaldi is not rigid; he uses a great deal of imagination and inventiveness in his concertos.

Vivaldi's instrumental work has a spirit of democracy in it and is bound up with the music of the people. He is not a slave to the so-called church style, but he makes use of its achievements. His sonatas are chamber (*i.e.*, secular) music in character and come close to the suite. The influence of the opera is sometimes clearly felt in his concertos, and this emerges in both the dramatic force of the style and in the expressive means used by the composer.

The nobility of the melodic line in the slow movements, the combination of severity in style, plasticity and emotion peculiar to them, their artistic profundity and humanity, attained by simple means, enable us to see in some of the Largos in Vivaldi's concertos (for instance, in Op.11 and 12) the prototype of the Bach arias.

The sparkle and liveliness of the fast movements, the determined drive of the first Allegros and the folk-dance character of the finales have a strong appeal by reason of their emotional impact. This is achieved on the whole with the help of extremely unpretentious technical devices.

It is impossible to dismiss the peculiar programmatic quality of many of Vivaldi's concertos. Of special interest in this respect are four concertos for violin and bow orchestra from Op.8 (circa 1725). Under the general title of *The Seasons*, each ("Spring," "Summer," "Autumn" and "Winter") is prefaced by a literary program, a sonnet. Vivaldi's way of thinking in pictures manifests itself likewise in his sonic and expressive devices that correspond to his perception of the life and scenery around him.[29]

Though his development not only of the sonic and expressive

aspects but also of the technicalities of violin art was considerable, Vivaldi never turned virtuosity into an end in itself. He used his excellent mastery of the technique of the instrument as an important means of artistic expression. Professor Livanova, who calls Vivaldi the classic of the violin concerto, remarks that his concertos, as distinct from Corelli's concerti grossi, are characterized not only by "free development of orchestral texture, . . . but also by the singling out of the concertante solo of the soloist's principal part, which would be executed with the brilliance of virtuosity. It was in the violin concerto that they found the most direct expression of the aspiration for instrumental virtuosity, analogous to the aspiration for vocal virtuosity in the operatic aria of the time . . . However," adds the author justly (and this is also true first of all of Vivaldi), "in the first stages of development the violin concerto had not yet sacrificed its artistic meaning to external virtuosity. The brilliant concerto writing was merely a fresh recognition of the 'grand' concerto music, which had surpassed the former 'chamber' music in dimension."[30]

The technical means of expression used by Vivaldi in his violin works are in accord with their musical content. To execute these works one needs not only good taste, but also sufficient skill; yet Vivaldi is far from anything like virtuoso excesses.

It is only occasionally that Vivaldi uses scordatura (concertos 6 and 12 in Op.9); from time to time he used finger extension to a tenth (concerto 8 from Op.8), anticipating Locatelli's technique. In the concertos of his Op.3 he restricts himself to five positions, while in others he goes as far as the eighth position. Vivaldi's bow technique is connected with a variety of lively, and especially syncopated, dotted rhythms in the fast movements of his concertos (and sonatas) and with a broad use of the arpeggio.

Many generations of violinists have been brought up on Vivaldi's music, in which they find the food they need to form their artistic tastes and to acquire the technical skill demanded by the idiom of the violin.[31]

Among the eminent Italian violinists that were contemporary to Giuseppe Tartini there stand out two: Francesco Geminiani (1687-1762) and Pietro Antonio Locatelli (1695-1764), Corelli's best pupils. Geminiani entered the history of violin-playing mainly due to his strongly pronounced urge towards expressiveness, and Locatelli for his bold innovations in violin virtuosity.

Geminiani began studying the violin under Carlo Ambrogio Lunati and later became a pupil of Corelli. Some say he learned composition from Alessandro Scarlatti. Until 1714 Geminiani lived in Italy (in Lucca and Naples), and after that (with the exception of the years 1749-1755, which he spent in Paris) in England. Here, as in Italy, he enjoyed renown as a concert performer who played in a lively, temperamental way[32] with a wealth of dynamic touches.

Ferdinand David

Francesco Geminiani

Guiseppe Tartini

Raphael's "Parnassus"

Geminiani was friendly with Handel and often played together with him.

In Geminiani's earlier compositions one can feel the influence of Corelli, whereas in his later works it is easy to detect the influence of Handel. Yet Geminiani's compositions (mainly sonatas for violin and bass and concerti grossi) show considerable originality. This is evident in the imagery, the forms of experimental exploration, the expansion of the dynamic means of expression (Geminiani was one of the first to introduce into violin music signs for graded dynamics) and in the significance that he attaches to various ornaments.

Geminiani's esthetic positions are clearly expressed in his pedagogical treatises, in particular the one on *The Art of Playing on the Violin*, published in London in 1751.[33]

"The Intention of Music," wrote Geminiani, "is not to please the Ear, but to express sentiments, strike the Imagination, affect the Mind, and command the Passions. The Art of playing the Violin consists in giving that Instrument a Tone that shall in a Manner rival the most perfect human Voice; and in executing every piece with Exactness, Propriety, and Delicacy of Expression according to the true Intention of Music."[34]

In his esthetic views Geminiani belonged to the trend represented in the 18th century, along with François Couperin, Johann Mattheson, Johann Quantz, Carl Philipp Emanuel Bach, Leopold Mozart, Giuseppe Tartini and Luigi Boccherini.

The views of these musicians were incorporated in the so-called "theory of affects." While reflecting the progressive desire to make the musical idiom expressive, and sometimes to give a "correspondence between music and effect," the followers of this theory not infrequently fell victim to a certain historical narrow-mindedness, an inability to understand the development of the effects themselves, with their clashes and their interpenetration. Hence, for instance, the somewhat naive and mechanistic interpretation of melodic ornamentation by Geminiani, who was prepared to associate every ornament or the way in which it was performed with a particular feeling.

Nonetheless, Geminiani came to conclusions that were progressive for the time in which he lived, when he considered that music is good if it expressed "movements of the soul" and bad if it "expressed nothing." As we shall see, these views were adopted and developed further by Giuseppe Tartini.

Geminiani's way of thinking in pictures is also evident from the fact that (according to his contemporary Charles Henri Blainville) he composed music with his violin in his hands and began by picturing scenes that stirred him profoundly and gave rein to his imagination.

Another eminent contemporary of Tartini's, Pietro Locatelli, was born in Bergamo and was, at the opening of the century, a pupil of

36

George Frederick Handel

Corelli's in Rome; then he became violinist and chapel-master both there and in Mantua (from 1725). After that he made immensely successful concert tours in various countries of Europe as a violin virtuoso, and finally, in 1732, settled down in Amsterdam, where he spent his remaining days.

Among Locatelli's compositions are solo violin concertos (with bass), trio sonatas, concerti grossi and violin concertos. Of greatest interest are his twelve concertos for solo violin accompanied by string quintet (Op.3), published in 1733 under the title of *L'arte del violino*. The greater part of these (nine of the twelve) are in three movements, with solo caprices after both fast movements (to which the performer might add a cadenza of his own), and this opened a new page in the history of violin virtuosity.

While Locatelli still largely followed the Corelli tradition in his first opus (the twelve concerti grossi, 1721), one can trace in his third the beginning of his path toward Paganini, who in his youth carefully studied his predecessor's caprices before creating his own famous compositions in this form. What was new in Locatelli's third opus was not only the nature of the content, but the violin technique, too.

Pietro Locatelli

Locatelli's twelve sonatas Opus 6 (1737) are very rich musically. They are melodically expressive, emotionally warm and daring in their modulations, which at times anticipates romantic harmony. The boldness of his rich and varied technical palette stands out here, too (the technique of the arpeggios, the staccato passages and others being of special interest).

Each of these sonatas concludes with variations. The variations in the last sonata (known in the revisions of Ferdinand David and Delphin Alard) bear the programmatic title of *Labyrinth of Harmonies* and have "Facili aditus, difficili exitus"[35] as an epigraph.

The concrete imagery of Locatelli's way of thinking can be felt in the programmatic titles of some of his works. He called one of his concerti a quattro, Op.7 (1741), *Il pianto d'Arianna* ("Ariadne's Plaint"). His "symphony" for a quartet (like his sonata that is known in the arrangement of Eugène Ysaÿe) is a "tombeau," that is, a piece of music written in memory of one departed (in this case, his wife).

Although Geminiani's work (like that of Corelli and Vivaldi) is very close in spirit to Tartini's, the latter was undoubtedly familiar with Locatelli's compositions, which were often published at the time; they could hardly have failed to come to the notice of a violinist and music teacher who was in the forefront of the Italian violin school of the period.

Tartini's outstanding artistic individuality and taste in music, his sensitive and keen perception of all that was most interesting in his field of art, enabled him to make creative use of and develop whatever was akin to his own views and purposes, to follow his own road and retain his originality as an artist in the realm of music.

Chapter Two

Life and Work of Giuseppe Tartini

 Beyond doubt, Tartini strove for the truest possible expression in violin playing, he wished to give his epoch the best possible example of style, in the broadest sense of the word.

Leopold Auer

YOUTH AND FORMATIVE YEARS

Giuseppe Tartini was born in Pirano (now the Jugoslav town of Pirano), a small, picturesque town in Istria, on the coast of the Adriatic. At the end of the 17th century it was populated by Slavs[1] and Italians. The people made a living by catching fish, growing olives, making wine and extracting salt. Among the townspeople there were many jewelers and talented builders (to whose artistry various old buildings and museum exhibits still bear witness), and also singers and musicians.

Among the places of interest in the town are the remains of the ancient turreted fortifications, a Minorite friary, an old Gothic church, a clock tower that is an exact copy of the tower of St. Mark's in Venice and the "Venetian" ("Benecanka"), a building still standing in the square named after Tartini, not far from the house where he was born. This building dates back to the 15th century and its history is associated with a romantic legend about a Venetian beauty.

The proximity of Venice, a city with which Pirano at that time maintained commercial ties, left an imprint not only on its architecture, but also on its mode of life. At the same time the life of Pirano and its inhabitants was influenced by various features of Slavonic culture, which flourished in the work of its master craftsmen, as well as in the musical traditions of the Slavonic people who lived there.

By the 18th century the glory of Venice and of Florence, the birthplace of Tartini's father, had waned. The domination of Italian and Austrian feudal lords led to the decline of the town of Istria.

The Florentine merchant Giovanni Antonio Tartini moved to Pirano in the late sixteen seventies, and in 1685 he married a local

Tartini monument, Piran

Tartini monument in Padua

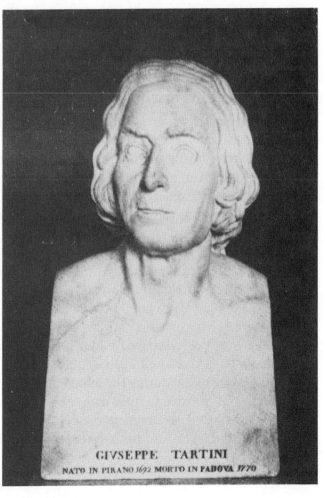

GIVSEPPE TARTINI
NATO IN PIRANO 1692 MORTO IN PADOVA 1770

Bust of Tartini

girl named Caterina Zangrando, whose family name had been known in Pirano as far back as the 15th or 16th centuries. Giuseppe Tartini was born on April 8, 1692. At that time his father worked in the offices of the Public Salt Works, and somewhat later as a syndic in a friary.

The childhood of the musician was spent in Pirano and in nearby Struegnano. Today it is hard to establish which of the musical impressions of Tartini's childhood bore fruit and took shape in his compositions; he naturally heard a good many Italian and Slavonic folk musicians and singers. The youthful Tartini may well have heard music at gatherings that he may have attended with his father at the famous "Dei Virtuosi" Academy in Pirano.

Giuseppe's father was preparing him for an ecclesiastical career. After receiving an elementary education at a church school (Scuola dell' Oratorio) in Pirano, he was sent to the Collegio dei Padri Scolopi delle Scuole Pie at Capo d'Istria (today the Jugoslav town of Koper) to study the humanities and rhetoric. Against his father's wishes, Giuseppe decided not to devote his life to the church, but to take up law. In 1708 he moved to one of the oldest towns in Italy, Padua (Padova), which, along with Istria, then belonged to the Republic of Venice. The town had long been famed for its old university, founded in 1222, which provided a high standard of education in jurisprudence. This attracted the young man, and in 1709 he enrolled in the university's law department.

Another place of interest in Padua was the Church of St. Anthony, completed in the early 14th century, and its del Santo chapel (basilica),[2] which was added to it in the 16th century. Masterpieces of Italian art, including paintings by Titian and Veronese, have been preserved in this church to the present day.

The Soviet writer Marietta Shaginian gives a vivid description of the basilica:

"There it stands, as if shaped by superhuman hands, like a gigantic toy, with an unbelievable completeness in its austere geometrical lines, with rounded domes amid the pointed ones, with a look of the Byzantine or at the least Oriental in it—there it stands, from top to bottom, in a kind of perfection of fulfillment, complete in itself, as if it were not fixed in the ground by its foundation, but had merely been placed, fully built, on the paving stones of the square, the most charming—no, that is the wrong word—the most convincing basilica of them all."[3] Giuseppe Tartini was to spend nearly half a century in the fine chapel of this church.

Vernon Lee[4] described Padua as a tranquil, sprawling town with canals overgrown with rushes, quiet gardens and deserted villas that only came to life during the annual fair of St. Anthony, when musicians and merchants from many towns and countries converged on the town. Operas featuring the best singers were staged there. The peace and calm of this western outskirt of bustling Venice, as

Basilica of S. Antonio, Padua

Basilica of S. Antonio in Padua

witnessed by Charles Burney, who visited Padua after Tartini's death, best explain why this town was chosen by the future musician, teacher and scholar as the place most eminently suited to his many-sided creative endeavors.

There is some evidence[5] that young Giuseppe had already displayed clearly his musical ability and his love for music in Capo d'Istria. At that time he was taking violin lessons; it was the instrument he had already enthusiastically taken to in his youth. Charles Burney writes that Tartini referred to the violinist Julio di Terni as his teacher. Later, however, di Terni himself took lessons from Tartini. It seems to be mainly to himself that Tartini owes his mastery of the violin. Having received elementary instruction early in life, he later set about perfecting his skill in a persistent and purposeful manner. He studied Corelli's compositions and listened attentively to the violinists he met (among them Veracini), emulating their achievements and developing them creatively but critically, discarding all that was alien to his esthetic views and adopting all that corresponded to his individuality as an artist.

In a letter addressed to Tartini, Gian-Rinaldo Carli, a close friend of his, wrote later (in 1744): "In your desire to devote yourself to music, you left your home and did naught but practice the violin eight hours a day."[6]

But complete mastery of the violin did not come to him as easily as all that. As a university student with a vivacious and sensitive nature, whose time was divided between law studies and music, he developed a passion for fencing as well. At one time it even seemed to him that fencing was his true vocation,[7] but this was no more than the romantic impulse of a young man, and it passed with time. Tartini's logical mind and sense of purpose, together with his growing involvement in music and the violin, soon took the upper hand and helped him to realize his true inclinations and become a professional musician.

Many things in Tartini's biography are still not clear; different sources give different and occasionally contradictory versions of various events and even entire periods of his life. It is hard to distinguish between the authentic facts in Tartini's life story and the numerous legends that grew up around his name.

According to some sources, Tartini, having conceived a passion for the Cardinal's niece, married her secretly in 1710; when pursued by her influential relatives, he was forced to flee from Padua to Assisi. According to other accounts, his wife, Elisabetta Premazone, was the daughter of the Cardinal's coachman. Be that as it may, Tartini left the university soon after his marriage, a step that aroused the displeasure of his family, who cut off all financial support.

One fact is beyond doubt: after being forced to leave Padua, Tartini spent two years (probably between 1713 and 1715) in the Minorite monastery at Assisi, where he worked assiduously to perfect his musical skills, and where he created his early compositions, which apparently included the initial version of his *Devil's Trill* Sonata.

There is another fact in the life of the talented musician that is not quite clear to this day. C. Conzati, the author of a biography of Tartini printed in Padua in the year of his death, asserts that Tartini took lessons at Assisi from "Padre Boemo," who was at one time an organist at the St. Antony Basilica in Padua. Padre Boemo was the name given in Italy to Bohuslav Matei Cernohorsky (1684-1742), the noted Czech composer and theorist and head of the 18th century Czech school of composition, who had also taught Christoph Willibald Gluck in Prague. Pierluigi Petrobelli, a competent contemporary authority and biographer of Tartini, also claims that the latter was guided in his studies at Assisi by Bohuslav Cernohorsky,[8] but this claim, supported by some and disputed by others, has received no documentary confirmation.

However, there can be no doubt as to Tartini's individuality and originality in musical thought and work, which on the whole he developed independently. Obviously, he heard much music and many musicians, but creatively assimilated and developed only what corresponded to his artistic inclinations and aspirations.

An important role in Tartini's self-education was brought about by his meeting with an older countryman of his, Francesco Maria Veracini (1690-1768), who was already an eminent violinist. Veracini was born in Florence and was famous far beyond Italy. He played with success in the interludes of Italian opera performances in London (1714), served at the Court in Dresden for a length of time (1717-1722), worked in chapels in Poland and Czechia (for Count Kinsky) and again in London (1736-1745). He must have met Tartini in Venice at festivities in honor of the Crown Prince of Saxony in 1716. There was something in the way that both of these violinists played that revealed a strikingly individual style. By that time Veracini had written his first sonatas which manifest certain novel elements, such as a melodic freedom in the flow of music, the "singing" quality of the tunes, a bold use of harmony and use of chromaticisms, doublestopping and ornamentation that were unusual for the period, thereby giving his sonatas a romantic coloring.[9]

All this could not but attract Tartini. He was especially impressed by Veracini's manner of playing, which was bold and vivid, with a smooth-flowing tone and an easy mastery of bow and finger techniques, including the trill.

His sensitive spirit and inquiring mind led Tartini to go into seclusion once again to absorb all the new things that he had heard from Veracini, to perfect his skill and return to Padua with a mature mastery of the violin.

If one is to bear in mind that by that time he was a fine violinist

Francesco Maria Veracini

(which is testified by his position at Assisi), it will become clear that such a decision required not only strong will-power and determination, but also a genuine love and respect for his art, an unflagging thirst for knowledge and a continual search for artistic perfection. All these were intrinsic qualities of Tartini's, and it was only four years later that he returned to Padua once and for all, having successfully accomplished the task he had set himself.[10]

According to Tartini, he played in the opera theatre at Ancona; his name is to be found among the musicians in the orchestra of the Ancona Opera as early as 1717. During the carnival of 1717-1718, as Pietrobelli noted, Tartini was first violin in the di Fano Theater. It is also known that in 1719 he was back at Assisi, where he was quite popular already. It is hard to say whether he then returned to Ancona (which was probably the case) or else stayed on at Assisi before returning to Padua. It is worth noting at this point the chance contacts Tartini had with Francesco Geminiani and Gaspare Visconti, followers of the Corelli school, which could only have strengthened his ties with that school.

However contradictory may seem the information available concerning this period, it was of immense importance in the biography of the violinist. He applied himself assiduously to his violin, playing it to perfection; he had not only assimilated creatively everything in Veracini's playing that attracted him, but also elaborated many new playing techniques.

During his studies Tartini paid special attention to the bow. Striving to broaden and enrich the tone (a desire to which his work in the opera theater must have led him), he arrived at the conclusion that it was necessary to lengthen the violin bow.[11] This enabled the bow to "breathe" freely, increased the flexibility of the stick and thus added considerable amplitude to the range of expression of the bowing technique.

According to some sources, Tartini reformed the bow in 1730. But if one is to agree with Andreas Moser that Tartini's *Art of Bowing*, requiring a perfection of the bow and a developed bowing technique, came into existence in the Ancona period of his life (this may have been the first version of the work, which may have been subsequently elaborated), it would be logical to assume that he had had a general idea as to how to improve the bow while he was still in Ancona.

Tartini's bowing palette became substantially broader and compared favorably not only with that of Corelli but with that of many other violinists of the mid-18th century too. The virtuoso bowings, in particular his "bouncing" strokes, required a surer grip (we must remember that at that time the bow was gripped not at the heel but at a certain distance from it),[12] and Tartini also fluted the wood of the bow.[13]

The operatic bel canto no doubt stimulated Tartini's amplification of the expression of the violin cantilena. Not only did he lengthen the bow that expanded its "breathing," he also thickened the violin strings somewhat, thus enhancing the intensity and quality of the tone. The expression of his playing was augmented by his original way of using the portamento device, which he had partly borrowed from operatic singers, but which he used in accordance with the specific sound of the violin.

Lastly, it was also during the Ancona period that Tartini discovered the acoustic phenomenon called "terzo suono" ("the third sound"), to the intoning of which he attached great significance. Later, in his treatises, he wrote that this happened in 1714. (It is worth noting that Tartini's discovery of the "third sound" could only have come about at a time when he was thinking out the technique of doublestopping.)

These problems will be dealt with in greater detail below. Meanwhile, what has already been said is sufficient to demonstrate the fruitfulness of Tartini's profound thinking, the purposefulness of his studies and the persistence of his investigations into the art of violin-playing, all of which characterize the Ancona period of his life.

THE MASTER'S MATURITY

Giuseppe Tartini arrived at Padua in the spring of 1721 a mature artist and versatile musician. His fame had reached Padua even before he arrived there. Tartini was immediately appointed first violin of the Basilica chapel of St. Anthony, or as it was called, the "Santo."

It was one of the best Italian chapels of the period; at the peak of its fame it consisted of twenty-four fine instrumentalists[14] and sixteen singers, and was known for its excellent ensemble and expressive performance.

Actually, Tartini directed the chapel and performed regularly as a solo violinist. In documents of that period he is called "sonator singolare" (the only, special musician) and "primo Violino, e Capo di concerto" (first Violin and leader of the orchestra). It was only in 1765 that the aging maestro was succeeded as leader of the chapel orchestra by Giuliox Menegini, a pupil of his.

Nevertheless, musical life in Padua was somewhat restricted. Receiving permission to appear in concerts in other Italian towns, Tartini performed successfully in Venice, Milan, Bologna, Livorno, Palermo and Naples. He visited Venice, where he not only played but also taught the violin. Among his pupils in Venice were Alessandro Marcello, brother of the noted composer Benedetto Marcello, and the talented violinist Maddalena Lombardini (to whom we shall return later). When Tartini appeared in the Chapel of St. Mark's, the first violinist gave up his place to his colleague from Padua and the latter delighted his audiences with his playing.

That Tartini was well-known beyond the borders of Italy is borne out among other things by the fact that in 1723 he was invited, together with the finest musicians in Europe, to play at the musical festivities in Prague on the occasion of the coronation of Emperor Charles VI. They were also attended by Carl Heinrich Graun, the Berlin composer and orchestra leader, Johann Joachim Quantz, a famous flutist, theorist and composer, Silvius Leopold Weiss, the lute player, Johann Josef Fuchs, the court composer in Vienna and author of the opera *Constanza e Fortezza* that was performed at the festivities, the prominent Italian composer Antonio Caldara and others.

The invitation to Tartini came directly from an influential member of the Hapsburg dynasty,[15] Count Kinsky of Czechia, a prominent patron of the arts, who maintained a fine chapel in Prague. One of the Czech musicians in Italy could have helped to procure this invitation. In accepting it, Tartini could hardly have been drawn by material interests alone, though during his work at the Basilica del Santo in Padua his allowance was very modest despite the fact that he occupied the post of leader of the orchestra. At the same time he was still relatively young and of an ardent and inquisitive nature and could not fail to be attracted by the prospects of performing in the very heart of Europe at an influential court that was famed for its patronage of the arts. Antonio Capri, a biographer of Tartini, makes convincing the assumption that what Tartini had heard of the success at foreign courts of such Italian musicians as Domenico Scarlatti and Francesco Geminiani played a certain role in Tartini's decision to go to Prague.

But if we recall that Tartini showed an interest in Slavic music, an interest stemming from reminiscences of his youth and possibly from his meeting with "Padre Boemo," which later expressed itself in the Slavic features in his work, it might be possible that in accepting Count Kinsky's invitation his purpose was to visit a center of Slavic music.

Giuseppe Tartini set out for Prague with a friend, Antonio Vandini, first cellist of the chapel at Padua.[16] In those days a violinist performing his own sonatas written for violin and bass usually travelled with a cellist who accompanied him with a single-line bass part. The bass part was not always performed on the harpsichord or the organ, in addition to the cello.

The role of the cello accompaniment was of keen importance in the absence of a keyboard instrument. A skillful accompaniment acquired great significance, since it necessitated a refined musical taste, a sense of proportion, an excellent knowledge of harmony and polyphony and a gift for improvising.

Arcangelo Corelli played with the cellist Francischiello, Francesco Veracini with Salvatore Lanzetti and Giuseppe Tartini with Antonio Vandini.

Domenico Scarlatti

Padre Giambattista Martini

Charles Burney

Sketch of a court concert

The friendship between Tartini and Antonio Vandini lasted for over fifty years. It was reflected in the compositions of Tartini, who wrote several concertos for Vandini as well as a number of interesting cello parts in his violin concertos. He was an excellent musician and composer and was especially famous for his expressive cello playing. His contemporaries highly appreciated his ability to "parlare" (speak) in the idiom of his instrument, for which he wrote several sonatas. After highly praising Tartini, de Brosses, who had heard both musicians, wrote in a letter from Italy in 1739: "I was no less gratified by the superlative playing of a certain Abbé Vandini who was with him."[17] Charles Burney, the British writer on music, was able to meet this famous cellist in his old age in Padua in 1770.

Antonio Vandini

Vandini was not only a colleague and partner of Tartini, whose tastes in music were similar to his, but was also a devoted friend.[18] In a letter to Padre Martini dated April 7, 1769, Tartini wrote of Vandini,[19] to whom he was linked by "fifty years of true and sacred friendship."

Unfortunately, no detailed description of Tartini's life and work in Prague has reached us. We know only that after the coronation festivities, he and Vandini worked in Count Kinsky's chapel until 1726, Tartini as a chamber musician, and that Tartini played in Prague's "musical academies." There he probably again met with Veracini, who played in the same chapel.

It was only natural that while in Prague Tartini should have associated with eminent Czech musicians as well as Czech violinists. These violinists continued to contribute to the further development of the Czech school of violin-playing,[20] among whose founders was Heinrich Johann von Biber, the famous violinist and composer. In Prague Tartini must have met Bohuslav Cernohorský again and quite possibly he associated with young representatives of Cernohorský's school too: Jan Zach, who played the violin, Frantisek Ignac Tuma, the famous gambist of that period, and others.

Recalling that the Paduan astronomer Gian Rinaldo Carli, a friend of Tartini's, had asserted that the latter took lessons with Cernohorský at Assisi, Igor Belza wrote: "Tartini almost met Cernohorský again in Prague in 1723-1726, and it may have been his studies with the 'Czech Padre' that helped the Italian violinist to master the composer's technique and theoretical knowledge, which he later elaborated in his well-known works."[21]

It is also possible that in that period he performed at concerts in Vienna together with the chapel where he worked.[22]

In Prague Tartini not only performed but also composed music too. It can be stated for certain that it was in Prague that he wrote his Violin Concerto (No. 89)[23] in A major in 1724. It was probably also in Prague that he wrote his Concerto in D major for gamba, possibly for the Czech gambist Kozec or Tuma.[24]

Despite the fame he enjoyed in Prague, Tartini had no intention of leaving Padua permanently. In his letters of that period he complained of the state of his health, which was affected by the northern climate, and asked that his position in the Paduan chapel be kept for him.

In 1726 Tartini returned to the Paduan chapel never to leave it again for any length of time.[25] On more than one occasion he received very flattering invitations to go to France, England and other countries, but invariably he turned them down.

In the famous Santo chapel headed in the twenties by the well-known musicians Francesco Antonio Callegari, Giuseppe Rinaldi and, later, by Francesco Antonio Vallotti, Giuseppe Tartini was able to find all that he needed to satisfy his musical interests. The best compositions were played there, mostly in the "church" style; however if instrumental concertos (for instance, Vivaldi's) were performed rather infrequently before Tartini's time, with his appearance such concertos became a tradition. The Basilica orchestra itself, which he headed for some half a century, served as a splendid "laboratory" in which he tried out the creations of his musical fantasy. The great number of violin concertos he composed and performed speak of the immense opportunities that his many years of work in the chapel offered him both as a composer and as a performer.

When Charles Burney visited Padua in 1770, soon after Tartini's death, the Santo Chapel consisted of eight violins, four violas, four cellos, two double-basses, two oboes and two horns.[26] However, in his concertos Giuseppe Tartini limited himself mainly to bow instruments and the part of the figured bass in the chapel was naturally given to the organ. The organist and the cellist (again Vandini) together accompanied him when he played sonatas.

Tartini very seldom played in other Italian cities. Besides his performances in Venice, one might mention his journey to Rome somewhere around 1740 at the invitation of the Cardinal, when he played in the presence of Pope Clement XII. The wonderful violinist was received with great enthusiasm in Venice, Milan, Florence, Bologna, Naples, Palermo and other cities in which he played on his way to Rome.

This was probably Tartini's only major concert tour; after that he lived and worked in Padua more or less uninterruptedly. In this respect he was like his older contemporaries Corelli, who was closely connected with Rome, and Vivaldi, who settled in Venice, and unlike most of the outstanding 18th century Italian violinists who sought to practice their art outside Italy.

Although Tartini occupied a place of prominence in the Paduan chapel, he received rather modest remuneration for his work there. At the same time he continued to give material support to his relatives in Pirano. However, it was not only this circumstance that compelled him in the years that followed to engage in the most varied types of musical activity outside his service in the chapel, working as composer, violin soloist, playing in orchestras and acting as conductor.

Tartini's gifts as performer and composer were combined with rare talent as a teacher and great ability in theory and research. His nature was an amazing fusion of strong emotional feeling and the capacity for profound thought and logical generalization, a romantic spirit and a rational mind. Besides playing and composing he was filled with a lively interest in the teaching of the violin and also in the science of music.

Not all of Tartini's works have been published, not all were completed, but all of them were the fruit of his inquiring and creative mind; they were all linked to the practical experience of an erudite and versatile musician.

In his treatises Tartini displays at times a closeness to Rameau in his desire to follow nature and study objective laws of musical harmony, in which he spontaneously proceeds from materialistic premises.

In 1754 Tartini's *Trattato di Musica Secondo la vera scienza dell'armonia (Treatise on Music Based on a True Knowledge of Harmony),* which he had written in 1750, was published in Padua. This work was criticized by his contemporaries mainly for its complex manner of presentation and frequent lack of clarity.

The main ideas of Tartini's work were outlined more simply and clearly in another of his treatises entitled *De' principi dell'armonia musicale, contenuta nel diatonico Genere (On the Principles of Musical Harmony Contained in the Diatonic Genre)* written in 1764 and published in Padua in 1767. Finally, his *Trattato delle appogiature . . . (Treatise on Ornaments)* that he had written before the middle of the 18th century, *i.e.,* before both of the above-mentioned treatises, was published posthumously in Paris in 1771 in a French translation. A treatise of his called *Delle ragioni e delle proporzioni (On Measures and Proportion)* found in the city archives at Pirano has not been published as yet. In this treatise, which Tartini wrote toward the end of his life, he attempted to explain a theory of his constructed on a mathematical basis.[27]

Some of the theoretical deliberations of the famous musician were reflected in his vast correspondence and polemics with musicians, philosophers and other learned people of the period, among them Martini, Valotti, Carli, Algarotti, Euler, Rousseau and, according to some sources, d'Alembert, who approved of Tartini's works.

A little over a year after he returned to Padua from Prague, Tartini established a violin school of his own which earned general recognition beyond the borders of Italy as well. By that time the great violinist had already accumulated a wealth of practical experience as a performer. After making a thorough study not only of the nature of the violin but also of the laws of violin playing that are

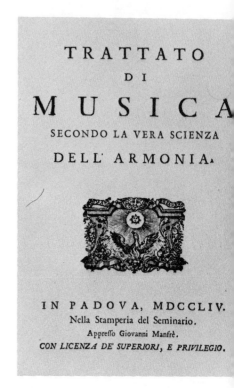

Title page of *Trattato di Musica*

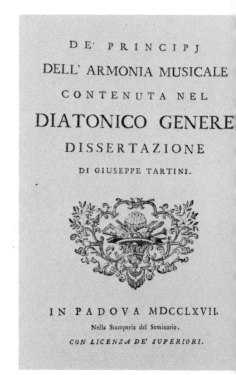

Title page of *De' Principi Dell' Armonia Musicale*

largely peculiar to this instrument, he experienced an urge to share his knowledge with his younger colleagues and to teach young violinists the fundamentals of his beloved art and eventually to further the shaping of his school and the progress of violin playing. It is interesting to note that Tartini taught his pupils not only how to play the violin, but also the theory of composition and counterpoint.

Soon the school founded by Tartini began to attract violinists from various Italian cities and from many other countries too. He became known as the "Maestro delle Nazioni" ("Teacher of Nations"). This high reputation was due to his accomplishments in teaching his pupils in addition to his inspired music, his consummate skill as a performer and all his qualities as an artist and as a person. History has kept for us the names of his numerous pupils, the most outstanding of whom was Pietro Nardini.

"One cannot speak of music at Padua without mentioning the famous Giuseppe Tartini, who has long been the first violin of Europe," wrote the well-known French astronomer J.J. Lalande, who visited Padua when the musician was still alive. "His modesty, moral standards and considerateness evoke as much respect as his talent; in Italy he is referred to as 'il Maestro delle Nazioni' both in regard to the violin and to his compositions . . . No one has impressed me more with his inspiration and the fire of his compositions than Tartini."[28]

DECLINING YEARS

Tartini possessed a rare capacity for work. Even in old age he continued to play his compositions in the chapel and gave lessons to pupils. True, in the sixties he appeared much less frequently in the church with his violin in his hands.[29] In those years Giulio Meneghini, a pupil of Tartini's, took the place of the celebrated musician more and more often. But he continued to devote up to ten hours a day to his classes.

In the last years of his life Tartini was often ill, frequently being bedridden for months at a time. In that period his predisposition to philosophical reflections sometimes took on an abstract nature, not devoid of a mystic coloring.[30] He was preoccupied with the category of harmony as expounded by the esthetes of the ancient world, among them the Pythagoreans.[31] Tartini, who had shown a heightened interest in mathematics and astronomy earlier in life, took great pains to discover the "law of eternal harmony" which would throw new light on the essence of music and its significance. The sensitive performer and musician in him came into conflict with the scholastic tasks he had set himself in his attempt to resolve them by means of abstract calculations of mathematically expressed relationships.

To a certain extent this was a reflection of the rationalistic spirit of the 18th century, a desire characteristic of advanced bourgeois

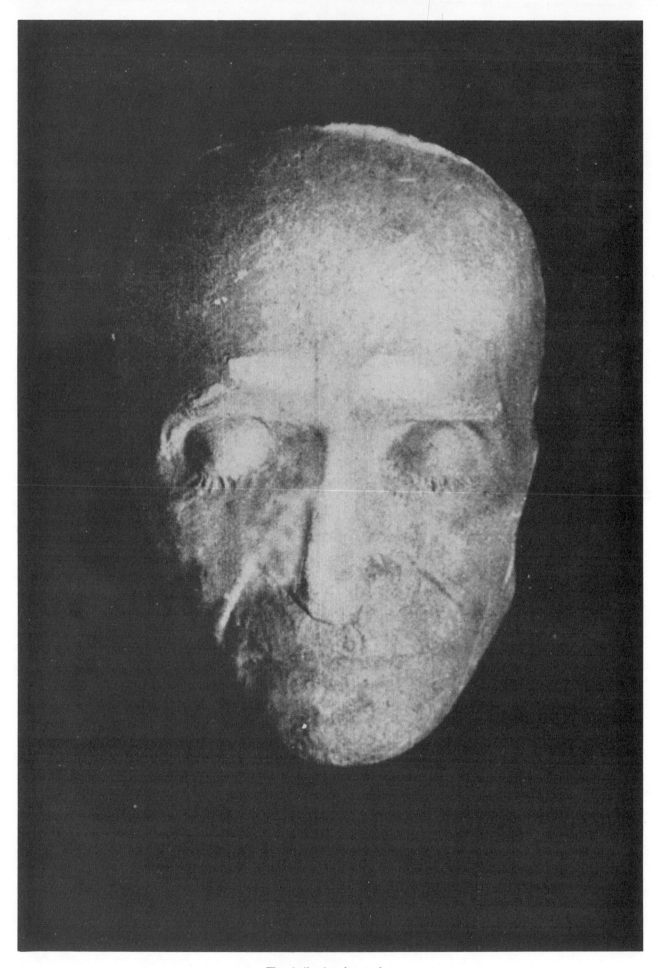

Tartini's death mask

Pietro Nardini

thinkers to "test" everything with the intelligence, on the basis of natural science and mathematics.[32]

In his declining years Tartini, as a child of his time, was to a certain extent influenced by the mechanistic philosophy so characteristic of his age, which led many of his contemporaries into the sphere of idealistic abstraction and metaphysics. But the interesting thing is that it had no bearing on the substance of Tartini's music. In the music he composed later in life his art remained living, humane and democratic. The humanism and sincerity of his emotional message, so typical of Tartini the artist, proved stronger than the introspection that corroded his rational thinking and consumed so much of his time and energy in the last years of his life.

Giuseppe Tartini died in Padua on February 26, 1770, in the arms of his best pupil and friend Pietro Nardini, and he was buried in St. Catherine's, next to his wife.

"He died universally regretted by the Patavinians, who had long been amused by his talents, and edified by his piety and good works," wrote Charles Burney in 1770. "There was a public function performed for him at Padua, March 31, 1770, at which a funeral oration was pronounced by the Abate Francesco Fanzago, and an anthem performed, composed for the occasion by Signor P. Maestro Valloti.

"His merit, both as a composer and performer, is too well known to need a panegyric here: I shall only say, that as a composer, he was one of the few original geniuses of this age who constantly drew from his own source; that his melody was full of fire and fancy, and his harmony, though learned, yet simple and pure; and as a performer, that his slow movements evince his taste and expression, and his lively ones his great hand. He was the first who knew and taught the power of the bow; and his knowledge of the fingerboard is proved by a thousand beautiful passages, to which that alone could give birth. His scholar, Nardini, who played to me many of his best solos, as I thought, very well, with respect to correctness and expression, assured me that his dear and honored master, as he constantly called him, was as much superior to himself, in the performance of the same solos, both in the pathetic and the brilliant parts, as he was to any one of his scholars."[33]

In 1806 the Paduans, who were connoisseurs of the arts, erected a monument in their city, where the splendid musician had spent the greater part of his life and which to this day reflects his glory.[34] This monument is one of the 84 statues standing in the square of the Parco della Valle (now Victor Emanuel II Square), portraying renowned Paduans. At Tartini's feet lie books and a violin.

The inhabitants of Pirano have also immortalized his memory. A statue of the renowned musician with a violin and a bow in his hands by the sculptor Antonio Dal Zotto was set up in 1896 in the only large square in the town, bearing the name of Tartini (now Tartinijevtrg).

Medal in commemoration of the 200th anniversary of Tartini's death

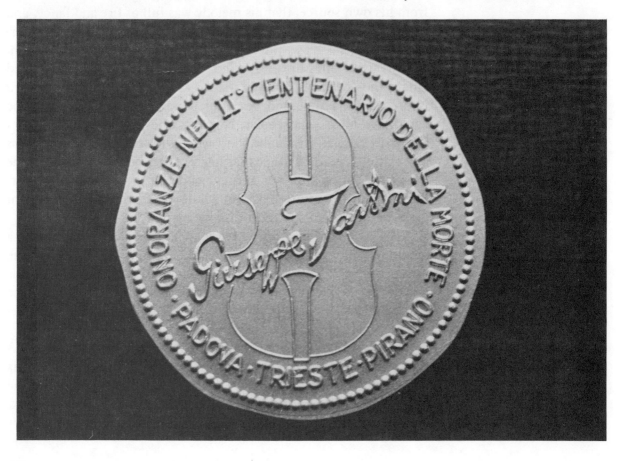

Chapter 3

Tartini the Composer

 With this sonata[1] began a new era for
the violin.

V.F. Odoevsky

GENERAL CHARACTERIZATION

It is a vast heritage that Giuseppe Tartini has left us. We owe to his pen no fewer than three hundred and fifty works, the majority of which were written for the violin.

Like Corelli and unlike Vivaldi, who wrote a considerable number of operas in addition to instrumental music, Tartini with very few exceptions (all occurring in the latter part of his life), composed exclusively instrumental music.[2] This was in spite of the fact that he played in the orchestra of the opera theater in Ancona in his youth, while in Padua itself there was a fine theatre that staged operas by the most outstanding Italian composers where one could hear the best singers of the time.

Tartini condemned composers of instrumental music who attempted to write vocal music, just as he condemned experts in vocal art who tried to compose for instruments. "These two kinds of music," he said, "are so different that he who is successful in one of them cannot be so in the other; each must remain within the confines of his own talent." He went on to say: "I have received offers to work for theatres in Venice, but I have never agreed to this, for I know well that the vocal cords are by no means identical with the violin fingerboard. Vivaldi, who wanted to work in both genres, was always booed in the one, whilst in the other he was completely successful!"[3]

Naturally Tartini could not have failed to feel the fruitful influence of the operatic bel canto, but he made no attempt to imitate this vocal style in his own compositions. He had a fine sense of the specific nature of the "singing" of instruments, particularly the violin, and this he used with great mastery.

It was to Tartini's time that academician B.V. Asafyev attributed "the breakthrough of the melodic line (principle) beyond the bounds of the vocal." "Bel canto singing," he wrote, "acquired a tendency to become 'bel canto playing' as well. The instrumental culture of the period mastered melody, from which entered the concertante style, both solo and ensemble."[4]

Special credit for this development is due to Italian violinists and cellists, whose example was followed by many other musicians. "Singing is the basis of all music," wrote G.P. Telemann, an outstanding musician of the 18th century, in his autobiography. "He who writes music must sing in everything he writes. Every would-be composer should learn from the Italians."[5]

Tartini's exceptional melodic gifts were combined with a rhythmical inventiveness, a fresh and frequently daring harmonic idiom, interesting polyphonic devices and a subtle feeling for instrumental means of expression; all this was organically welded into one artistic whole, permeated by a unity of feeling and thought, ingenuous and spontaneous in its musical embodiment.

Most of Tartini's manuscripts are to be found in the music archives of the San Antonio chapel in Padua; some of his works are in other archives, others have not been discovered to this day. Only a very small part of his musical heritage has been published. The first collection of Tartini's concertos appeared in 1728 in Amsterdam; it was there that his sonatas were first published, four years later.

In addition to the main body of his compositions for the violin and those in which there are violin parts, Tartini left us a few odd compositions for viol da gamba, for cello and for flute.

Tartini's gifts are most distinct in his violin music, which he performed himself and had his numerous pupils perform.

No accurate description of his performance has come down to us. Knowing the traditions of the times, we may be sure that it must have added considerably to and enriched the content of what has reached us in the form of written music. His creativity as a composer and violinist materialized in the unity of his activity in both fields, an activity which incorporated his creative imagination (flights of fancy), his inspiration and skill. His capacity for profound feeling, his ability to express these feelings in his art, the gift of artistic imagination and a tendency to think, musically, in terms of pictures determined the content and character of the work of this talented violinist and composer.

Tartini was undoubtedly at one with the advanced musicians of the time who upheld the well-known esthetic teaching, later called the theory of "affects," whose source can be traced back to ancient times.[6] The supporters of this theory tried to reflect strong feelings, stirrings of the soul "emotional states" in their music. As Romain Rolland remarked, "at that time they had come to a clear realization of the expressive and descriptive force of music."[7] Both composers and performers strove for a "correspondence between music and affect" *i.e.,* truthfulness of expression. And if, as a result of the narrowness of their historical outlook, some of them thought of affects without any regard to their development (as did Quantz with his "principal affects" or Geminiani with his naive idea that practically every ornament was associated with a certain affect), others, among them Tartini (Luigi Boccherini, too), strove to rise above this narrow-minded and mechanistic conception, for they understood the need for a "joint accord of movement" between music and affects, in other words, their life and development.

At all events, in his creative work Tartini adhered to the most progressive interpretation of the affects theory existing in the 17th and 18th centuries, which "in musical art was the theoretical expression of the growing interest . . . in emotional life and its artistic depiction."[8] Together with Luigi Boccherini, his younger contemporary and compatriot, he might have said, "I know well that music is made to speak to man's heart; that is what I am trying to achieve, if I can: music devoid of feeling and passion is insignificant."[9]

Tartini's distinctive way of thinking and feeling in pictures told on all of his artistic work and in particular can be observed in the original, programmatic features so peculiar to his music. The imagery in the way of musicians' thinking in the 17th and especially the 18th century led them to search for a source of inspiration and mood, for a concrete support for their creative imagination, and this took on a different shape for each of them. Some found a stimulus for their creative work in paintings, others in literature, still others in conscious and not infrequently artificial excitement of emotions and ideas.

Thus, for example, Biber prefaced his violin sonatas (1674)[10] with painted miniatures of a biblical nature ("Mysteries from the Life of Mary"), using them as a kind of epigraph; they served as sustenance for his creative flights of imagination.[11] Vivaldi placed a sonnet before each of the concertos of his eighth opus (1725) bearing the programmatic names of "Spring," "Summer," "Autumn" and "Winter," and he conveyed the content of the sonnet in music by making wide use of devices imitating sounds.

When about to begin composing music, Geminiani would try to stir his imagination by imagining to himself profoundly emotional, dramatic or even tragic events that gave rise to some affect or other. He considered it beneficial not only before composing but also before performing to stimulate his feelings and arouse his imagination by reading some truly great poetical work. The spirit of the times caused him to understand the connection between affect and creative work in a somewhat mechanistic fashion, but behind this conception lay a progressive desire to express feelings and passions in his music.

This desire in musicians to find a support for their compositions in affects aroused by poetical word images was to a great extent shared by Tartini both as composer and as performer.

According to his contemporaries, Algarotti and Arteaga, he drew inspiration from reading Petrarch's poems. Another contemporary and compatriot of Tartini's, Fanzago, declares that the musician was especially enthusiastic about the romantic dreams of Metastasio,

Tartini's house in Padua

Giuseppe Tartini

Petrarch

whose plots and librettos were used in the 18th century by Araja and Paisiello, Berezovsky and Bortniansky, Myslivecek and Mozart, in the operas they wrote.

Tartini prefaced some of his works by verses by Metastasio and other authors, whose names for the most part have not been established (that some of these verses are by Tartini himself is also a possibility). In a number of his violin concertos he wrote the verses beneath or above the music, showing the rhythmical correlation of the syllables and the notes.

It is here that we get an insight into Tartini's artistic methods and into his way of understanding the "affect theory." Although the programmatic quality of Tartini's music was far from assuming the form of concrete images that it had acquired from Vivaldi, and although, unlike Vivaldi, Tartini hardly ever went in for picture or sound imitation, this "programmaticality" can occasionally be felt in his titles. It is to be found in the names of Tartini's violin sonatas: *The Devil's Trill, Didona Deserted,*[12] *The Emperor* and *The Dear Shade.*

But compared to Vivaldi, Tartini's programmatic leanings are less obtrusive, less noticeable to the listener. They are doubtless more closely bound up with the musician's personal feelings, which he had no wish to reveal or make explicit to the listener; they are more subjective, at times intimate. Tartini's individuality in this respect is also due to the fact that the programmatic in his work is conveyed, not by means of outer, external representation in sounds, but only by the general mood of the music, by its warmth and emotion, and lyricism and romantic elation peculiar to it.

The listener might find considerable aid from promptings in the mottoes used by Tartini or in his writing beneath the text. As a rule, he put these verses in cipher, cautiously concealing the real state of his feelings, expressing them with the help of music alone. This speaks of Tartini's modesty as a musician and artist, his sensitivity, his aversion to imposing upon others the innermost programmes of his compositions.

Tartini wrote these mottoes in verse in a cipher he himself invented, and for some two hundred years it remained a mystery to investigators and gave rise to all kinds of stories, which intensified the mystical element in depictions of Tartini, exaggerated though it already was. It was only a little over thirty years ago that Tartini's cipher was cleverly decoded by Minos Dounias, a Greek violinist and musicologist.[13] The interesting find is that the vast majority of the verses that acted as an inspiration to the ecclesiastical musician, as Tartini's post proclaimed him to be, were wholly secular and lyrically subjective as to subject matter; some are deeply lyrical, others dreamy and idyllic in mood, still others spirited and romantic.

One explanation of Tartini's ciphered mottoes probably lies in the fact that he was simply in no position to disclose the worldly nature of the conception and musical realization of works that were designed for performance in church. In many of Tartini's musical compositions there is a contradiction between the secular, democratic content and the "ecclesiastical" form, which Tartini was able to fill with new matter expressive of human emotions and moods.[14]

In Tartini's music there is no direct depiction of the mottoes he gives; here it is only a question of conveying the nature of the affect expressed in the verses or aroused in him when he read them, a question of the musical embodiment of a mood created by the poetic image.

The piece of poetry written in under the music naturally determined the metrical and rhythmical make-up of the tune; sometimes it affected the intonations, which then bore a resemblance to the intonations of expressive speech.

Here are some examples of Tartini's mottoes, which are to be found in over twenty of his concertos and in many of his sonatas as well: "For God's sake, my dear idol, do not treat me cruelly and ungratefully; as it is, heaven is making me pitiful and miserable" (the Andante of a violin concerto); "My dear one, remember, if I should happen to die, how devoted to you was my soul" (the Grave of a violin sonata); "Spreading out his net beneath the leaves, the hunter hid himself and blew his horn sweetly" (a pastoral part in a violin concerto); "The swallow returns from afar in the spring to see its nest again" (a pastoral scene in a violin sonata); "I was dreaming by the lake and waiting for the wind to abate; but I felt I was still enthralled by the storm" (a violin sonata); "Seized with the horror of the storm" (the Allegro of a violin sonata), etc.

The fact that Tartini turned to poetic images is a manifestation of his desire to attain a maximum of expression, to break through the abstract and scholastic da chiesa norms of the baroque epoch and to assert the principles of a new, profoundly humane and democratic musical style.

A considerable role in Tartini's compositions was played by the influence of folk music. The intonations of folk songs, the characteristic rhythms of folk dances and even the specific features of folk performance (with the improvising peculiar to it) were used by him in his own creative interpretation.

He gave considerable space to folk songs in his *Treatise on Music*, written in 1750. "Each nation," he writes, "has its own songs, many of which arose from old tradition, though many are created afresh in harmony with the prevailing spirit. As a rule, they are extremely simple; one might even remark that the simpler and more natural they are, the better they are assimilated."[15]

Tartini's interpretation of Italian folk songs and dance music that were particularly close to him in spirit and artistic taste was sensitive and lively. Much of his music absorbed their expressive tunes

Tartini monument, Piran

Title page of Leopold Mozart's *Violinschule*

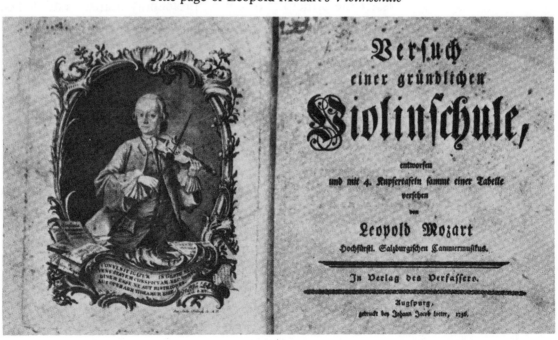

Pietro Metastasio

Tartini manuscript with his cipher

and enchanting rhythms. Having once heard from a Venetian gon-
dolier an appealing improvised and melodious song, he wrote it
down at once. Here is one of these jottings by Tartini:

Adagio quasi Recitativo

On another occasion the sensitive and impressionable musician
heard some gondoliers singing a song with words from a poem by
Torquato Tasso, the 16th century Italian poet.[16] Tartini put down
this song and included it as the introductory movement of one of his
solo sonatas for the violin (the second sonata in C major, according
to Brainard[17]), and he wrote Tasso's text under the notes:

Aria del Tasso

It is this tune, somewhat modified and with the same text from
Tasso written under the notes, that is used to open the third movement of Tartini's Sonata in D major (the Second D major Sonata according to Brainard):

Aria del Tasso

In both sonatas these movements are called "Aria del Tasso." It is
of interest to note that the second movement of the first of these
sonatas is based on a Venetian song; the movement is in fact entitled
Canzone Venetiana:

Canzona Venetiana

In the second of the sonatas referred to above, the "Aria del Tasso" is followed immediately by the Furlana; the use of the tune of this Italian folk dance, which was at that time very widespread, bears witness once more to the democratic leanings in Tartini's musical idiom:

Furlana

Tartini was greatly interested in the music of other nations too. He had always felt the appeal of Slavonic folk songs and dances. As has already been said, as a child he would listen entranced to the music and singing of the Croats and Slovenes that inhabited his native Istria. In later years, when Tartini spent the summer months with his relatives in Pirano or Strunjan, he no longer confined himself to direct emotional perception of the ingenuous Slavonic songs or folk dancing with their characteristic rhythms; he analyzed their peculiarities and used them in his own interpretation.

A Croat authority, F.X. Kuhac, finds intonations.[18] In the treatise referred to, Tartini enlarges upon the Dalmatian folk songs that according to him "have no definite intervals, but flow in a prolonged, improvised tune, now rising, now falling."[19]

Very likely it is the folk music of the southwestern Slavs that Tartini draws upon in his use of improvised melodic phrases with an augmented 2nd, which according to him creates an "excellent impression."[20]

Fine examples of this are to be found in the following passages from the first movements of concertos No. 114 and No. 28 and the finale of concerto No. 115:

Folk elements in Tartini's work, especially Slavonic, are evident not only in the song-like tunes, but also in the characteristic dance rhythms. In his *Treatise on Music* Tartini points out several times the folk origin of dancing and its significance for the development of music.

Interesting examples of dance tunes and rhythms that are in the Slavonic spirit can be found in the first movement of Tartini's Concerto in E major (No. 46):[21]

Another instance of Tartini's Slavonicisms is the beginning of his Concerto No. 111 in A minor, written in his first period. Both the rhythmical pattern and the intonation structure point to Slavonic folk influences:

11 **Allegro assai**

The interest that Tartini entertained for folk music and its strong appeal for him are undoubtedly related to his innate urge towards natural simplicity and imitation of nature. He considered that both the folk song and folk dancing were born of nature, as opposed to all that was artificial. "Ma la natura ha più forza dell' arte," ("but nature is stronger than art"), he writes in his Treatise. He especially values the simplicity of expression peculiar to folk music, because it is "closest to nature."[22]

Here Tartini speaks with the voice of his epoch (many of his ideas are similar to those of his French contemporary Jean-Jacques Rousseau) as one of the musicians who did so much towards overcoming the conventions and canons of the art of the preceding period to help in the birth of a new art, democratic and profoundly humane.

In doing this, Tartini, as can be seen in particular from his *Treatise on Music,* was guided by the "buon gusto" (good taste) that was born of human nature and controlled by the human mind. It is worthy of note that Tartini recognizes the change that "good taste" undergoes with the development of human society; thus, he takes account of the difference between the "good taste" of ancient times and that of his own time, the eighteenth century.[23]

Christoph Willibald von Glück

In looking to nature for a model in art, Tartini displays his comparatively progressive interpretation of the well-known imitation theory, one that is close to the views of his younger contemporaries, the French Encyclopedists, and also to those of Glück and Grétry. Naturalism is alien to him; he shows an understanding of the creative essence of art, and there are realistic tendencies in the way he seeks support in nature and in live human emotions.

In turning to a discussion of Tartini's works, we must recall that in his time the art of improvisation was of considerable significance, and that this was only partially designated in the music and in a very relative way at that. One can imagine how much more colorful, lively and expressive Tartini's own execution of his work must have been as compared with what was merely printed on paper. It was the

Tartini monument in Piran

Tartini's birthplace

Torquato Tasso

Maddalena Lombardini

dynamic coloring and timbre, the agogic shifts, the varied strokes, the manner of playing the ornaments, chords and arpeggios, the cadences, etc., that lent real life to the music and the artistic images in it.

Together with all this, when one listens to Tartini's music one senses a lively feeling for form that is peculiar to him, a feeling that is at the same time logically meaningful; it is this that accounts for the classical grace of his music.

The main forms of music used by Tartini were the concerto, the solo sonata (with and without bass) and the a tre and a quattro sonatas. His contribution towards their development was considerable.

THE CONCERTOS

In the main, one can agree with Minos Dounias, who did research into Tartini's music and divided his work into three main periods, the first from 1721 to 1735, the second from 1735 to 1750 and the third including the last twenty years of his life.

This division is justified by the fact that each period is characterized by specific features. However, in adopting it, borderlines of the periodization should be accepted with reservations, for there are certain peculiarities of Tartini's style that run through the whole of his creative work, from beginning to end. Among them are such features as the expressiveness, lyricism and fineness of his melodic line, the logical grace of form, the exceptional conformity of the means of expression, not only to the musical content but also to the nature of the instrument as well. It goes without saying that these qualities were not resistant to change; in many ways they developed within the framework of each of these roughly outlined periods.

Out of the hundred and twenty-five violin concertos by Tartini listed in Dounias' thematic catalogue, forty-eight belong to the first period, which was one of creative penetration and generalization of the attainments of the Italian violin school in the 17th and 18th centuries. For all Tartini's originality in his musical gifts and way of thinking, this is a period in which he continued a trend that was related to Corelli and his school. One might say that Tartini summed up all that had been accomplished by the Bologna and Roman violin schools over many, many years. In this period, without doubt, he also made a careful study of Vivaldi's work, especially the form of the concerto that the latter had been bringing to perfection. The interest that Veracini's art aroused in him was already noticeable. His acquaintance with this talented compatriot's perfect technique in playing the violin could not but leave its mark on a man like Tartini, who was so sensitive to all that had any bearing on his musical ambitions, and to a certain degree this affected the technical side of his own compositions.

Tartini paid special attention to the technique of his instrument in his compositions of the thirties, whereas in the twenties he had occupied himself largely with matters of form. His investigations in the first period produced much that is of interest from this point of view. The number of tutti and soli in the fast movements is not fixed, although more often than not there were the four tutti and three soli that were later to become conventional.

Tartini's compositions of the first period already display the opening or outlining of new perspectives that later influenced the development of the image-content, the musical idiom and the means of expressive violin technique.

The concertos of this period still retain features of church style that appear now in the severity of the general character of the music, now in the elements of restrained passion, now in the fugued structures and the imitations, which at times resembled Corelli's style:

In music composed in this period Tartini not infrequently makes use of an extremely simple type of imitation in which only two violins take part, the second imitating the first and playing a third lower:

A curious thing is the modal, melodic and rhythmical kinship of the piece cited above, the beginning of Tartini's Violin Concerto No. 60 that was written in the 1720's, to the beginning of Boccherini's Cello Sonata that appeared forty years later:[24]

It is not difficult to find elements in Tartini's compositions that resemble Corelli's work in intonation and rhythm. Suffice it to refer to Tartini's frequent use of a rhythm and intonation figure repeated in sequences with syncopation in the second half, a device characteristic of Corelli. For instance, let us compare the first bars of the Allemande in Sonata Op. 5 (No. 8) by Corelli and the Concerto in A major (No. 90) by Tartini:

At this early period we already find in Tartini's work the lyricism, fervor and energy of musical idiom that characterized Vivaldi. For example, it is not at all difficult to catch the closeness between the first movement of Vivaldi's well-known violin Concerto in A minor and the first movement of Tartini's Concerto in A minor (No. 111):

This was a period during which Tartini was advancing beyond the "church" style and developing "chamber," worldly, democratic elements in his music. These elements stand out distinctly in the expressive, unaffectedly lyrical, at times elegaic sphere of the middle slow movements, with their romantic imagery that are permeated with features of the dance movements of the suites (courante, jig, minuet, gavotte, Siciliana) in which one can easily trace a closeness to folk sources:

"After returning from Prague [*i.e.*, in 1726–L.G.] Tartini attempts to give more depth to the emotional content of his music," Antonio Capri says of the composer. "His Adagio in particular acquires a more intense singing quality. Due to its melodious expressiveness, the highest voice comes more and more to the fore, with clearer details. The increasing musical completeness of the Adagio lends it a new poetical meaning, and this brings it close to Vivaldi."[25]

However, one cannot speak here so much of a closeness to Vivaldi's style; it is more of a creative and independent interpretation, a development of Tartini's own leanings towards a poetic way of thinking in images.

The fact that Tartini turned very early on to a three-movement form of the concerto—fast, slow, fast—as had Vivaldi, was undoubtedly progressive. This is the form that Tartini used for most of the hundred and twenty-five violin concertos listed in Dounias' thematic catalogue.[26]

Like Vivaldi, Tartini's form of the violin concerto was still very close to that of the concerto grosso (in fact it is sometimes difficult to distinguish the one from the other). However with Tartini there began to take shape from the very beginning a type of specifically solo violin concerto: the violin is used as a solo instrument, accompanied by string orchestra, with the addition of a keyboard instrument (usually the organ) to play the part of a general bass. True, later Tartini hardly used a general bass, especially in solo episodes, since the fullness of sound of a quartet renders it superfluous. As compared with Vivaldi's, Tartini's concertos are distinguished by a tendency to limit the role of tutti and enhance the importance of the solo instrument.

A certain role in Tartini's instrumentation was also played by such factors as the instruments that made up the orchestra in the Santo chapel and the acoustics of the basilica. The bow quartet, whose voices were gaining greater and greater equality, could naturally be complemented by hautboys and French horns.

Tartini saw no impediment to his creative imagination in the three-movement concerto cycle that was a tradition with him. Within the limits of this form—in the first and most effective Allegro of the slow and usually lyrical middle movement and in the lively finale that bears so strong an affinity to folk music—he shows great originality and a wealth of creative thought and feeling.

Extremely characteristic of his first period is his Concerto in E major (No. 46) that has come down to us in the form of an autograph. This early work of Tartini's is already marked by expression in its thematic material, by skillful composition, by elegance of structure and clarity of form, which is that of a three-movement cycle combining the qualities of contrast and unity.

The first Allegro is built upon a theme with a lively, spirited rhythm that sets the tone, a joyous one for the whole movement (see example 9). The syncopated rhythms that are used extensively after this (and that are characteristic of the finale as well) underline the gaiety and grace of the music which without any doubt reflects folk influences (see examples 10, 22):

One cannot fail to notice the Slavic nature of the dance tunes and rhythms in the main theme of the movement (see example 9) and particularly in its further development (see example 10). We shall come back later to the Slavic elements in Tartini's work, but in the meantime let us note that they already constantly recur in his first period (see, for instance, the theme of the finale in his Concerto No. 111).

The second movement of the Concerto in E major (the Adagio in B major) is written in the rhythm of a Siciliano:

This is an example of Tartini's simple, expressive melody. Above the solo part of the text it says: "In the sea, in the forest, in the stream did I seek my idol, and I found him not." True, the simplicity and directness of the melodic line is somewhat broken by violin passages and ornaments, which was characteristic of Tartini's work at this period. We may note that in this movement the concertante instrument is accompanied only by two violins (or a violin and a viol) with no bass part.

The Adagio ends with a short cadenza ("in a single breath") by the solo violin:

This recitative makes the beginning of the lively, rhythmically stressed finale stand out in contrastive, which corresponds to the mood of the first movement; it has the same animation and spirit:

In this movement the downward motion of the harmonic melodies is interesting:

In this example one's attention is attracted by the original designations for the dynamics (piano, più forte) which confirm the fact that at this period Tartini was already making use of the crescendo effect. With respect to dynamic shades, Tartini was in no way behind Geminiani and Veracini, who used special graphical signs in the thirties and forties to indicate loudness and softness. At the end of the finale he wrote out an expanded thirty-two-bar solo cadenza ("a capriccio")[27] in which the virtuoso capacities of the violin were used brilliantly.

In his first period Tartini makes frequent use of such capriccios (especially in the finale of his concertos). These are at times lengthy episodes (sometimes growing into independent movements) in which a variety of ornaments are extensively used (figured passages, trills, grace-notes, turns, arpeggios, etc.). Unlike Locatelli, Tartini constructs his capriccios on a thematic foundation, which he elaborates skillfully (sometimes polyphonically), enabling the performer to display his own virtuosity in the process of developing the musical idea. In a number of his concertos Tartini restricts himself to marking "a capriccio" in the manuscript, allowing the performer to improvise on the theme.

Below we give an example of this original capriccio of Tartini's from the finale of the Concerto in E major (No. 46) that we have just been discussing:

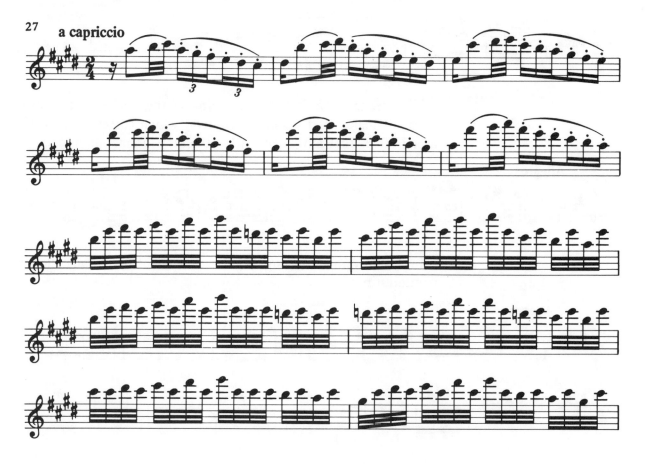

Cadenza

The capriccio leads directly to a sixteen-bar coda that rounds off the whole concerto. Sometimes Tartini finished his capriccios with cadenzas (short virtuoso constructions based on the dominant were unconnected with the thematic contents of the work).

In the 18th century, as we know, cadenzas were gradually growing into broad improvisations, thus breaking with their original basis of the work. For performers without taste or senses of proportion they became an end in themselves, a way of showing off their virtuosity at the expense of the integral artistic conception of the work.

In his *Treatise on Ornaments* Tartini condemns such cadenzas, which are closer to capriccios, although he admits that since they please the listeners one must be able to play them. Minos Dounias has established that there are no capriccios in Tartini's work after 1740.

To conclude this review of Tartini's Concerto in E major it must be stated that in both the fast movements the part of the violin is marked by a distinctly expressed virtuosity which intensifies the vitality of the music. The performer must above all have complete mastery of the bow and the various strokes (including the "flying staccato"), high positions, passage technique and doublestops.

Concerto in B minor (No. 124) is close in style to this work. The themes of the movements (Allegro, Grave, Allegro) are shown in the following example:

Especial expressiveness, pathos and warmth characterize the middle movement.

Among the very few modern editions of Tartini's concertos of this period is the Concerto in A major (No. 92) edited by Robert Reitz,[28] including his own cadenza in the first movement. This version is apparently close to the original. In the second (slow) movement, where the editor offers a version that is an attempt at reconstructing the type of performance of the Adagio that was current during Tartini's lifetime, he accompanies it by the composer's original text. In performing this kind of music Reitz undoubtedly enriched it by livening the melodic line with ornaments of his own improvising, in accordance with the esthetic principles of the times.

The concerto consists of an Allegro ma non molto, an Adagio and an Adagio assai. The first movement, with its four tutti and three soli, is full of the joy of life, and this is emphasized by the character of the melody, by the varied, occasionally syncopated rhythms and the frequent use of trills. The tuneful and thoughtful Adagio contrasts well with the extremely animated movements, after which the merry, graceful finale stands out in high relief:

The following example is the beginning of the Adagio in the contemporary edition of R. Reitz:

One of the best concertos of Tartini's first period is Concerto in D major (No. 51) which has been re-issued in our times by Michelangelo Abbado, with the original cadenzas.[29] Here are the opening themes of the three movements:

The appeal of this concerto comes from the extreme care with which it was written, the great perfection of form that was exceptional for the period. The developed soli with their distinct outlines that make it impossible not to feel the solo nature of the concerto (a feeling enhanced by Tartini's own cadenzas in the very fast movements), and the varied yet unified content of the cycle make this work well worth including in the modern performer's programme.

The first movement, the Allegro (or, as Abbado calls it, the Allegro deciso), in which Antonio Capri discerns elements of Handel, is light-hearted and sunny. The following episode with its shift to A minor (a kind of second subject) forms a striking artistic contrast to the first subject:

Then follows an Andante written in a parallel (relative) minor key (called Cantabile by Dounias and Grave by Abbado), one of the most expressive movements in the Paduan master's concertos; its appeal lies in its warmth and sincerity, coupled with its exalted fervor, in which Capri remarked a concentration that he likened to that of Bach.

The finale (an Allegro, called Allegro Grazioso by Abbado) is a lively jig with frequent polyphonic devices.

Below are Tartini's original cadenzas for the fast movements of this concerto:

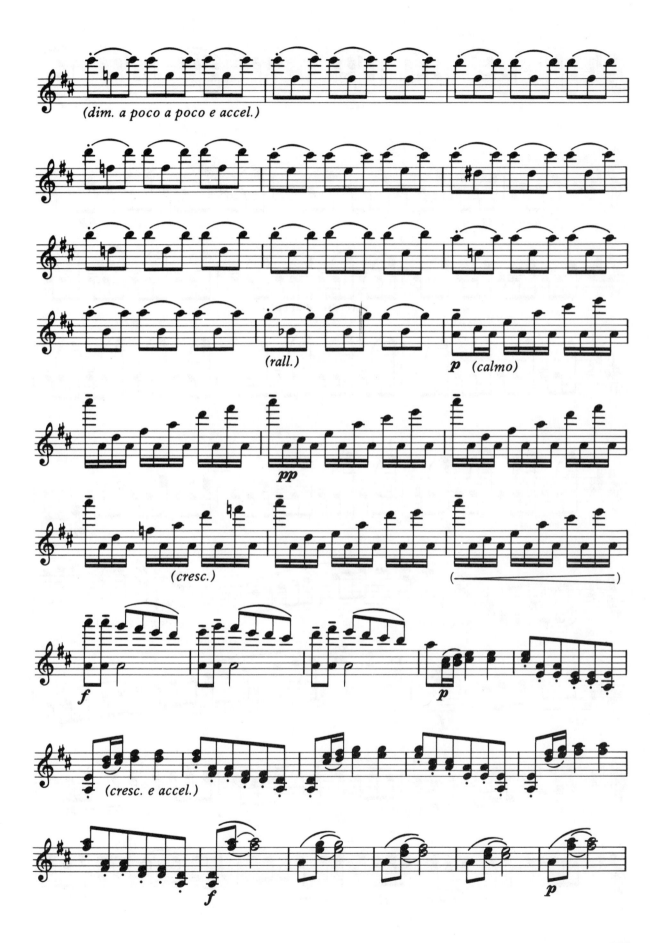

83

84

It was in the second period of his work as composer (1735-1750), when he arrived at artistic maturity and reached his creative peak, that Tartini to a great extent discarded his adherence to baroque. Both the concertos and the sonatas of this period are more profound in content and more perfect in form; in many ways they herald an approach to the 18th century classical style.

His melodic line became more flexible and plastic, his themes and images more clearly outlined; the predominant importance of the sequential "threading" of motifs, imitation formulae and "fugued" constructions gradually receded. A certain role in this process was played by influences emanating from the opera, to which Tartini himself was no alien, though he never composed in this genre.[30] In speaking of the influence of the opera, one must bear in mind that this applied not only to bel canto, but equally instrumental overtures and entr'acte music, or as it was called, symphonies (sinfonia), and to dances as well. Dynamic means of expression, syncopated rhythms, the so-called "Lombard style" and even such devices as the trill, to say nothing of the expressive "speaking" pauses woven organically into the melodic line, were all largely used in operas of the Neapolitan and other Italian schools. This could not fail to show, to some extent, in the compositions of a musician as sensitive to the esthetic demands of the time as Giuseppe Tartini.

In the thirties Tartini had paid tribute to the development of virtuoso principles; subsequently he paid more and more attention to depth—and not only depth, but also artistic simplicity—in expressing human feelings. In 1743 his friend Gianrinaldo Carli (1720-1793), professor of astronomy at Padua University, who was also born in Istria, wrote that Tartini placed nature above all else as an object for study by the artist; at the same time Tartini "showed me that art was capable of portraying human passions and arousing them."[31]

These trends were naturally a response to the needs of the constantly growing numbers of listeners and were a sign of the direction in which the composition of music was going towards democratization, towards clarity, simplicity and expressiveness of the musical idiom, which was capable of acting upon the sensibility of the human soul.

In the flowing, plastic melodies of Tartini at this period, of special importance are the influences of folk melos, and in particular the intonations peculiar to Slavic folk music, which, as has already been said, were felt at times in his earlier works.

Reacting to the dispute between the supporters of the gusto melodico melodic style and the supporters of the (gusto armonico) (harmonic style) which was characteristic of this epoch, Tartini inclined to the former, especially in his second period, and made many original contributions to the development of melodic expression and the melodic formation of subjects. In a number of his compositions he attempted to overcome the "squareness" (the eight-bar structure) of the theme, its thematic sequentiality, its abstract fugued character; his themes became more expressive and individualized. The emotive elements of expression that characterize the theme were given greater depth and clearer outline, whatever the theme, whether in the style of vigorous march, lyrical contemplation or a graceful dance. The sphere of thematic ideas was itself broadened, and this Tartini achieved by making the themes poetical and by using his inventive powers in the fields of melody and rhythm. All this undoubtedly contributed to the democratization of the gifted musician's work.

A contemporary of Tartini's, the well-known French music writer and cellist Charles Henri de Blainville, showed a preference for expressive music close to nature, in the style he called "genre cantabile," to which he said Tartini's music belonged. He wrote: "There are works of purely instrumental music that are so true that they seem to have been prompted by words, feelings, images or pictures: it is thus that I visualize the music of Tartini, whose truthful language of musical phrases is based on the purest melody and his skill in making the violin sing."[32]

We find the opinion of this subtle and observant 18th century musician fully justified upon acquaintance with the works of the mature Tartini, with the concertos and sonatas of his second period.

There is nothing accidental in Tartini's desire at this time to use

Wolfgang Amadeus Mozart

more modest techniques and modes of expression. This in the final analysis is also connected with his growing desire to be closer to nature, to find simple and natural ways of expression. "I try to be as close as possible to nature," he wrote to his friend, the poet Algarotti, in 1749, "I do not recognize as art what does not imitate nature."[33]

At this time Tartini would often desist from using the highest positions, frequent doublestops, speedy tempi and conspicuously florid ornaments, which he now used only when their character and proportion corresponded to the affect. Simplicity and purity in expressing feelings and thoughts meant cutting down merely virtuoso devices. This occurred at a period of life when he was one of the best violinists. His fame had spread far beyond the borders of Italy, and he was renowned for his complete mastery of the art not only of singing expressively on the violin, but also of finding the greatest ease in surmounting difficulties encountered by the virtuoso.

With the deepening of expression in Tartini's compositions the role of dynamics increased substantially. In this he followed the same path as his compatriots Veracini and Geminiani. According to the theory of affects in music (both operatic and instrumental) dynamic nuances were no longer limited to contrasts (the "echo" effect); so-called "terraced" dynamics appeared, and after that gradual shifts. There can be no doubt that in his search for the greatest possible musical expression, the closest possible approach of music to human nature, human emotions and the expression of human speech, Tartini used varous dynamic colors. True, in his manuscripts dynamic nuances were comparatively rarely marked (as, for instance, in Concertos Nos. 46, 54 and 115), which gave the performer a free choice.

As for the form of Tartini's concertos (those written in the years 1735-1750), it is, with certain exceptions, based on the conventional three-movement cycle. In most cases the first movement consists of four tutti and three soli with the tonal sequence Tonic-Dominant; Dominant-Tonic. In the forties Tartini frequently uses a reprise of the exposition of the first tutti and of the first solo instead of a new exposition.

In the main Tartini followed the monothematic principle in composing the first movement (the two-theme Sonata-Allegro crystallized in the work of his younger contemporaries, Mozart and Viotti, who created the classical violin concerto), but he resorted to a development of the elaboration part of the movement, whose center of gravity is usually found in the third tutti in the dominant or a parallel (relative) to tonality. The opening tutti was not limited to a simple preparation for the solo; it was now more independent, had more freedom and at times acquired its own meaning and emotional significance.

The second movement of the concertos of this period to a considerable extent lost a certain "academic" quality it had and sometimes also its dramatic monumentality. The movement became more lyrical and subjective, and this was reflected in the tempo notations at the beginning of the movement (Andante or Adagio cantabile instead of Adagio) and the concomitant mottoes ("Misera anima mia").

The element of virtuosity is concentrated in the part of the solo violin. The modest accompaniment is usually reduced to mere harmonic support and stands in sharp contrast to the rich tutti sound of the bow quartet (to which wind instruments are sometimes added).

After a careful study of the manuscripts of Tartini's concertos, Dounias actually cites only one case of orchestration for wind instruments.[34] This was the Concerto in D major (No. 39), in which the score of the accompanying orchestra consisted of the following voices: an hautboy, two horns, two violin parts, two viol parts and two bass parts (most likely cello and double bass). The exposition of the first movement of this concerto in the score (example 41) is of great interest, for it discloses Tartini's superb mastery of the technical modes of expression of the orchestra of his time; it was on a level with the orchestration of Sammartini and Boccherini, Stamic and Myslivecek. The example cited is evidence of the fact that Tartini was abreast of the times in this respect:

However, with few exceptions, Tartini remained true to his principle of a less "flamboyant" style in his use of orchestral accompaniment (less flamboyant for the period, naturally) and as a rule he confined himself to a bow quartet. This is largely explained by the very nature of his concerto music, which was lyrical and graceful and contained elements of improvisation in the ornamentation (especially in the slow movements). There is also some truth in Dounias' contention that the modesty of the accompaniment in Tartini's concertos was also due to the specific acoustic conditions in the Santo basilica.

To the second period of Tartini's work belongs his Concerto in D major (No. 28) for violin, bow orchestra and two French horns that were added later. It has come down to us in an edition by E. Bonelli,[35] and with the latter's cadenzas, as Concerto No. 57. The editor inserted in the score of the fast movements parts for two horns and a kettledrum (in addition to the parts for two french horns). The texts for the opening bars as given by Dounias and Bonelli differ in one or two places; it is most probable that the editors used different manuscripts:[36]

This concerto is one of those works of Tartini's that, for their musical qualities, well deserve to be brought back to the repertoire of the modern performer. It is simple, clear and yet expressive music. The vigorous, animated fast movements find a subtle contrast in the lyrical shades of the middle slow movement, which is in D minor.

Folk influences can be felt in this concerto. They can be heard in the characteristic intonations, rhythms and dynamic shades (the "echo"). It is interesting to note the use in all the movements of an augmented 2nd (an example of which has already been cited from Tartini's Concerto in A minor (No. 114)); this lends special expression to his melodic line and is an indication of his bonds with folk melos of the southwestern Slavs.

Of the modern publications of Tartini's concertos in his second period we might likewise single out his Concerto in E major for violin and bow orchestra (No. 53), which has reached us in Hermann Scherchen's edition.[37] The fast movements are full of the joy of life. They are related thematically by their intonation basis—a tonic triad in a major key. The first movement, the Grandioso (Allegro in the original), has, especially in the ritornello tutti, a flavor of hunt music (caccia) and recalls the sound of the hunter's horn or fanfare:

In this movement the episodes with digressions into neighboring minor keys (C-sharp minor, F-sharp minor) are most expressive. The "echo" effect is characteristic of their dynamics.

The second movement, the Andante, is full of expression; its melodies are close to that of highly emotional speech. It reminds one of the musician's skill of "speaking" in the language of his instrument that is so greatly valued by the Italians:

The finale, the Allegro grazioso (Allegro assai in the original), contains elements of folk dance music and folk humor; it sparkles and radiates grace and elegance:

Tartini's third period, which embraces the last twenty years of his life (1750-1770), was given to the concerto. It is marked not by the quantity of music that he produced (of his hundred and twenty-five violin concertos only fourteen belong to this period), but by its quality.

The distinguishing features of the concertos of this period were characterized by a dignified simplicity and a plasticity and finish of the melodic line. Tartini's break with the treatment of the solo violin as an instrument for demonstrating brilliance in virtuosity (a break that began in the previous period) now became complete. It is most unlikely that this simplification of technique in Tartini's later concertos should be due mainly to the failing strength of the aging musician.

At this period Tartini's desire to get close to nature (whose laws he attempted to trace in music, too) and his desire for naturalness of expression—together with his reaction to the widespread excess of virtuosity of the times, to the overburdening of tunes with ornaments and to the "senseless coloraturas in vocal music" that Dounias justifiably refers to[38]—could not but show in the style of his later concertos.

While rejecting a certain ostentatiousness and floridity in the melodic line, Tartini infused more life into its harmonic setting, which became more varied and interesting at the modulation level (see concertos Nos. 42, 45, 54). Harmony began to play a more noticeable role in characterizing the musical images, and this sometimes unexpectedly lends features of romanticism to Tartini's pre-classical style. This is borne out by the appearance in his work of chromaticisms, plagal phrases, occasional juxtaposition of tonalities remote from each other and even dissonances.

The slow movements in his Concertos in C major (No. 14), D minor (No. 45) and A minor (No. 115) may serve as examples of the sincere expressiveness of Tartini's music in the third period. They are all in minor keys and are marked by flowing melody and pure, exalted lyricism:

Tartini's choice of key, as with many of his contemporaries, was guided by the affect which had been selected as the groundwork for the music. Most of his violin concertos (one hundred and nine of the hundred and twenty-five given by Dounias) were written in major keys, in accordance with the custom of the times. Let us recall that out of the twelve concerto grossi by Corelli only two are in minor keys, that all the concertos by Boccherini that have been preserved (for cello and for violin) are in major keys and that of all of Mozart's numerous concertos only two (for the pianoforte) are in minor keys.[39]

To offset this, the minor movements of the concertos in major keys (and sometimes even the minor episodes in the major movements) acquire a special charm by contrast; they are touchingly human and warm in their intonation and their unaffected sincerity. Folk intonations can be heard in the second movement (in A minor) of Concerto in A major (No. 109):

51 **Adagio**

A Larghetto in A minor from another Concerto in A major (No. 110) belonging to the third period also brings to mind folk intonations, possibly Slavic ones:

52 **Larghetto**

In his *Treatise on Music* Tartini himself characterizes the affect expressed in the minor key as being "languid, melancholy and sweet" ("L'armonia di terza minore e languida, malinconia è dolce") and the one in the major key as being "strong, joyful, bold" ("L'armonia di terza maggiore è forte, allegra, ardita").[40]

However, Tartini does not seem to have come at once to this differentiation of the expressive modes of the key (a differentiation undoubtedly connected with the "affect theory"), or else he did not always keep to it. One can judge this from the beginning of his violin Sonata in F major (Op. 1, No. 2). Here, in spite of the major key, Tartini emphasizes the sorrowful nature of the Adagio by using the special notation "lugubre."

In Tartini's last compositions there is a noticeable increase in the role of dynamics, to which he attaches great expressive significance. We have already noted the sparing use of dynamic notations in most of his manuscripts. Like Bach and many other composers of the 18th century, the choice of dynamic coloring was often left to the performer. However, Tartini himself as a violinist was said by his contemporaries to have made extensive use of various dynamic shades.

Whereas Tartini had mainly used the f and p signs for episodes with echo-like dynamics in concertos of the previous periods, he now used them more broadly in accordance with the particular musical phrase. Dounias cites an interesting example from the finale of the Concerto in E major (No. 54), in which a sudden "piano" in a cantabile episode of this fast movement helps to set off a harmonic shift:

As can be seen in the excerpt cited below from the first movement of the same concerto, Tartini uses here (while changing to a different key) a notation that is dynamic and esthetic in character, "dolce piano":

And this is how Tartini marks a phrase requiring a gradual dynamic increase:

In this example the notation "dolce" is also of interest for it is given after the "piano–forte–fortissimo" at the beginning of the fall of a melodic line immediately following a rise. Tartini himself did not write out the "crescendo" and "diminuendo" notations, although he used these dynamic devices in playing and required them of his pupils. However, we do come across the notations "piano–più forte" even in his works of the first period (as we have had occasion to see in the finale of his Concerto in E major (No. 46)).

True, even in his last compositions Tartini allows himself the use of the "echo effect" in repeating identical phrases, but as in the opening tutti in his Concerto in B minor (No. 125), for instance, the contrast is produced not as a sharp opposition ("forte—piano"), but as a softened counterpoise, which he marked as p and più p:

Some of the concertos of the last period are also extent in modern editions. Among them are a Concerto in D minor (No. 45) and one in A minor (No. 115).

The first of these has come out in an edition by Emilio Pente.[41] There is a disc with an excellent recording by Joseph Szigeti in an edition of his own.[42] This version contains cadenzas by Szigeti in which he displayed a subtle understanding of Tartini's style.

The concerto begins with an Allegro at a moderate pace; the first tutti is fairly well expanded and forms a kind of first exposition which is then further amplified by the solo violin. The music in this movement has sweetness and warmth combined with inner animation. In the theme itself one can hear the intonations of expressive speech, which sometimes acquire a lively, elevated and pathetic character:

A rhythmical enrichment of the texture lends life to the music:

There is a great appeal in the sincerity and rare emotion (sensitivity) of the Grave in this concerto that is akin to the first movement of the *Devil's Trill* sonata; the music is heartfelt and elegiac:

At the same time the music in this movement has an exalted passion and a severity of melodic pattern that make it akin to Bach's grave and adagio.

The spirited finale (Presto) is not without an element of folk dance:

This concerto, which has been published again and again, has come down to us in an edition compiled according to an autograph by Rudolph Baumgartner.[43] In this edition all the editor's directions for the performer, written with a fine feeling for Tartini's style, are put in brackets. This gives the performer a clear idea of what the original manuscript (kept in the Paduan chapel) was like. The concerto in this edition was performed for the first time by Wolfgang Schneiderhan with the Swiss chamber music ensemble Festival String Lucerne led by Rudolph Baumgartner.

Joseph Szigeti's candenzas for this concerto[44] are the following:

Tartini's Concerto in A minor, published in 1929 by Mario Corti in his own edition, [45] is no less deserving of use than the preceding one both in modern teaching and in concert repertoires. While mainly keeping to the original, the editor made several changes in the texture of the orchestral part (the clavier), thus evincing a due understanding of Tartini's style.

This concerto too consists of three movements, but Tartini introduced a new element into the conventional pattern with his original and unusual construction of the first movement: two contrasting episodes alternate four times, one of them a lyrical and touching Andante cantabile and the other an energetic Allegro assai that is perhaps closer in spirit to Vivaldi than to Corelli:

True, we come across the division of one movement into several contrasting episodes in Corelli's music, too (in his first sonata from Op. 5, for instance); but while this was more likely the influence of the older canzona, with Tartini it was the result of his search for a new form. This may also be the explanation both of his intensification of contrast and of his introduction of elements of development, especially in his exposition of the second theme (Allegro assai). It is not difficult to discover a tendency in the first movement to resort to bithematicism, which had become an essential principle in the classical sonata form. Tartini himself used this structure of a movement in the finale of his *Devil's Trill* violin sonata, in which there is a triple contrast between the soft and poetic Andante and the energetic Allegro assai, emphasized by trills.

In the concerto we are now considering, the contrast is intensified not only by differences of tempo and meter (a three-beat rhythm in the Andante cantabile and a four-beat rhythm in the Allegro assai), but also by the specific features of the melodic line in both episodes reflecting the difference in their emotional content: the smooth downward motion at the beginning of the Andante cantabile, the lyricism and the "speaking" pauses in the second half, the energetic nature of the music and the determined rhythmically stressed movement of quavers in the Allegro assai, that are remote from each other.

Each new appearance of the two contrastive episodes in Tartini's music is by no means a literal repetition. While the Andante cantabile changes mainly in tonality, the second theme (the Allegro assai), is genuinely elaborated and expanded, especially the third and fourth times it appears.

The poetic and expressive Andante cantabile written in the minor dominant forms the second movement of the concerto:

64 **Andante cantabile**

The finale (Presto and in Corti's edition Allegro mosso) begins with a vigorous motion which alternates with smooth passages and dance rhythms that lend it the character of folk music.[46]

Giuseppe Tartini wrote several concertos for other instruments, too, which in style and form were close to his violin concertos. Of these, recent editions have been published of his concertos: in G major for the flute,[47] in A major for the cello and in D major for the gamba, the latter having been arranged for the cello in addition. The best known of them are the last two concertos, which have come down to us in several editions.

The concerto for the gamba and orchestra was most likely written during Tartini's stay in Prague and may have been intended for one of the Czech or foreign gamba players there.[48] We must recall that in Italy at the time the gamba was hardly used; additionally, the concerto genre was by no means characteristic for the gamba, for it was little suited to this instrument's modes of expression.[49]

The technique used in the Concerto in D major and in particular the negligible number of doublestops and chords, together with the total absence of the alto clef (so usual in compositions for the gamba), leads one to suppose that Tartini intended it for performance on the cello. At all events, Tartini's gamba concerto may be regarded as a chance interlude in his work.[50]

There exists a possibility that the cellist Antonio Vandini had earlier played the gamba (which may be deduced from the fact that in a picture of him that has been preserved, he is shown with his cellos, but holding the bow in the manner of a gamba player) or else he played both instruments, in which case Tartini's concerto might have been composed for Vandini.

Tartini included a bow quartet and two horns in the orchestra. The traditions of the time decreed that violas and horns participate only in tutti.

Unlike the majority of Tartini's concertos, the concerto for the gamba begins with a developed slow movement (Largo in Rudolf Hindemit's edition), followed by an Allegro, a Grave and the Allegro. Although the Largo may be regarded as an expanded preamble to the first Allegro, we still have a four-movement cycle which was most unusual for Tartini. The themes of all the movements are given below:

The artistic merits of the music of this concerto appeal to cellists to this day. This is particularly true of the "lyrical center" of the concerto, the Grave, which is marked by exceptional depth and feeling. This movement may also be performed as an independent piece. Incidentally, there is a phonograph recording of it in an inspired interpretation by Pablo Casals, who composed a short cadenza of his own for the movement.

The fast movements of the concerto are not without their virtuosity; the cadenzas at the end of each movement give it the character of concert music.

Below is the cadenza from the finale:

Whereas the concerto for the gamba is stylistically close to the concertos of Tartini's first period of work, the cello concerto probably belongs to the second period. It was published in 1937 according to the original, which is in the Music Archives of the Basilica of St. Antony in Padua (it is the only cello concerto by Tartini in this collection).[51] R. van Leyden, the publisher, considers that the concerto appeared around 1740. There are certain elements in the composition, especially in the fast movements, which indicate that the baroque style still felt in Tartini's first period was now a thing of the past, yet the presence of a basso continuo (cembalo) shows that there is a connection of this concerto with his first period.

The concerto was undoubtedly written by the composer for his friend Antonio Vandini and they probably performed it together time and again in the Santo chapel. There are both bow and keyboard instruments in the accompanying orchestra. According to the practice of the time, the first desks alone played solo parts; the violas took part only in the tutti sections.

The composition consists of three movements: a light, sparkling Allegro, with dotted rhythms, trills and echo-like dynamics to enhance its characteristic features; a lyrical Larghetto, with a shade of elegy, written in the corresponding minor key, A minor (the best part of the concerto); and the final Allegro assai, full of animation and grace:

Performers choose this concerto even today. After a hundred and fifty years of oblivion it was played for the first time according to the manuscript in Padua by Arturo Cuccoli (and conducted by O. Ravanello). In the edition by R. van Leyden mentioned above, it was first performed by Richard Krotschak, who added his own cadenzas.

The renewed interest in this concerto of Tartini's in our time was spurred on by the performance of it by many modern cellists. These performances show that the concerto occupies a merited place alongside concertos by Leo, Vivaldi and P.E. Bach in pre-classical cello music.[52]

To conclude our review of Tartini's concertos we quote his French contemporary, the well-known writer on music, Pierre-Louis Ginguené (1748-1816): "Giuseppe Tartini, who may rightly be called great, has accomplished a double revolution, both in the concerto style and in his performance on the violin. It is impossible to overestimate his noble and expressive tunes, his learned traits that are yet so natural and at one within the melodic harmony, his unbounded artistry in melodics without that spirit of slavishness and pedantry that are to be found even in Corelli himself, who engages in counterpoint more than singing; no carelessness, no affectation, no triviality; the majesty without pomp of his first allegros; the touching and pathetic expression in his adagio, the singing that you cannot but connect with feeling and in which you can hardly fail to notice the embodiment of human speech; lastly the prestos, brilliant and varied, animated, but without frivolity, merry, but without extravagance, such are in general the character and form of Tartini's concertos."[53]

THE VIOLIN SONATAS

According to Brainard's data there are nearly a hundred and seventy-five sonatas by Tartini for violin and bass.[54] In addition to these, he wrote numerous sonatas for solo violin and also trio and quartet sonatas.

Let us take his sonatas for violin and bass. While giving Tartini his full due as author of the violin concertos, Andreas Moser, historian of violin art and for many years assistant to Josef Joachim, writes: "It is his violin sonatas that are Tartini the composer's greatest glory. It is not only that they are of importance as the foundation of violin art; at the same time they represent the peak of 18th century Italian violin music. The fast movements show his almost inexhaustible powers of invention in the formation of plastic themes, and the slow movements have a rich bloom that is equally suitable in expressing profound sorrow and happy spiritual content under a clear blue sky. Added to this is the exemplary structure of the sonatas as a whole (they are for the most part restrained in form), and their great harmonic wealth, which is expressed in veritably amazing capriccioso phrases."[55]

The first collections of Tartini's sonatas were issued in Amsterdam in 1732, 1734 and 1743.[56] In spite of the fact that many reprints and new editions of the sonatas were published in Tartini's lifetime, [57] the bulk of his sonatas, like the concertos, are still in manuscript and have never appeared in print.[58]

On the whole, Tartini's sonatas might come under the same general three-period classification as his concertos,[59] but one must take into account not only the gradual evolution in the style of his music that cannot be fitted into strict chronological classes but also the specific features of the genre.

In his *Twelve Sonatas* that were published as Op. 1 by Le Cene in Amsterdam in 1734, Tartini followed the style and compositional devices characteristic of Corelli's sonatas Op. 5, as did the latter's pupils Geminiani and Locatelli. As we know, Tartini himself played these sonatas and used them in teaching.

According to Dounias, who made a study of Tartini's work, at that time: "Corelli's elevated style and elegiac pathos were closer to him than the passionate idiom of Vivaldi, from which he adopted the form alone."[60] But unlike Corelli's sonatas, in which the number of movements fluctuates between three and five, Tartini's sonatas, with few exceptions, have a three-movement cycle,[61] usually in a sequence of slow − fast − slow.[62]

In Tartini's scheme of slow − fast − fast he infringed the principle of agogic contrast by putting the two fast movements next to each other. He sought to contrast these two movements by making them different in character, in meter and in rhythm. Tartini's scheme was used by his fellow countrymen Locatelli and Boccherini, also by Stamic, Graun and Quantz in composing their sonatas.

Among the few exceptions in Tartini's three-movement sonatas are the 24th in G major, the 11th in A major and the 11th in A minor (according to Brainard),[63] which had a sequence of fast − slow − fast.

Unlike the concertos (in which the slow movement is in the dominant tonality or in the tonality of the parallel or relative minor), the opening tonality in Tartini's sonatas nearly always remains constant in all the movements.[64] However, the impression is not one of tonal monotony, for the exposition of the thematic material inside the movement is in the parallel or dominant tonality of the same keynote, with a return to the tonic at the end of the movement. For example, the tonal scheme Tonic-Dominant; Dominant-Tonic, which was characteristic of the old Italian sonata of the pre-classical period, is used quite often. Sometimes other contrasts in tonality are encountered; for instance, the second half of the second movement of the Sonata in B minor (in the edition by E. Pente and C. Angemini) begins in A major and it is only later, through D major, that it returns to B minor. In the more expanded sonatas there are clear signs of elements of development and recapitulation.

The guiding principle in Tartini's sonatas, as in his concertos, is contrast between the movements of the cycle and a tendency to use elements of contrast inside separate movements, which is a symptom of the approach of some of his sonatas to the classical style.

In the first six sonatas Tartini adheres to the more severe da chiesa style (though not so consistently as Corelli), whereas the second six contain features of the da camera style and are close to the suite genre. The last sonatas show a stronger individualization of the theme and features of subjective lyricism in the slow movements; the polyphonic structure of the fast movements gives way to a homophonic-harmonic structure and the first and second movements are given a primarily two-part construction.

The slow movement, especially in the first six sonatas, is in the form of a smooth-flowing introduction, sometimes dramatic in mood:

The Allegro that follows this retains Corelli's fugual style; it is the exposition of a fugue in three, sometimes in four, voices:

This movement sometimes ends in a short, slow coda (an Adagio), whose functions are to demarcate both Allegros and to act as a setting for the fast finale that follows it.

The latter is usually colorful and lively. It has a great deal of grace, features of folk dance and the motion of the jig. Tartini prefers a six-beat to a twelve-beat meter:

In Tartini's first twelve sonatas it is impossible not to feel his individual traits distinctly, and also the appearance, however hesitant as yet, of features belonging to a new, more democratic style (despite their undoubted relationship to the style of Corelli and the persistence of baroque elements).

Charles Burney wrote that Tartini "changed his style in 1744 from extremely complex to graceful and expressive."[65] This remark by Tartini's erudite contemporary is extremely significant. However, Dounias is right in not accepting an exact date (1744) for the appearance of the new style, separate features of which can easily be found in Tartini's works of an earlier period. These features continued to develop towards the point where the 18th century classical style was to crystallize. Tartini made a great contribution to the emergence of this style.

All traces of the division into the da camera (secular) and da chiesa (church) styles disappeared in Tartini's later sonatas. Tartini discarded the conventionalities of the da chiesa style, though he made creative use of some of the elements, and left behind the limitations of the dance suite, though making a similarly creative use of its folk elements. He created his own kind of violin sonata, the best of which came close to the classical instrumental sonata of the 18th century.

The most interesting of the *Six Sonatas* (Op. 2) published in 1743 (by Le Cene in Amsterdam) is the Sonata in E minor (the 7th in E minor according to Brainard). It has survived in the arrangement of E. Pente and is in the repertoire of David Oistrakh and other modern violinists. Its strength lies in its musical qualities, the moving lyricism of the first movement (Grave, and in Pente's version Largo), the radiance, grace and rhythmical variety of the second movement (Allegro, and in Pente's version Allegro Capriccioso e non Vivace) and the vigor and the folk-dance character of the finale (Presto). The following examples show the subject of all the movements of this sonata:

76 Grave

77 Allegro

78 Presto

It must be said that for all the liveliness and the alternately graceful or vigorous character of the fast movements, they do not lose the warmth and lyricism of the first Grave. This is what gives unity to the cycle while preserving the contrast between the separate movements.

The expression of the middle movement that is written in classical finished form is embodied in the intonations of the melodic line and in the rhythmically animated motion. It is emphasized by such notations (in Pente's arrangement) as grazioso, dolce, espressive, posato, sentito.

The greatest expression is to be found in the first grave, which comes close to the slow movements in the Bach concertos (to the middle movement in A minor of his Violin Concerto in E major, for instance). That Tartini himself liked this movement can be deduced from the fact that he transposed it into F sharp minor and made it into the middle movement of his Concerto in A major (No. 103).

The sonatas in Op. 2 show on the whole an increased tendency to have a singing quality and a stately simplicity. The movements with a dance-like character (the finales) become clearer and more finished. The solo violin part is given greater musical development while becoming more limited from the point of view of virtuoso proper. The bass part becomes simpler and figuration disappears; the role of the bass part is reduced to a harmonic support of the solo voice. The harmony itself is also somewhat simplified. Alteration continues to act as an important mode of expression but is more restricted in its use.

A great deal of what has been said about Tartini's concertos applies to his sonatas as well. This is true of the content, the form and the musical idiom. In the sonatas, just as in the concertos, one feels the great influence of folk music and this broadens the sphere of expression in Tartini's work.

The democratization and individualization of Tartini's music gave depth to the content. It is interesting to note the changes in the very principle of subject-formation which were especially characteristic of his second period. More and more often, Tartini moves away from a purely sequential repetition of the nucleus of the motive. In the late thirties he seeks to introduce some kind of modification of the ornament (expressive "speaking" pauses, a new shade, etc.), into each new appearance of the principal motive, even when the construction of the subject idea does retain elements of sequentiality.

Gradually the polyphonic style gives way in the fast movements to the monophonic. Tartini moves away from the fugal principle of constructing the allegro, replacing it with a two-movement form of reprise with a tendency to develop the three-movement classical allegro (the elements of variational repetition and of the rondo form become more distinct and original).

For the slow movements Tartini shows signs of a preference for the terms andante cantabile, aria cantabile (or simply cantabile), andante affettuoso, larghetto affettuoso (or simply affettuoso), etc., to the terms largo, adagio, grave, etc. This preference of his shows Tartini's desire for a more strongly emotional and esthetically meaningful style of music and of its exposition. We also see this desire in the names of the fast movements of his sonatas—allegro cantabile, allegro con spirito, tempo majestoso.

The jig is not the only dance form used by Tartini, although by far it is the most frequent. He also uses the Siciliana and the minuet and occasionally the gavotte and the furlana, while in the Sonata in A major (No. 23) (according to Brainard's catalog) he called the second movement "A la Francese."

The following are subjects from some of Tartini's other sonatas:

82

The following is an example of the so-called "speaking" pause:

83

One can get an idea of a later collection of Tartini's sonatas (Op. 5) from a modern edition in an arrangement by Bonelli.[66] There are six sonatas in the collection. Only one of them is in four movements, and all the others are in three. It is of interest to note that in sonatas with a fast—slow—fast sequence the middle slow movement is written in the parallel tonality (C major in the first Sonata in A minor and D minor in the fifth Sonata in F major).

The music of the Adagio in the fifth sonata is very expressive:

84

The finale of the first sonata is full of animation and grace:

85

The finale of the third Sonata in A major and that of the sixth Sonata in B-flat major are worthy of note. They are composed in the form of a subject with variations (there are eight variations in the first one and four in the second). The variations contrast in character, motion and texture. The following examples show the opening bars of the subject and variations from the finale of the sixth sonata:[67]

86

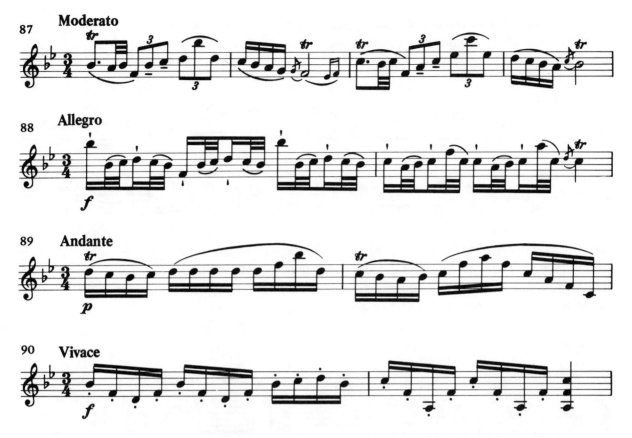

In the sonatas of the last period (remember, the division into periods is tentative) one can sometimes perceive a shade of secret pain, melancholy and resignation; but such moods are more often than not superseded by radiant lyricism, hope and vitality.

In the music of Tartini's later sonatas one can find a reflection of his desire for a deepening of expression, for simplicity and sincerity which are qualities that bring him close to the classical style.[68]

Let us examine in somewhat greater detail Tartini's two sonatas in G minor, the most popular in the repertoire of the violin.

The most interesting of his violin sonatas, which shows that even at a very early stage he was capable of compósing expressive music, is his Sonata in G minor (No. 10) from the first opus.

This sonata was given the romantic programme name of *Didone abbandonata (Dido Deserted);* in some editions it is preceded by a verse by Metastasio which had inspired him to compose the sonata. Many consider it in no way inferior to the *Devil's Trill,* although it does not actually come up to that sonata in depth, emotional fullness, psychological penetration or technical virtuosity.

Dido Deserted consists of three movements: an Affettuoso (an Andante or Larghetto in some editions), a Presto (with the addition of the words non troppo in some editions) and an Allegro (sometimes marked comodo). A number of arrangements give another slow movement between the two fast movements that is not in the original.[69]

The first movement has an appealing lyricism and stirring melos. Elements of pathos mingle with the moving sorrow of this movement:

91 **Affettuoso**

In this comparatiavely early sonata of Tartini's, ideas (images) and subjects are already to be found in the first movement placed side by side for the sake of contrast. Right after the stirring lyrical opening of the movement comes an episode in a major key with a scherzo-like sharpness that serves as a still brighter setting for the principal lyrical idea:

92 **Affettuoso**

And what a contrast is to be heard in the Presto non troppo following this movement! The contrast is achieved, in spite of the fact that it is a continuation in the former key, by the vigor and resolution of the music, its impetuosity and drive. Enrico Polo, who made an arrangement of the sonata, even discerns in this movement a "tragic fury":[70]

93 **Presto**

The finale is composed in the rhythm of the jig, but the dance character in it is softened by the preponderance of a smooth movement and the somewhat sorrowful shade of the music:

94 **Allegro**

110

The artistic merits of the sonata spring from the vivid imagery of its content, the expression in its musical idiom, its well-constructed form and the fact that it is exceptionally well suited to the nature of the violin with its cantilenic and virtuoso qualities. All this makes it eminently suitable for inclusion in both modern concert and teaching repertoires.

It is another sonata by Tartini that enjoys the greatest and undoubtedly the most deserved popularity. This is the Sonata in G minor that is also known by the programmatic name of *The Devil's Trill*. Tartini considered it his best work. J.J. de Lalande tells the following story that he heard from Tartini himself: "One night in 1713 he (Tartini — L.G.) dreamed that he had made a contract with the devil, who happened to be in his service. Whatever Tartini wanted was granted to him, and all his wishes were anticipated by his new servant, who gave him his violin to see if he could play anything harmonious. But what was Tartini's surprise when he heard a sonata so original and lovely and performed with such perfection and meaning that he could never have imagined anything like it! He experienced such amazement, admiration and delight that he was breathless; this strong emotion woke him up and he immediately seized his violin in the hope that he would be able to remember at least part of what he had heard, but in vain. The piece that Tartini composed then is indeed the best of all that he has ever done, and he calls it *The Devil's Sonata*. But the former one that amazed him was so much higher that he would have broken his violin and given up music forever if only he could have."[71]

Though this story would seem to indicate that the sonata appeared in 1713 when Tartini was barely twenty-one, the date justly arouses doubts in the minds of many of those who have made a study of his work (among them Andreas Moser, Antonio Capri and Paul Brainard).[72] Actually the artistic content of the sonata, the profundity and finish of its ideas, the harmony and originality of form and the manner in which technique is used all speak of the mature period in Tartini's work. Andreas Moser expresses the supposition that *The Devil's Trill* could not have appeared before 1730; Paul Brainard writes that the sonata could hardly have been written before 1740.

At the same time Michelangelo Abbado advances an argument that cannot be ignored. He says that after hearing Tartini perform his compositions in Prague in 1723 Johann Joachim Quantz stresses among other things the Italian master's skill in playing double trills. Since this device does not occur in any other of Tartini's known works, Abbado is prone to think that the sonata had already been

Legend of the Devil playing

written at that time, that is, in 1723. Certain peculiarities of form (the division of the middle movement into two parts and the repeated change of tempo in the finale) show the affinity of this sonata (or so he thinks) with the work of Tartini's first period.

All this is further complicated by the fact that the autograph of the sonata no longer exists. It would be logical to assume that Tartini wrote the first version of the sonata in his youth and then returned to his composition again and again, perfecting and polishing it until he achieved the maturest version that we know today (one that has firmly established itself in the classical repertoire of the violin). This perfecting of the sonata very likely went on while the composer himself played it and while he taught his pupils how to play it.

As for the dream that according to Tartini played such as important part in the creation of this sonata, we must refer to Pavlov's teachings on the activity of the higher nervous system to show that there is nothing of the mystical in it; the explanation is completely materialistic.[73]

With Tartini the musical idea of the sonata must naturally have matured long before the dream came to him. He had already worked hard on the trill, conceiving it not only as a technical device but as a means of musical expression. The esthetic beliefs of his time undoubtedly prompted him to give thought to the expressive possibilities of this device and to the affects to whose musical embodiment the trill might contribute. It was no accident that he made wide use of the trill (to which he later devoted so much attention in his *Treatise on Ornaments)* in many other compositions for the violin.

It is therefore natural that the trill that filled Tartini's thoughts to such an extent should have become a kind of "sentry point" in his dream, for he possessed a strong sense of imagery and a highly developed imagination. His observations, feelings and the conclusions he came to during his work and other activities little by little accumulated. Sooner or later it was inevitable that they should lead him to something qualitatively new in his art—to the sonata that resulted from all this. All that was needed was a trigger to set it off, in this case the musician's fantastic dream; the excitation of the "sentry points" in the dream stimulated his creativity when awake.[74]

Naturally, what Tartini put down when he awoke was far from what he had heard in his dream (as he says in his own account of it), but the powerful impression the dream had produced on him was capable of inspiring this romantic man and arousing his creative spirit.

In speaking of the romantic name of the sonata, Konstantin Rosenschild writes: "In this 'Pathetic Sonata' of 18th century Italian violin music, there really is something 'demoniacal', to use the concept in the broad esthetic manner of that period, in the sense of being possessed by violent passions with all their turbulence and transports, perhaps oppositions, a state caught and put into music by the artist."[75]

The sonata consists of three movements. It begins with a Larghetto affettuoso, written in the rhythm of a siciliana. The music is highly poetical and exalted, full of soulful lyricism and repressed sorrow. In the melody of this movement (as in the short final Adagio, the coda of the whole sonata) Tartini's skill in intensifying the melodic expression by chromatic modes is clearly demonstrated. The listener is enchanted by the song-like music and the dreaminess; at the same time one can sense an underlying excitement which comes out in harmonic accentuations (diminished seventh chords). The Larghetto affettuoso is one of the best pieces in the 18th century violin classics:

Larghetto affettuoso

95

The second movement, the Tempo giusto (Allegro), is vigorous, bold, at times dramatic in character:[76]

96 **Tempo Giusto della Scuola Tartinista**

The further use of a short trill on semi-quarters lends the music a sharp, rhythmically stressed shade.

Lastly, the finale of the sonata (which in early editions is called "Sogni dell Autore") consists of two parts, contrasting in content, that alternate three times: a Grave [77] and an Allegro assai.

The Grave is characterized by breadth of melos and is song-like and at the same time pathetic:

97   **Andante (Grave)**

Contrasting dynamics are characteristic of this movement.

In the Allegro assai the music assumes elements of determination, will power and temperament:

98   **Allegro assai**

It is in the Allegro assai that Tartini so skillfully uses the trill. There is a background of continuous trills in the higher voice against which the expressive articulation of the lower voice is heard:

99   **Trillo del diavolo al pie del letto** *)

As we have said, the Grave and Allegro in the finale that are repeated three times are modified each time, creating an impression of life and development in the main idea.

Whereas the second and third Grave (Andante) differ in tonality alone (the tonality of the minor dominant in the second and the principal tonality in the third), the first Grave, with the same character and the same mood, is like an independent episode. This enabled the authors of some of the later arrangements to make a third movement preceding the finale; however, this can hardly be what Tartini had in mind. He had intended it as a cycle in three, not four, movements. The first Grave (Andante) is interpreted by some researchers and performers as the lyrical center of the sonata, but it must not be separated from the following Allegro assai, which when consecutive form a striking dramatic contrast.

Below we give the third appearance of the Grave (Andante) and the beginning of the last appearance of the Allegro assai:

The finale ends with a four-beat Adagio, full of expression and passion:

The fact that the separate movements of the sonata are related to each other both in intonation and harmony[78] (a relationship to be found not only in the slow movements, but in the opening motives of both fast movements as well, as we see in examples 96 and 98) contributes to the unity of the whole cycle.

There is one more circumstance, at first sight a superficial one, that makes this sonata stand out from Tartini's numerous works as something exceptional. The characteristic features of the principal idea of the first movement of the sonata (defined in the opening phrase by the intonational, rhythmical and harmonical structure Tonic-Subdominant-Tonic) are repeated in a number of Tartini's other compositions. One can see the relationship between intonation and harmony very clearly if one compares the opening phrases of *The Devil's Trill* and *Dido Deserted* (examples 95 and 91).

The same thing can be noticed at the beginning of the Grave in Tartini's Concerto in D minor, No. 45 (example 59).

As we know, the principal theme of the first movement of *The Devil's Trill* is played in a minor key for four beats; beginning with the fifth beat, which has the same intonational, rhythmical and harmonical structure as the first, the theme is played in the relative major key:

Transformation of an opening phrase into a major key is to be found in the Andante cantabile of the Sonata in D major (No. 4 in Brainard), in the Andante larghetto in G major of the Concerto in C major (No. 12) and in some other compositions of Tartini's:

As Abbado remarks, there is a distinct intonational and harmonic resemblance to the *Devil's Trill* sonata in the Largo Sonata Op. 2,

116

No. 1 (published in 1743),[79] where it is to be found not only in the opening phrase but also in its further development in the major key:

In addition to this, there is also a similarity to be found if one compares the first bars of the finale of this sonata and those of the second movement of *The Devil's Trill*.

All these and other examples go to show that the intonations, themes and ideas of *The Devil's Trill* were no exception in Tartini's works; they had gripped the composer's imagination for many years. He seems to have been especially attracted by the contrast between the elegiacal and the lyrical qualities as well as the heroic and the vigorously determined.

The Devil's Trill may be regarded as Tartini's creed in art, as a generalization not only of the ideas, images, meaning and emotional content of his work, but also of its specific melodic, harmonic and rhythmic idiom, and of certain devices in composition and execution.

The sonata was first published by Jean Baptiste Cartier in his *Method (L'Art du Violon ou Collection Choisie dans les Sonatas des Écoles Italienne, Française et Allemande)*, that came out in Paris in 1798 (and the second edition in 1801).[80] After that it fell into abeyance for over half a century. In 1855 it reappeared with a pianoforte accompaniment in arrangements by Henri Vieuxtemps[81] and Robert Volkmann. These editions marked a return of interest in Tartini's work generally and not only in his *Devil's Trill*.[82] At the end of the 19th century and at the beginning of the 20th there appeared a large number of arrangements of this sonata, in particular by Joseph Joachim,[83] Fritz Kreisler, Leopold Auer and Georgi Doulov, which show the continued appreciation of this splendid composition.

In a collection of cadenzas published in the Soviet Union, there are eleven for *The Devil's Trill*, including those by Henri Vieuxtemps, Leopold Auer, Joseph Joachim, Fritz Kreisler and Michael Erdenko.[84] Jan Kubelik's cadenzas still remain in manuscript.

A specific place in Tartini's works is occupied by some sonatas and separate movements (particularly variations) for violin without accompaniment that have survived in manuscript. In Padua alone there are about thirty of these sonatas as well as manuscripts of his

Henri Vieuxtemps

sonatas in libraries and archives in Austria, Germany and the U.S.A.

The original manuscripts by Tartini are more often than not a single line recording a violin part; some of them have a second line for the bass part which is either not written out or else roughly sketched in.

These sonatas, of which there are several dozen, are to this day somewhat of a mystery. A certain amount of light has been thrown upon it by Brainard, who made a close study of Tartini's sonatas, in an article entitled "Tartini and the Sonata for Unaccompanied Violin."[85] Actually it was Tartini himself who gave a clue to the solution of the problem in a letter to Francesco Algarotti (then chamberlain in the court of Friedrich II in Berlin) dated February 24, 1750. On Algarotti's advice, Friedrich ordered several compositions from Tartini. The composer sent some of them to Berlin (sonatas for solo violin that Tartini called little sonatas, "piccole sonate"), accompanied by a letter in which he wrote: "These little sonatas of mine that I am sending you are provided with a bass part for the sake of tradition (per ceremonia). . . I play them without the bassetto, and that is my true intention."[86]

King Frederick II of Prussia

At that time the word "bassetto" was used in place of cello. Thus we find in this letter a clear indication of the fact that Tartini really did prefer to play the "little sonatas" or sonatas for solo violin unaccompanied, unlike the usual performance of his sonatas accompanied by the cello alone or with the addition of the organ.

It is naturally quite possible that occasionally and probably even frequently a cellist as accomplished as Tartini's constant partner, Antonio Vandini (who had mastered the famous violinist's style to perfection), may have improvised the accompaniment. It is also possible that Tartini may have added a second voice where this was required to enrich the harmony or clarify the modulations, and that Tartini himself played both voices. This would have been in keeping with a practice that was widespread in his time (that of improvising) in which both as composer and performer he was very skilled.[87]

The expressive Andante in B minor cited by Brainard, with its added doublestops and chords (which Tartini could have performed alone while playing the sonata), sounds extremely convincing:

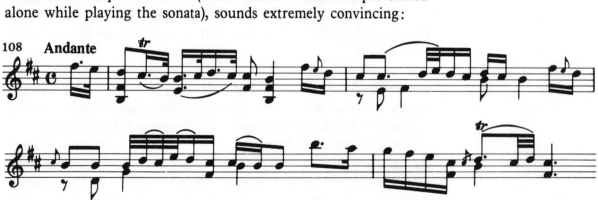

The original script of this piece is this:

109   **Andante**

Of course, the arrangement printed above should not be regarded
as the only one that is in accord with Tartini's conception, nor is it
likely that he himself played everything without any changes at all.
However, in his compositions for unaccompanied violin one can see
both his imaginative flights and his belief in the abundant expressive possibilities of the violin, and also—which is very important—a manifestation of his desire to free himself of the cramping
practice of basso continuo.

With his gift for improvisation, Tartini made skillful use of the
polyphony of the violin in performing his "little sonatas" without a
bass. As an instance of this, let us cite the beginning of the Andante
cantabile from his second Sonata in E minor (according to
Brainard):

110   **Andante cantabile**

It is unlikely that Tartini was familiar with Bach's solo violin
sonatas and partitas. Yet Tartini, who was a contemporary of Bach,
had an amazing understanding of the expressive possibilities of the
solo violin and an extraordinary skill in using these modes, which
enabled him to make a valuable contribution to the genre. Tartini's
solo sonatas without bass that have survived are sufficient to give us
an idea of their great artistic value. His gift is shown in the plasticity
of the musical idiom and the beauty of the melodic line, the majestic

119

Johann Sebastian Bach

A late portrait of Tartini

Bust of Tartini

simplicity of the content and the laconism of the form. In this genre Tartini can be said to have expressed more clearly than anywhere else his desire to rid himself of all artificiality and get as close as possible to nature. It was these aspirations that he expressed in his letter to Algarotti of November 20th, 1749.

Tartini's music for unaccompanied violin without any doubt at all was a reflection of folk influences. This is confirmed not only by its simplicity and laconism as already mentioned, but also by the fact that it is clearly folk in character. Suffice it to say that a movement of one of Tartini's sonatas (that we have cited) bearing the name of the Italian folk dance furlana is included in one of the sonatas for solo violin. Likely enough Tartini found the idea of the very genre of music for unaccompanied violin in the folk music he heard.

OTHER COMPOSITIONS

There is, among Tartini's compositions for violin and bass, a sweet poetic Pastorale in A major which was added to the edition of the first opus of his sonatas (published in 1734) and also an Andante affettuoso that has come down to us in a free arrangement by Bonelli[88] which is captivatingly expressive.

Tartini's fugues for violin,[89] published separately, are also worthy of note. Like other fugal movements in his sonatas, they display his polyphonic skill.

Although Tartini's principal style in composing was homophonic and harmonic, his fugues are of interest both from the point of view of music generally as well as technically. The value of these works in teaching especially should be recognized (which by no means belittles their importance as independent works of art); in particular it is advisable to use them in preparation for learning Bach's solo violin fugues.

One of these fugues of Tartini's, that in G major, the second movement of Sonata Op. 1 (No. 4), has been written in an excellent arrangement by Cesare Barison (Leipzig, 1912). The second movement of Sonata in A major Op. 1 (No. 1) became popular in a free arrangement by Fritz Kreisler (Mainz, 1913):

122

Both these fugues are in three voices; the two higher voices belong to the solo violin and the third to the bass. The theme of the Fugue in G major (which is one of Tartini's numerous Slavonicisms) has the character of a folk dance. The theme of the concluding Presto of Sonata No. 5 in the collection by E. Pente and M. Zanon is very close to it.

As an example of Tartini's use of the genre of variation we can take his theme (Andante cantabile ma non largo) with three variations (Lo Stesso tempo, Allegro e Giga, Allegro non presto) that form the fourth movement of the Sonata in G major.[90] It is preceded by a Largo, an Allegro amabile and an Allegro. The first bars of the theme and the three variations are shown in the following examples:

Tartini is more consistent in using the principle of variational development in a piece called *Minuetto Variato* (in A major) arranged by Pente. Zanon wrote the pianoforte part according to the original bass, just as he did in a number of sonatas by Tartini that he published. This graceful minuet was written in the form of a theme with eighteen contrasting variations.

There is another composition by Tartini that attained an incomparably greater measure of popularity. This is his *L'Arte del Arco (Art of the Bow)*, written in the form of variations for violin and bass (the latter being a constant factor both in the theme and in all the variations). The Gavotte from Corelli's Violin Sonata in F major Op. 5 (No. 10)[91] served as the theme for this composition. The following example shows the theme with the bass part, which is invariable in all fifty variations:

Tartini seems to have written this composition in the first period of his work, probably at Ancona, and, if so, before 1721. True, it is possible that the first variant of the variations may have been altered by the author later on.

David Boyden, a modern historian of violin art, quite rightly sees the prototype of Tartini's *Art of the Bow* in *50 Variations* from a collection of Johann Jacob Walther's work entitled *Hortulus Chelicus* (1688) and in Corelli's *La Folia* (1700).[92] Musically, Tartini's composition surpasses the first of these and technically the second one. It characterizes a new and higher stage in the history of violin art.

We will come back to this composition of Tartini's; for the moment we would simply like to stress the fact that its artistic and virtuoso (technical) qualities are very high. Each of the variations is a miniature piece of music in which the various devices for the performer are not presented in a formal or schematic way but as material that is musical in every sense.

Early editions of this work of Tartini's that came out in France in the forties and the fifties (during the musician's lifetime) contained only thirty-eight variations.[93]

The first complete edition containing all fifty variations only appeared after 1782 in Naples (Marescalchi) under the title of *L'Arte del Arco o Siano Cinquanta Variazioni per Violino e sempre collo stesso Basso sopra la piu bella Gavotta del Corelli*, Op. 5.

Charles Auguste de Beriot

The early interest in this composition both in Italy and beyond its borders is demonstrated by its inclusion in a collection compiled by J. B. Cartier *(L'Art du Violon . . .)* which was published in Paris in 1798 under the title of *L'Art de l'Archet par Tartini, gravé sur un manuscrit de l'auteur appartenant à J.B. Passeri.* Whereas there were only thirty-eight variations in this edition, the second edition of Cartier's *Méthod* (1801) already contained all fifty variations.[94]

The interest the violin world took in this composition continued to be lively. The music stimulated the appearance of numerous *airs variés* (in particular those of Charles Bériot and Henri Vieuxtemps). Arrangements of *The Art of the Bow* are known by Ferdinand David (fifty variations), Hubert Leonard (ten variations), Alberto Bachman, Fritz Kreisler (three variations in all, of which only one belongs to Tartini; the theme, too, is substantially changed), Sam Franko, Elena Genyeva and others.[95]

Among Tartini's compositions there are quite a few trio-sonatas written for two violins and bass.[96] In the author's lifetime six sonatas Op. 8 were published in Paris (1749), twenty-four sonatas (including twelve sonatas Op. 3) in London (1750, 1756), a number of sonatas in Amsterdam (c. 1755), etc. This speaks of the early popularity of Tartini's trio-sonatas in which the principal role is played by the two violins while the bass part is taken by a cello with the usual addition of a keyboard instrument (basso continuo).[97]

Proof of the vitality of these works of Tartini's and their persisting musical value is amply furnished by phonograph recordings made of one of his trio-sonatas by David and Igor Oistrakh (one with the pianoforte, the other with a harpsichord).

Finally, one must recall several quadro or sonate a quattro by Tartini that can be regarded as prototypes of the classical quartets for two violins, viola and cello. Michelangelo Abbado writes that as one of the first authors of such compositions Tartini "merits the same respect as Scarlatti and Vivaldi,"[98] while Paumgartner avers that Mozart "was inspired to write his first quartet by the Italian Quattro as composed by Sammartini, Boccherini and Tartini."[99] This was in the year in which Tartini died.[100]

In reviewing the heritage left us by Giuseppe Tartini, there are several conclusions to be drawn. Tartini's works for bow instruments mark an important milestone in the history of musical culture, in the history of the development of the sonata, the concerto and the chamber orchestra from the pre-classical style to the 18th century classical style (with the expression, humanity and democratism that belongs to it).

Tartini's music, with its artistic merits, its depth and imagery, its expressive melodic idiom, its rhythmic wealth, its clear, simple form and its talented use of instrumental expressive modes, takes a well-deserved place on the programmes of modern performers and enjoys extensive use in the practice of modern music teaching.

125

Chapter 4

Tartini
the Violinist, Performer
and Teacher

 **Tartini has always been to me a
source of achievements with the
violin.**

Joseph Szigeti

The investigator comes up against exceptional difficulties when
he attempts to reconstruct the image of a performer of music who
lived at a time when there was as yet no method for mechanically
recording his musical performance. In order to gain insight into the
multifaceted activities of Giuseppe Tartini, one has to resort to the
accounts of his contemporaries, his pupils, his compositions for the
violin. The latter, when analyzed as to the violin techniques
employed, may reveal some of the author's traits as a performer. It is
necessary to refer to what Tartini himself wrote in his treatises and
in his well-known *Letter to a Pupil* and to what has been passed
down by word of mouth.

In the first place it must be stressed that Tartini's performance as
a musician cannot be treated as something separate from his creative
work as a composer, just as Tartini the teacher cannot be separated
from Tartini the performer. Tartini's principles in performing and
teaching, like his principles in composing, were based on a realization of the humanism of art, its need for content and on his desire to
be as close as possible to nature, without artificiality or affectation.
They were based on the recognition of the capability of art and
hence of the performer of this art to delight his hearers, to arouse
and inspire them, to express through its performance human feelings and experiences. This was in complete accord with the advanced esthetic views of the day and was partly reflected in the so-
called theory of affects.

"Good musical taste" ("buon gusto musicale"), which according to
Tartini is displayed both in composing music and in performing it,
is a product of human nature and must be guided by one's ("sommo
giudicio") "highest judgment." Tartini, who realized the creative
nature of the art of performance—which in his time was permeated
with elements of improvisation—stresses the importance of "good
taste," which must be an essential component of musical performance and determines the truth of the expression.[1]

Hic fidibus, scriptis, claris hic magnus alumnis,
Cui par nemo fuit, forte nec ullus erit.

Giuseppe Tartini in 1761

The fact that Tartini was both composer and performer determined the unity of his principles and views on the arts of composing and performing. As a composer he registered much that was prompted by performance, quite possibly ideas that arose while he was improvising; his imagination and inspiration as a composer set him new artistic and technical tasks in his role of performer. However, these tasks never came into contradiction with the possibilities of the violin, whose nature he had grown to know so well.

"Expression is a quality with the help of which the musician feels keenly and conveys with energy all the ideas that he must convey, and all the feelings that he must express. There is one expression of composition and one of execution, and it is their concurrence that results in the most powerful and agreeable musical effect."[2]

This sentiment, expressed by Tartini's contemporary, Jean-Jacques Rousseau, is from an article by the latter called "Expression" in his *Musical Dictionary* and can well be applied to the Italian violinist and composer.

SOUND: THE TECHNIQUE OF THE RIGHT HAND

In finding, as did Rousseau, a criterion for the beautiful in nature, Tartini attached the greatest importance to the art of "singing on the violin." Though Tartini never composed music for the opera, he could not have failed to come into contact with the influence of the operatic bel canto with its warmth and uplift, its portamenti and various melodic ornaments and the influence of expressive human song. Also of influence were the chamber and folk songs, especially the Italian and Slavic songs that were so familiar to him.

"Non suona, ma canta sul violino"[3] was what his contemporaries said of Tartini's playing. This is confirmed by the numerous compositions in which he uses the expressive violin cantilena.

In this respect, as in several others, Tartini was developing the precepts of Arcangelo Corelli's school, remembering the "singing" of Corelli's bow, the song-like slow movements of his violin sonatas and also the broad "breath" of his pupils' bows, especially that of Giovanni Battista Somis.[4]

However, following the spirit of the times and his own esthetic convictions, Tartini went further than Corelli. This was in the content of the violin's "singing"; its "objective" character was replaced by a more subjective and emotional use of the expressive mode, which was also more lyrical and soulful.

The importance that Tartini attached to the song-like quality and to the development of a broad violin tone can be seen from one of the principal exercises that he recommended in his *Letter to a Pupil*. It consists of so-called "sons filés," ("sustained tones"); exercises in these sounds have since then become a stable element in violin teaching.

In *Regole per ben suonare il Violino (Rules for Playing the Violin Well)* by Tartini and rewritten by his pupil Giovanni Francesco Nicolai,[5] Tartini differentiates two manners of playing: *cantabile* and *sonabile*. According to him, the singing manner of playing *cantabile* required slurring and coherence, as distinct from *sonabile*.

Tartini used to say to his pupils, "Per ben suonare bisogna ben cantare" ("To play well it is necessary to sing well").[6] Without doubt this applied both to the *cantilena* and to the technical passages that Tartini wished to hear not only well played, but also well "sung."

In all the evidence of Tartini's singing style of playing there is only one seemingly contradictory note to be found, and that is in the last sentence of an assessment by Johann Joachim Quantz, who heard Tartini play in 1723 in Prague. True, it was only thirty years later that Quantz wrote it; thus it is not so much an immediate registration of an impression still fresh in his mind, as it is a recollection of the remote past. It is quite possible that his fading memories of the event may have been overlaid by his new views and his new esthetic criteria. Even so, his assessment was in the main a delighted one. However, let us refer to Quantz' *Autobiography*, which was published in 1755 by F.W. Marpurg, and see what it was that Quantz actually said.

"When I was in Prague, I also heard the renowed Italian violinist Tartini, who was then in the service of Count Kinsky. He really was one of the greatest of violinists. He produced a beautiful tone from his instrument, and possessed an equal mastery with his fingers and the bow. He played the most difficult things perfectly and effortlessly. He can play a trill and even a double trill with all his fingers equally well. Both in fast and slow pieces he added many double-stops and took pleasure in playing the top register. However, his performance was not moving, nor was his taste refined—more, it seemed just the contrary of good vocal style ("Singart") . . ."[7]

Legitimate doubt is cast upon this last assertion by many students of Tartini's work, for it is contradictory to all the other appraisals of his performance by contemporaries. It is certainly not a question of Quantz' having been in low spirits when he was listening to Tartini (as supposed by W.J. Wasielewski), nor merely of the possibility of Tartini's not having been in the right mood that day for playing movingly or, like any other youthful virtuoso, having wished to make an impression by his technical skill (according to A. Moser).[8]

Minos Dounias and Antonio Capri, who see the reason for Quantz's assessment in his esthetic positions, have a more considered approach. Two years before the publication of his *Autobiography*, Quantz printed his *Method of Playing the Flute*,[9] that was widely read. This book is much more than a purely instructional work intended for flute-players alone; it is a valuable memorial to the art of performance in the 18th century and contains many important esthetic principles.

In this book, too, there is a certain amount of prejudice against Tartini's style (without actually naming him Quantz makes it clear who he means). Quantz speaks of him as "one of the first and greatest masters in the performance of difficulties on the violin," with such an original taste, that "it is impossible to imitate him in singing," saying that this taste "belongs only to violinists who have very little idea of what a genuinely good vocal style means."[10]

But Quantz' reasoning was not only directed against Tartini; it speaks of his prejudice against the whole of the Italian style of playing. We must recall that this was the time of the lively polemic between the Italian and the French schools of music, and German musicians would sometimes come out very sharply against Italian music. Quantz levelled his criticism at Tartini as a representative of the Italian style of music, for he considered this style to be not only expressive and profound, full of life and daring, but also somewhat quaint, bold and arbitrary.[11]

Quantz can hardly have had any motives for a personal dislike of Tartini. Even when he criticized some aspect of his style, he could not refrain from giving him his due as an outstanding violinist. Any criticism of Tartini's style as a performer (in the same book) he applies rather to Tartini's pupils, implying that they had misunderstood their master and had "either learnt his style incorrectly, or—as a result of differences in their manner of perception—had made this style even quainter."[12] And nonetheless, Dounias' conclusion as to the insufficient objectivity of Quantz' judgment of Tartini is well founded. As Dounias writes: "It arose from the whole spiritual situation in Germany around the middle of the century and should be accounted for by the position of the German musicians, who were depressed at the time by the predominance of foreign art."[13]

There can be no doubt that Michelangelo Abbado is right when in his research into Tartini's works he finds "more eloquent and unprejudiced" evidence of the exceptional expression and song-like quality of Tartini's style in the compositions of the latter (especially in the *cantabile* and mournful ones)[14] and often in his adagios, which are soulful and song-like in the Slavic manner.

In spite of the influence of vocal art that we have already noted, the song-like qualities of the Tartini style of bowing had their own instrumental specific features. For all the similarity of the sound of the violin and the human voice, that of the violin has its own expressive peculiarities close to those of the human voice,[15] but by no means coinciding with them. The peculiarities of vibrato, portamento and articulation in performance on the violin that are connected with the art of bowing, dynamics, etc., were things for which Tartini had a profound understanding. He gave them full play in his art, in complete accord with the nature of the expressive modes of the violin.

130

Tartini did not simply sing on the violin, he sang expressively. According to his contemporaries, when Tartini heard a violinist who played well, but formally, he remarked, "It's beautiful, it's difficult, but it says nothing to the heart."[16] When talking of the cellist Antonio Vandini and wishing to stress the extreme expressiveness of his manner of playing, contemporaries said that he was skilled in "speaking" on his cello. There can be no doubt that Tartini also possessed this skill in a high degree. His singing on the violin had a rare expressiveness, a wealth of dynamic colors, a beautiful vibrato, which he played on a par with other ornaments designed to intensify the melodic expression, and it was refined in artistic taste.

It is of interest to note that Tartini achieved this exceptional expression in his performance, according to some accounts, with a relatively soft tone and with a comparatively limited use of vibrato (of which in greater detail further). What helped to create the expression was the rare profundity of the playing and important qualities such as sweetness and warmth of tone (no wonder Carlo Gozzi talks of Tartini's "sweet violin"!), exceptional purity of intonation, accomplished articulation of the musical phrase, complete mastery of bowing, and "speaking" bowing (that accorded with the element of declamation in poetic human speech).

Charles de Brosses, a French contemporary of Tartini's who heard Tartini play when he was passing through Padua in 1739, called him Italy's first violin and wrote that "it [his playing] was the best he had ever heard for the exceptional purity of his tones, not one of which was lost, and for his perfect accuracy. However, his playing lacked brilliancy."[17]

This last remark might have been provoked either by the music used by Tartini that day, which did not require brilliancy, or by some comparison that occurred to him with some "brilliant" French violinists who were popular at the time. The Italian musician and the French traveler would seem to have held different esthetic views. Tartini's compositions are evidence of the unusually high development of his technique. The whole point lies in the fact that Tartini, both as composer and as performer, did not use it for the purpose of displaying his virtuosity, but in order to carry into effect various musical expressive tasks with the aid of this technique. One cannot help mentioning here the brilliance of the violin technique that he used in many of his compositions. This is further confirmed by Charles Burney, the 18th century British musicologist, who wrote that the Tartini school possessed more finesse, expression and perfection than brilliance.[18]

Although Burney did not have an opportunity to hear Tartini, he did hear some of his pupils, who, with their many other qualities, did not possess a powerful tone. He characterizes Pietro Nardini's tone, for instance, as "even and sweet; not very loud, but clear and certain," and goes on to say, "He has a great deal of expression in his slow movements, which, it is said, he has happily caught from his master Tartini. As to execution, he will satisfy and please more than surprise; in short, he seems the completest player on the violin in all Italy, and, according to my feelings and judgment, his style is delicate, judicious and highly finished."[19] This is what Burney says of André Pagin, one of Tartini's best French pupils: "He has a great deal of expression and facility of executing difficulties; but whether he did not exert himself, as the room was not large, or from whatever cause it proceeded, I know not, his tone was not powerful."[20] At the same time Burney finds more fire in a German pupil of Tartini's, Josef Holzbogen, in addition to his purity of tone, than in his other pupils.[21]

Carl Lipinski

Some researchers are of the opinion that the relative softness of tone in Tartini's playing is connected to a certain extent with the "Italian" way of holding the bow well away from the heel. This manner was described as "Italian" by Michael Corrette in his *Method*[22] and was likewise used by Francesco Geminiani and Pietro Locatelli. However, judging by a picture made at the time, Francesco Maria Veracini (and also Leopold Mozart) already held the bow right at the heel, so it is probable that Tartini did the same.

It must be borne in mind that the odd pieces of information given above should be treated with caution, for even if we set aside their possible subjectivity, they are insufficient for us to form any categorical conclusions as to whether the absence of loudness applies to Tartini's school as a whole. There exist other facts that cannot be ignored. The famous Polish violinist Karol Lipinsky (1790-1861) (who gave recitals in Italy many times) mentions a Giulio Meneghini, Tartini's pupil and successor in the chapel at Padua, who was nicknamed "Giulio Tromba" ("Giulio the Trumpet"), most likely for the strength of his tone.[23] But let us see what Tartini himself has to say. This Italian master's *Rules for Bowing*[24] shows that he was by no means indifferent to strength and fullness of tone. He says, "The bow should be held firmly between the thumb and forefinger and lightly by the other three fingers, in order to produce a strong, sustained tone. To increase the tone, press harder on the bow with the fingers and also press down the strings more firmly with the fingers of the other hand."[25]

From this we see not only how mindful Tartini was of the problem of the dynamics of tone and his interest in its strength, but also how correct was his understanding of the physiology of the process of increasing the sound. This is connected with a pronate effort (implied when he says "The bow should be held firmly between the thumb and forefinger") and of the interdependence of pressure efforts in both hands.

As has been said, Tartini paid due attention to dynamic shades; he connected the strengthening or softening of the tone with expressive aims or with the development of some emotion.

Tartini attached great importance to the expressive value of ornamentation, especially in the *cantilena*. There still exist manuscripts of some of his compositions in their "pure" (unornamented) form (so that he could improvise the ornaments) and also some with ornamentation. These show the role he assigned to the latter in enriching the expressive force of the melody and in giving it life. In his *Trattato di Musica* (1754) Tartini wrote that "good taste" nevertheless depended less on ornaments than on the performer's ability "to produce a tone sweetly, to soften or increase it, to sustain the tempo, etc."[26]

Tartini's interest in dynamics was displayed in his use of various shades in his own execution; at the same time it was expressed in the gradually expanding dynamic sphere of his compositions.

Lastly, a great deal can be deduced from a motto attributed to Tartini, which he allegedly wrote in large letters on his music stand: "Strength without convulsiveness, flexibility without laxity (slackness)".[27] It follows that Tartini was not against strength of tone resulting from exertion of greater pressure on the bow; what he objected to was excessive, convulsive pressure.

Tartini's views on bowing are revealed in a letter written to him in 1744 by a friend, Gianrinaldo Carli, professor of astronomy at the University of Padua. He wrote: "To your reflections are due the merits of many of the beautiful things and of the phenomena that have been discovered in music, among them also those which you explained to me with such wisdom and willingness when I asked you two years ago to explain to me why it was that the more you press the bow to the string, the less audible is the sound at a certain distance, while at close quarters this sound becomes more piercing, harsh and unpleasant than usual. You told me then that by skillfully moving the bow horizontally across along the string we produce horizontal and clear vibrations in it, which in their turn produce consequent exact sound waves that enable the sound to spread to as great a distance as possible. But if, on the contrary we move the bow by pressing perpendicularly on the string, two different vibrations arise, one perpendicular and the other horizontal; one hinders the other, and they destroy each other. The resulting air wave is no longer simple and straight, but vertical and indefinite; therefore at close quarters the sound can only be harsh and noisy, it cannot spread as in the first case to an equal distance. I learned then why your violin is different from all other violins and why the sound produced by your bow is so pleasing and sweet."[28]

To add to what has already been said, Tartini's proposal for lengthening the bow (which among other things was done for the purpose of intensifying the sound and broadening the melodic breath) opened new horizons for the development of dynamic, increased the "cantability" and enriched the bowing technique (see further: Tartini's *The Art of Bowing*).[29]

Johann Joachim Quantz

Jean Philippe Rameau

Thus we can form an idea of Tartini's ideal for a full, strong tone. As for the "brilliance" and "fire" and "energy" in his art, clear evidence of this is to be found in his compositions for the violin. It is hard to imagine, for instance, how the fast movements of the *Devil's Trill* could be executed without "energy" or "fire." As to the "brilliance" of his passage technique (the fingering and bowing), there are many episodes in his compositions that bear witness to this, also in his examples of "artificial cadences" in his *Treatise on Ornaments.*

Yet the finesse, expression and perfection mentioned by Burney are without doubt the principal features of Tartini and his school in their style of execution. This is also the opinion of Stefan Arteaga, who wrote of his contemporary Giuseppe Tartini: "Having studied the art of down and up bow, slower and faster bowing, and pressure, he was able to produce the sweetest and loveliest tones."[30] This characteristic of the Italian master's playing is complemented by the authors of *Methods of the Paris Conservatoire* (Paris, 1802), Baillot, Rode and Kreutzer, who wrote that under Tartini's bow the violin becomes a "harmonious, sweet instrument, full of grace."

As we know, Tartini was highly accomplished not only in producing a beautiful singing and expressive tone and a rich dynamic palette, but also in virtuoso technique, with rapidity of fingering, a brilliant trill, passage technique (including the doublestop and the chord) and an extraordinarily developed and elaborate bowing technique. He used all these qualities exclusively to attain an artistic aim: to achieve the maximum of expression in his execution. By combining them in one harmonious whole while playing he created a complete and finished style of execution that drew general attention.

Tartini considered the mastery of bowing technique the basis of his method, and wrote about this in 1740 to Padre Martini.[31] He begins his advice in his *Letter to a Pupil,* written twenty years later, in the following way: "Your principal practice and study should, at present, be confined to the use and power of the bow, in order to make yourself entirely mistress in the execution and expression of whatever can be played (o sonabile) or sung (o cantabile), within the compass and ability of your instrument."[32]

From this letter, as from his *Rules for Bowing,* it follows that Tartini devoted a great deal of attention to the *attacca* of the tone and a complete mastery of the down and up bow (in any part of it) and in any dynamic shade. He attached great importance to the correct "distribution of the bow." According to a contemporary, he sometimes used two bows while teaching: one of them had its stick divided into four parts, and the other into three.[33]

Tartini's palette of bow strokes is worthy of special mention. Its wealth can be deduced from the great variety of bowing techniques he used in his compositions. These bow strokes were marked very sparsely in the score in Tartini's time, and the choice was often left to the performer, so that Tartini's manuscripts are not very revealing in this respect. However, there are several important things to be observed here.

Whereas Corelli virtually confined himself to détaché and legato bowing, Tartini undoubtedly used both staccato and "bouncing" ("hopping") strokes, even if he did not denote them by special and differentiated marks. True, in his *Rules for Bowing* we do come across the term "flying staccato" (Example 27).

In this capriccio, as in the finale of the Concerto in A minor, one may assume that sautillé bowing is used:

For all of these bowings of Tartini's, as we know, it was necessary not only to lengthen the bow, but also to flute the bow stick so that it could be gripped more firmly, which was required both for virtuoso bowing technique and for dynamics.

We can find an elementary explanation and indications in writing for a sharp, short bow stroke (staccato or martelé) in his *Letter to a Pupil:*

Another example occurs in his *Treatise on Ornaments:*

In the Allegro from his Concerto in F major (No. 64), the manuscript of which is in the Paris Conservatoire, he gives indications (vertical wedge-shaped marks over the notes) to show the sharpness of the bow stroke (marcato, staccato):[34]

121 **Allegro**

Tartini probably had in mind staccato or spiccato in the Allegro of his Sonata in G major (No. 24 according to Brainard's catalogue); here there are also wedge-shaped marks under or over the semi-quavers:

122 **Allegro**

At that period a non-legato manner of execution was used either in the absence of a slur mark or when there were small vertical strokes, wedge-shaped marks or dots over the notes. Such denotations are used here and there in the *Treatise on Ornaments*:

123

124

125

126

127

128

After giving nine different examples of "artificial cadences" in which the notes climb to an octave, Tartini says: "This figure can be performed by a voice or an instrument. For the voice, the notes are slurred (legato); for an instrument, detached (sciolto)":[35]

129

portamento con trillo

portamento

In this example which we have reproduced according to Nicolai's manuscript, the word "portamento" is superscribed in the sixth variant (with dots under the slur) and the words "portamento con trillo" in the seventh. In the corresponding part of the French edition (1771) on which Jacobi's publication is based, this is specified further by the words "portamento d'arco" since the word "portamento" alone would imply the technique of the left hand (an audible glissando) and not that of the bow.

An obvious example of Tartini's use of the portamento d'arco or the declamational bow stroke portato is to be found in the finale of *The Devil's Trill*, where it is only with this stroke in bowing that the articulation required can be accomplished in the lower voice, that sounds against a background of uninterrupted trilling in the upper voice (example 99).

Another variety of this declamatory bowing is used in the Adagio of his Sinfonia in F major (No. 3):[36]

Tartini would sometimes use in his compositions specific devices for bow instruments, such as bariolage (a passage in which two strings take part alternately, one being open), simply open strings, or "leaps" across strings:

Tartini used the arpeggio technique, in which the style of bowing and the varying rhythm were left to the performer (though he used it much less than did Vivaldi):

Tartini preferred to use broken chords, though he does use chord technique as well (see below). Of interest is the following example

140

from Tartini's Sonata in A major (No. 4 in Brainard's catalogue), where the chords are broken in the score; the autograph of this sonata bears the inscription "Composed in the style in which Prette plays the Portuguese guitar":[37]

The variety in Tartini's bowing strokes is due to the variety of rhythm in his music. Many of his compositions are striking in their rhythmical inventiveness:

Fine examples of rhythmical richness are to be found not only in Tartini's sonatas and concertos, but also in his *Art of Bowing* and his *Treatise on Ornaments* (especially in the section on cadences), of which we shall speak further; they are mainly of the character that he calls *sonabile*.

Tartini took pleasure in using various kinds of syncopated fabric that create certain difficulties in bowing:

Sometimes he combined syncopation and dotted rhythm:

Tartini makes extensive use of intricate passage technique on several strings; at the same time the bowing difficulties are frequently combined with difficulties for the left hand:

"The Lombard style" is characteristic in the last example. There are times when Tartini's bariolé bowing leads to "hidden polyphony":

The device of "throwing" the bow across the strings in a fast tempo is fairly characteristic of his bowing technique:

Here are two more examples of bowing technique that are typical of Tartini, which are to be found in the manuscripts of his concertos:

All these extremely varied bowings and others bear witness to Tartini's exceptionally rich bowing technique and to its organic ties with the musical phrase.

An observation made by Minos Dounias is of great importance. He found that Tartini's slurring of strokes coincides with that of phrases, as for example in the following extract from the first movement of Concerto in D minor (No. 44):

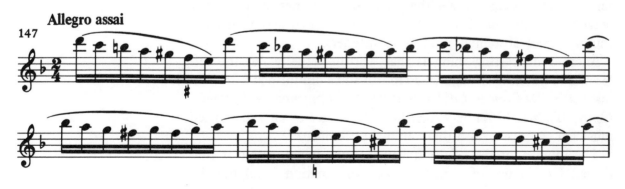

Altogether, the amount of attention that Tartini devoted to the character of bowing strokes and their correspondence to the musical phrase once more demonstrates his desire for expression, his desire to subordinate execution techniques to the achievement of this aim. In this respect Tartini stands out as a great representative of an art that is called upon to express human emotions and moods, to express "affects" in music.

Pierre Lahoussaye (1735-1818), a pupil of Tartini's and an eminent French violinist who was very highly appreciated by Giovanni Battista Viotti, said this of his master's playing: "It is impossible to express in words the surprise and delight that was aroused in me by his accuracy and the purity of his tone, the charm of his expression, the magic of his bow, in a word, all the perfections that won my heart and became an example for me."[38]

TECHNIQUE OF THE LEFT HAND

It is now time to talk of Tartini's technique for the left hand. What has been said of the expression, beauty and song-like quality of his tone is certainly connected with his technique for the left hand. It was characterized by exceptional purity and accuracy in intonation, and a warmth of vibration which, as we shall see from the *Treatise on Ornaments,* he never abused, as he never abused the ornaments he used as a means of enriching melodic expression.

The purity of Tartini's own intonation was stressed in the appraisals we have quoted on Quantz, de Brosses, and Lahoussaye. The purity and accuracy they talked of applied, naturally, not only to the production of sounds, but also to intonation as an essential mode of expression.[39]

In his *Treatise on Ornaments* Tartini speaks of the nature of "perfect intonation" that should be executed "with mathematical precision."[40] According to the modern theory of Nikolai Garbuzov on the zone nature of hearing sounds of different heights,[41] the intonation of performance is not based on a mathematically precise structure, but on a zone structure that comprises a large number of intonational variants. It is clear that in his practice Tartini used various intonational variants lying within the bounds of some interval zone. The opinion he expressed (quoted above) is valuable only for the way it demonstrates the keenness of his perception of the height of a tone and his ability to intone in such a way that the sound seemed absolutely pure to his listeners.

Another interesting thing is that Tartini actually felt the difference in intoning an augmented fourth and a diminished fifth.[42] In his treatise *De Principi dell'Armonia Musicale Contenuta sel Diatonico Genere* (Padua, 1767) he wrote that "the finger of an experienced musician can distinguish this minimal difference."[43]

The intense interest of the Italian violinist in intonation is confirmed by his use of a *terza suono* (combination tone) that he discovered to verify the purity of the intonation in doublestops. "If you can't hear the bass," he told his pupils, "it means that your thirds or sixths are not perfect in their intonation."[44]

While Corelli did not usually go beyond the third position, Tartini used nearly the whole fingerboard. We know this from the appraisal of Quantz that we have already cited: "He took pleasure in playing in the uppermost register." But one is easily convinced of the fact that Tartini used high positions by a glance at his compositions. If we recall that in Tartini's time the fingerboard was shorter than it is today, his use of the seventh, eighth and ninth positions can indeed be appreciated as playing "the uppermost register." This practice was of course in complete accord with Tartini's desire to broaden the melodic range of the violin.[45]

We shall now give a few examples. The eighth position is used, for instance, in the finale of his Concerto in A major (No. 92):

We come across the same position in his Concerto in E major and in several sonatas (sometimes with an extension):

Tartini uses the ninth position, for instance, in a solo capriccio in his Concerto in E major (No. 46) and in the finale of the Sonata in A major (Op. 1, No. 5), and here, in this upper register, he adds a trill to the notes.

Here is an example of the use of doublestops in the ninth position, from the first movement of Concerto in E minor (No. 55):

In speaking of Tartini's technique for the left hand it is impossible to pass by its connection with the technique of ornamentation that he developed so highly and used so widely. Not only the trill, with its brilliance and variety of tempos, but also every imaginable kind of grace note and mordent that Tartini often used in his compositions are evidence of his masterly agility in fingering. We also find this type of technique in numerous legato passages in his sonatas and concertos (as well as in the cadences in his *Treatise on Ornaments*):

The use of fast non legato passages requires that the performer possess a developed coordination of the movements of both hands:

154 **Andante**

We have already reproduced on these pages similar passages with the use of several strings, which complicates the performer's task considerably. Here is one more example:

155 **Andante**

Andreas Moser finds a convincing example of finger-extensions in the following excerpt from a sonata by Tartini. (Not only Locatelli, but Tartini also was Paganini's predecessor in this technique.) In this sonata tones are combined on adjacent strings in legato to form a tenth:

156 **Allegro**

A twelfth scale, played in legato on adjacent strings and requiring considerable extension of the fingers, has had doubts cast upon it by Andreas Moser, who thought it possible that in the early edition upon which the cited extract is based there may have been mistakes in the indications for slurs:

157 **Allegro**

The following example from the first movement of the Sonata Op. 5 (No. 5) is extremely interesting:

158 **Moderato**

Tartini's mastery in using doublestops, particularly thirds, sixths and even tenths, was considerable. He used them both in slow tempo, which produced the impression of an expressive vocal duet, and in fast virtuoso tempo:

The following excerpt from the first movement of his Concerto in B minor (No. 124) may serve as an example of a tune combined with a second voice:

Interesting doublestops are also to be found in the first movement of Concerto in E major (No. 46):

Tartini possessed an excellent mastery of violin polyphony, examples of which we can find in *The Devil's Trill* and other violin sonatas and concertos of his:

Special mention should be made of an interesting device that was used by Tartini in the finale of his *Devil's Trill*, where, against a background of trilling in the upper voice, elements of the theme are heard in the lower voice.[46] In this example, too, we find an extension of the third and fourth fingers on a lower string.

Let us also recall Tartini's skillful chord technique, examples of which are given below:

Tartini particularly liked to use his chord technique in his "little sonatas" and played them without any accompaniment.

It would appear that Tartini no longer used the thumb of his left hand to play certain kinds of chords (on the lowest string) as some of his contemporaries still did. Neither did he use the scordatura that was so widespread in the 17th and 18th centuries and consists in tuning up the violin temporarily to notes other than the normal to produce chords that could not otherwise be played. The scordatura was much used by the violinists Biagio Marini, and Heinrich Ignaz Franz Biber; it was also used by Antonio Lolli, Pietro Nardini, Bartolomeo Campagnoli and others.

Tartini is known to have used the scordatura only once. In one of his sonatas (Sonata in A major (No. 16) according to Brainard's numbering) the violin is tuned this way: A E^1 A^1 E^2:

In the first movement of Tartini's Concerto in D major (No. 16) there is an interesting example of three-voice chords forming triads placed close together, which as we know cannot be played on a violin.

In giving this example, Andreas Moser expresses the supposition that Tartini did not intend all these notes to be played simultaneously, for it cannot be done. He intended them only to give the illusion of being played so.[47] Tartini could have achieved this by playing the lower notes as a double grace note. It might have been done as follows (a way which in an Allegro tempo requires considerable skill):

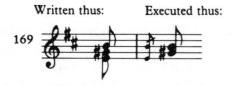

The expressive means of execution used by Tartini and the various types of violin technique and devices that he employed (reviewed above) display his profound understanding of the nature of his instrument. All these things in an exceptionally harmonious combination characterize the style of execution of the Italian

150

violinist who so skillfully used his wealth of technique as an important mode of musical expression.

As has been said, it is by no means easy to form a complete or true picture of all of the details and elements of Tartini's art in execution, even the important ones. It is known, for example, that many things were of immense importance in his expressive performance—the peculiarities of his articulation of the musical phrase, his dynamic and agogic subtleties, his characteristic accents, improvised ornaments, etc., that is, all that goes to make up the life and breath of musical execution and is seldom marked in musical notation.

What can be affirmed is that historically Giuseppe Tartini's style of execution and his violin technique were evolved from the attainments of the art of violin-playing in Italy in the 17th and the first half of the 18th centuries. They marked a new stage in the development of that art and played no small part in the further progress of violin culture not only in Italy, but far beyond its borders.

This was largely due to the fact that as a musician Tartini was advanced in his esthetic standpoint and always proceeded from a profound realization of the humanity and expressive force of musical art, and of the art of the violin in particular.

INSTRUCTIONAL WRITINGS

If one wants to get a better idea of Tartini as a violin player and teacher, one must make a study of those of his works that deal not only with esthetics, but also with instruction. We have already spoken of the indivisibility of these two sides of his musical activities. In writing his theoretical and instructional works Tartini proceeded from practical premises. He sought to give them a practical turn, and for this purpose he made use of his wealth of practical experience, his artistic taste and his talent as a teacher.

His first writings in this sphere were practical manuals for his pupils ("Lezioni pratiche per violino") which they usually copied out themselves and partly transcribed from dictation. Afterwards Tartini would add to them, touch them up, then give them a final polish, after which the manuals would sometimes turn into finished treatises. Most probably this was the way his renowned *Treatise on Ornaments* came into being.

The melodic expression of Tartini's music, as we know, was greatly enhanced by his extensive use of ornaments which required of the performer not only highly developed taste but also a degree of technical skill. Therefore we shall try to paint in a more complete picture of Tartini and his style of execution from this angle. As an objective basis we can take Tartini's *Treatise on Ornaments* that he apparently wrote between the years 1735 and 1750[48] (at a period of intense activity both as performer and teacher), which was translated into French and published in Paris only a year after his

151

death.[49] For a long time before its publication this *Treatise* was widely used in manuscript form (especially by Tartini's pupils) and it seemed to have been designed mainly for purposes of instruction.[50] This work has come down to us in copies made by his contemporaries.

Tartini's *Treatise* does not only reveal the way he executed the

170

various ornaments in practice. In many respects it displays the general trend of his style of execution, the way he sought to show the connection between these devices and the way in which he achieved the greatest expression possible.

In our time, too, notwithstanding all the evolution in the art of execution over the past two centuries, Tartini's *Treatise* still has a great deal to say. It enlightens performers and arrangers of Italian instrumental music of the 18th century (particularly music for bow instruments). It can help also to avoid interpretations of ornamentation that might go counter to the composer's idea of the music.[51]

It is difficult to overestimate the importance of this *Treatise* in the 18th century, at a time when much in the execution of the music was left to the performer's taste and was connected with the art of improvisation. There have been musical performers without sufficient taste, feeling for style or theoretical knowledge of music who have erred gravely when using ornaments of all kinds and who have endlessly abused this expressive mode.[52] This is probably the reason that Tartini began to write them out fairly carefully at a certain stage.

An eloquent instance of these abuses of ornaments can be taken from the following extract from Jean Baptiste Cartier's *Method*, that illustrates the common 18th century practice of using ornaments. Cartier gives several variants for the execution of a single bar from an adagio of Tartini's.[53] In the last few variants it is quite impossible to make out the principal musical phrase, which has somehow been dissolved in the conglomeration of ornaments.

As compared with example 170, the following one (example 171), also from the 18th century, is more rational. It is the execution of a musical phrase from an adagio by Nardini:

The advanced musicians of the 18th century who left behind them *Treatises* or *Methods* were, besides Giuseppe Tartini, Francesco Geminiani (1739), Leopold Mozart (1756), Carl Philipp Emanuel Bach (1753, 1762) and Johann Joachim Quantz (1752),[54] devoted a great deal of their attention to ornaments and stressed their expressive significance.

However, one cannot help noticing certain differences, sometimes quite serious ones, in the interpretation of ornaments by Tartini, C.P.E. Bach, Quantz and others. These differences are not only an expression of their individual tastes or the teachings of the various national schools they belonged to; they are mainly due to the fact that Tartini had in mind performance on the violin, Bach on a keyboard instrument and Quantz on the flute. A performer on a bow instrument would have insurmountable difficulties to overcome and would be unable to help distorting the music if he attempted to interpret some of the ornaments by blindly following the directions set forth in the *Method*.

These differences in treatment of various ornaments in treatises even within the same country or epoch (for instance, those of Quantz, C.P.E. Bach, and Leopold Mozart) were pointed out by Joachim. In a chapter called "On Execution" in the third volume of his *Method* he rightly saw the reason for the differences in the specific requirements of each instrument, in the difference between the esthetic views of the Italian, French and German (both North German and South German) schools and their gradual development and also in the differing individual tastes of the performers, which he regarded as "the product of his [the performer's] upbringing and background."[55]

Bust of Tartini

In the 18th century an opinion prevailed among certain musicians (one of whom was Francesco Geminiani) that in accordance with the theory of affects, each ornament was capable of expressing a certain spiritual state, an affect. However, in aiming at the greatest possible expression in music and its execution, many musicians approached the problem metaphysically, comprehensibly due to historical limitations. Thus Geminiani wrote in his *Method*, which was published in London in 1751, that the mordent (appogiatura) "is proper to express several Passions, as for Example, if it be perform'd with Strength, and continued long, it expresses Fury, Anger, Resolution, etc. But if you play it quite soft, and swell the Note, it may then denote Horror, Fear, Grief, Lamentation, etc. By making it short and swelling the Note gently, it may express Affection and Pleasure."[56]

Giuseppe Tartini took a considerable step forward in his conception of the expressive force of the ornament. Like Geminiani, he found it alien to his way of thinking to transform the use of ornaments into a purely decorative device unconnected with the inner nature of the music itself. Both musicians were fully conscious of the expressive powers of music and musical ornamentation, but Tartini was better able than Geminiani to rise above a mechanistic and naive understanding of these powers.

Tartini found inspiration in the poetry of Petrarch, Tasso and Metastasio, and he would create a musical image in his mind to which he then gave shape in his music and its execution.

154

It was not only the idea and the theme of his music that Tartini sought to individualize, but also the shape they would take in execution, and this included the performance of ornaments. With Tartini the choice of ornaments and the manner of execution were determined by an understanding of the music to be performed and the feeling, idea, experience or, as was said in those days, the affect that it expressed.

The life of the image predetermined Tartini's live, creative execution of the music and his rejection of mechanical and formal use of ornaments. He does not restrict himself to making subtle distinctions in the use of the various ornaments in slow ("serious and mournful") movements and in fast, lively and merry movements. He seeks to individualize their execution within each of these types, too, in accordance with the principal "affect" of the particular musical phrase.

In his *Trattato di Musica* (1754) Tartini wrote: "I can approve of the proper use of musical ornaments in many tunes, but I have never been able to understand the use of exactly the same ornaments in all tunes. I am firmly convinced that every tune that truly corresponds to an affect of words must possess its own individual and original manner of expression, and consequently its own individual and original ornaments."[57]

tioned, there is an interesting example taken from a manuscript in the archives in Padua which records the (apparently improvised) slow movement from one of Corelli's sonatas (Op. 5, No. 9) as executed by Geminiani (the middle line) and Tartini (the last line). This example gives us some idea of Tartini's application in practice of several ornaments (diminution, embellishment of melodic tones, trills, grace notes) that he sets forth in detail in his *Treatise on Ornaments*:

172

The original (Corelli):

The use of Tartini's *Treatise on Ornaments* by modern musicians has been made easier by the new modern edition in German, French and English by Erwin R. Jacobi. He appended to this work of Tartini's a facsimile of an Italian manuscript copied down by a pupil of

Tartini's, Giovanni Francesco Nicolai,[58] and discovered only a few years ago by Pierluigi Petrobelli in the library of the Benedetto Marcello Conservatoire in Venice. In addition to the main text of the *Treatise* the manuscript contains an extremely interesting instructional work of Tartini's, *Rules for Bowing (Regole per le Arcate)*, with which Nicolai's manuscript begins and which we will consider further.[59]

Another manuscript copy of the *Treatise* was found in Italy at about the same time as this one and is now in the University of California.[60]

There are sufficient grounds to suppose that the first edition of the *Treatise* to be published in Paris was based on a manuscript belonging to another pupil of Tartini's, Pierre Lahoussaye, a Frenchman, who was most likely the one who translated it into French.

Let us try however briefly to give an idea of the contents of Tartini's *Treatment on Ornaments*, for this will help to give a better understanding of his style of execution and some of his esthetic and instructional principles.

In the first part of his *Treatise*[61] Tartini considers various kinds of grace notes, trills, tremolos (as he calls vibration) and mordents; in the second natural and artificial "figures" ("modi", that is, devices or ways of using ornaments) and natural and artificial cadenzas. Whereas the first part deals with the main ornaments used in music, the second part gives the principles of free ornamentation.

Tartini describes grace notes (appoggiature)—long and short, rising and falling—of which he considers the last to be the more natural. A long, descending grace note (which, like the others, is executed with a single stroke of the bow with the principal note) is given half its length; if the main note is dotted the grace note is given two thirds of the whole length. In such cases Tartini says that the bow must begin the long grace note softly, increase it gradually until halfway through its length and decrease it again to the main note. Since the grace note fell on a stronger beat in the bar, the importance of the main note needs a short trill to emphasize it.

173

Unlike a number of other authors who wrote on ornamentation, Tartini connects the character of the long grace note not only with rhythm and dynamics, but also with the essence of the music itself.

156

"The effect of such grace notes," he writes, "is to give the expression melodiousness and nobility. Thus, they suit all slow, mournful tempi. If they were used in gay, quick tempi, known as the 'Lombard style,' their brilliance would be dimmed and the liveliness of such tempi would be weakened."[62]

"The effect of short, passing grace notes," he goes on to say, "is to sharpen and brighten the expression. It is very different from that of long grace notes, which merely make it sing more. Short, passing grace notes should therefore not be used in slow, mournful pieces, but only in allegros, or at most in those marked andante cantabile."[63] And here Tartini gives an example of how to execute short grace notes:

Tartini finds grace notes that proceed by leaps especially suitable for "cantabile, grace and patetico pieces":

Especially important in modern practice are Tartini's directions as to the correspondence of long grace notes to slow, cantabile pieces and rapid ones to lively, vigorous pieces.

Andreas Moser rightly sees a clear example of how this principle of Tartini's, which is connected with his esthetic views, can be completely misunderstood in the interpretation of grace notes made by Robert Reitz. In his arrangement of the Allegro of the Violin Concerto in A major, in spite of Tartini's distinctly expressed directions, he uses a long grace note:

One can hardly imagine the thought entering anyone's head to treat the grace notes in the third bar of the Allegro from *The Devil's Trill* as long ones, for it would be in complete contradiction to the energetic and determined character of the music.

From grace notes Tartini goes straight on in his *Treatise* to trills. "The trill," he says, "is an ideal ornament in music; but it must be used as salt is used in cookery. Too much or too little salt spoils the result and it should not be put in everything one eats."[64]

In his *Treatise* Tartini recommends beginning the trill on the higher note, as did C.P.E. Bach and L. Mozart after him. But later he discarded this dogmatic rule and in his *Letter to a Pupil* (in accordance with the development of musical practice) he speaks of the advisability of beginning a trill with the main note.

Tartini makes a strict differentiation between the trill of a whole tone and the trill of a semitone. He pays special attention to the speed and dynamics of the trill and their connection with the expressive aims of the music and recommends beginning the trill slowly and softly and then gradually increasing its speed and strength. The following quotation reveals the esthetic undertones of this recommendation:

"The slow trill is suitable in serious, pathetic and sad pieces; the moderate trill in moderately gay ones; the fast in pieces which are gay, lively and swift. A good player must practice and master trills at all these speeds. It is clear that a trill in a cheeky, swaggering allegro must not be the same as in a grave or an andante malinconico, nor one on the E string the same as one on the G string."[65]

These last words show that Tartini made the character of the trill dependent on the timbre of the string and the register. He considered a long trill suited to the end of a musical phrase in a cadenza and pointed out the difference of trills on half and on full close cadences. Tartini considered a short trill possible in ascending and descending scales and arpeggio-like passages. He objected to a trill being made an octave higher, apparently a common practice among violinists of those days.

After that, a specific type of semitone trill is described. It is not produced by the raising and lowering of the finger, but by making a rapid rippling motion of the whole hand, resembling the movement made for vibrato. Tartini recommends this kind of trill in playing melodies that are passionate in character.

Tartini stresses the melodiousness of the following trill and its accordance with nature:

Then he gives examples to show his conception of how to use the trill according to considerations of rhythm and bowing:

Tartini warns against trilling on the first note of any strain and against putting two trills on two successive notes, except when one wishes to make a "chain of trills." An example of the use of such a chain is to be found in the first movement (written in Tartini's first creative period) of a Concerto in G major:

In giving examples of trills in scales of dotted notes, where trills can come either on the long notes (a dotted quaver) or on the short ones (a semiquaver), Tartini remarks that the first kind makes the expression more melodious *(cantabile)* and the second sharper *(sonabile)* and more daring:

Though the *Treatise* deals with the mordent after vibrato, it seems more advisable to speak of it now, since it is organically close to the grace note and the trill.

The mordent (a term used by Tartini to cover two different kinds of ornament) that consists of three small ascending or descending notes (of which the author prefers the latter) joined to the main note is, says Tartini, an ornament given by Nature and Art and should be played very fast and lightly. As the mordent is a kind of accent giving emphasis to the main note, it should not be placed on single notes outside the bar or on any other that the performer does not in-

159

tend or need to emphasize. He gives the following examples of the mordent:

182

183

According to Tartini, the mordent "makes the main note more lively, bold and fiery." For this reason from its very nature the turn is more suited to quick, light music *(sonabile)* than to merely smooth strains *(cantabile)*. When we want to use it in such strains it does not suit every kind but only andantes and allegros when we wish to give "spirito nell' espressione" ("fire to the expression"). It should never be used in slow, sustained or mournful strains."[66]

Tartini also gives another kind of mordent consisting of two, four or six small notes resembling a trill, but differing from it in that the main and the lower note alternate:

184

"The mordent is much used in bright, lively pieces. It is bad in slow, mournful ones."[67]

Finally let us turn to vibrato which (as has been said the *Treatise*) includes the ornaments[68] together with the grace note, the trill and the mordent and the tremolo (from the Italian tremare, meaning tremble). The tremolo is based on an imitation of the natural vibrations of a string that has been struck. Tartini says that to reproduce it on the violin, the viola or the cello, a finger is pressed on the string and is caused to vibrate by a movement of the wrist. The finger does not leave the string, though it is raised a little.[69]

Tartini uses a wavy line above the notes to denote vibrato, varying the line according to the changes in the speed (and amplitude) of the vibrato:

185

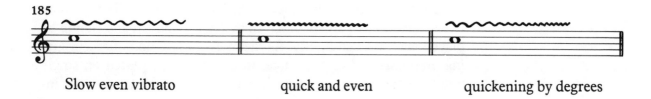

Slow even vibrato   quick and even   quickening by degrees

160

Today every violinist and cellist as a rule plays with almost continuous vibrato, whereas in Tartini's time this was looked upon as a sign of bad taste. In his *School for Violin* Leopold Mozart ironically says of such violinists: "There are musicians who constantly tremble on every note, as if they were in a fever. The tremolo (*i.e.*, vibrato — L.G.) should only be used where nature requires it."[70]

In our days a special notation is needed for playing without vibrato, "non vibrato," when the composer wishes to make the musical phrase restrained, austere or non-emotional (we find such cases in compositions by Bartok, Prokofiev, Stravinsky, Britten and others); but Tartini, Geminiani and Leopold Mozart (and later even L. Spohr[71]) sometimes marked the music specially for episodes that required vibrato.

Tartini considered vibrato more suitable for an instrument than for the voice. He rejects its use as an ornament in *messa di voce* since it requires special purity of intonation, which especially with singers may be spoiled by vibration. "This ornament," he writes, "makes the final note of a phrase sound excellent, when that note is long. It flatters both the *suono (tone) and the canto (melody)*."[72] Tartini also finds that vibrato sounds excellent on long, syncopated notes, both on single and doublestops. In this connection he speaks of making the vibration stronger on relatively strong beats in the bar, which is contradictory to our conception of the essence of syncopation:

186

The second part of Tartini's *Treatise* is devoted to so-called free ornamentation, where much is left to the taste and skill of the performer, to his feeling for style and his gift for improvisation. The inclusion of such sections in 18th century treatises came as a reaction on the part of advanced musicians and teachers against the arbitrary conduct of many performers who were devoid of a sense of moderation and ability or desire to understand the style of the music they performed, which they disfigured with unsuitable and tasteless ornaments.

Nevertheless, in setting down his rules, Tartini is far from being dogmatic and leaves a great deal to the performer's gifts, taste, imagination and ability to improvise.

Tartini makes a distinction between natural and artificial "modi" ("figures") and natural and artificial "cadenze" ("cadenzas"). He uses the term "natural figures" to denote those melodic ornaments that are a gift of nature and are often sung by "people who have no knowledge of music, who sing for their pleasure very gracefully".[73] Tartini affirms that figures such as those he sets forth in the *Treatise* exist among the people in large numbers. Many of them he no doubt heard from the people he had lived among in his childhood in Slovenia and Italy:[74]

Tartini cites sixty-two examples of "natural figures" and remarks that "they are simple and taught by Nature, and we shall come to do them without study, application, practice or thought."[75] There is no doubt that Tartini himself used these figures extensively when performing.

Tartini contrasts "natural figures" to "artificial figures," which come into being as a result of the composer's skill and are therefore innumerable. He says "they depend on good taste and can only be used in places which are in themselves melodic."[76]

"Artificial figures" should not be used "whenever the subject of the composition and its details have a particular intention or sentiment. The music must not be altered in any way and must be expressed as it is. This arises quite often and therefore tasteful artificial figures are restricted to only a few places."[77] Tartini finds these places in cadences, or, to be more exact, before the first of two notes forming a cadence.

Natural, and to an even greater extent, artificial cadenzas are more imaginative for they are closely allied to the art of improvisation.

"Natural cadenzas" conclude a musical phrase *(cantilena)*; the "harmonic cadenzas" belonging to them must correspond to the bass (nor may they form parallel fifths and octaves) and they must always be played "in strict time."[78] Here are a few examples of a "natural cadenza":

189

190

191

The *Treatise* gives an enormous number of similar cadenzas and their variants.

Of "artificial cadenzas" Tartini says that they are known as "those by which any piece of music, either slow or fast, is brought to a close. This term indicates final cadenzas on which the singer or instrumentalist stops at will without regard to the beat, and makes them last as long as he wishes or as long as he can prolong them."[79] The place where the cadenza is played is indicated by a pause sign over the penultimate note of the cadence.

"This kind of cadence," says Tartini, "is nowadays a capriccio rather than a cadence because nowadays every singer or instrumentalist feels entitled to lengthen it, and with such different expressions that it is unreasonable to speak of a 'cadence' but rather should one say 'whim' or capriccio . . ."[80]

Tartini was against excessively elaborated capriccios, which would sometimes be even longer than the compositions or movements for which they were designed and with which they had very little in common thematically. Locatelli, as we know, wrote such capriccios for his concertos Op. 3 (*L'Arte del Violino*, 1733), two capriccios for each of his twelve violin concertos.

Unlike Locatelli and other contemporaries of his, Tartini (who usually played a capriccio in the finales of the concertos he wrote at some time before 1740) used one of the main themes of the concerto (or elements of it) in his capriccio. He elaborated it polyphonically with melodic ornaments, rhythmic and bowing modifications and doublestops.

Above we have given examples of cadenzas in an elaborated capriccio and a short cadenza "in a single breath," from Tartini's manuscript of his Concerto in E major (No. 46). Minos Dounias tells us that such capriccios are to be found in quite a number of Tartini's concertos of the first period (Nos. 46, 47, 61, 75, 90, 124 and others).[81] Sometimes the manuscript is simply marked "a capriccio" (or "cadenza"),[82] which implied improvisation by the performer on the pedal point.

Various progressive musicians spoke out, as did Tartini, against the abuse of the capriccio and the cadenza by many of the singers and instrumentalists of the time, who would make them inordinately long and unconnected in style and intonational structure with the main piece of music. However, audiences enjoyed solo virtuoso capriccios and cadenzas and were attracted not only by the virtuosity of the soloist, but also by his ability to improvise. Tartini wrote in his *Trattato di Musica* (1754) that one and the same audience might pay little or not attention to the composition itself, but always showed a lively interest in such (usually improvised) cadenzas.[83] In his *Treatise on Ornaments* he says: "As listeners today like hearing this kind of thing, however disorderly and unsuitable, one must know how to write it."[84]

After this, Tartini speaks of artificial cadenzas that are tasteful. "Instrumentalists have more freedom and facility than singers, because there are many figures and runs suitable to instruments which the voice cannot perform . . ." [85] He gives a number of examples in which ornaments and figurated passages are based on scale-like and arpeggio-like sequences.

A number of examples contain bowing variants (examples 129, 192):

There are interesting examples based on the pedal point (in C major) which serves as a background for the soloist to perform chromatic shifts that are digressions; here is one of them:

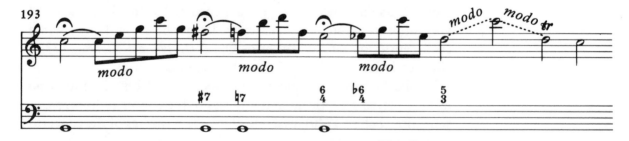

The following are some of the most developed cadenzas (examples 136, 194, 195):

Throughout the *Treatise* one can trace the author's constant attempts to relate the use of ornaments to the nature of the requirements of the music and to the nature of the instrument (or voice) in accordance with good taste and a sense of moderation. Tartini strives to reveal the expressive possibilities of the various ornaments; the peculiarities of their execution to a great extent characterized both his taste and his style of execution.

The ornaments we have considered were ones that he used extensively in his own compositions, contributing to their melodic development and their rhythmic (and bowing) qualities. They required melodic expression and a high degree of mastery of natural and virtuoso violin technique, in short, the very qualities that so strongly characterized the performance of Tartini himself.

Tartini's *Rules for Bowing* are written on a distinctly instructional level, which justifies the consideration of this manual immediately before the *Letter to a Pupil*. At the same time both of these documents also show several traits of Tartini's own manner of execution.

He begins with a clear differentiation of *cantabile* (the song-like character of music and its execution) and *sonabile* (its lively instrumental character). The former is distinguished by smoothness in motion and transition and must be played without any pauses between the notes; the latter does not go step by step, but by leaps, with the notes detached from each other. Tartini stresses the connection between the manner of execution and the subject of the music: "Since music expresses sentiments ('affects'), it is important to keep these separated."[86] And further we read: "To ascertain the character of a piece and whether it should be played allegro or andante (these terms meant not only tempo to Tartini, but their character, too—allegro meant gaily, in a lively fashion, joyfully, and andante meant smoothly, uninterruptedly, in a flowing manner—L.G.) observe whether the rhythm of the accompanying parts is the same as that of the principal part; if so, the piece is *allegro*. If, on the other hand, the parts do not all have the same rhythm, then the piece is *cantabile.*"[87]

Tartini attaches great importance to the smoothness of the bowing, to the necessity to keep to the style and character of the musical phrase. He recommends that the bow be placed on the strings gently at first (obviously due to the fact that the bow was held at a distance from the heel) and that the pressure be increased after that. The bow was to be gripped firmly with the thumb and index finger and held lightly with the other fingers "in order to produce a strong, sustained tone."[88]

Tartini is known to have used not only smooth (détaché, legato), but also sharp, "bouncing" bowings. In his *Rules for Bowing* he uses the term "le note pichettate," which is apparently close to spiccato.

"As regards bowing," Tartini says, "there are no definite rules for determining whether one should begin with a down-bow or up-bow. On the contrary, all passages should be practiced in both ways, in order to gain complete mastery of the bow in both up and down strokes."[89] Thus Tartini rejected the mechanical rule that some musicians of his time still observed, according to which the strong beat in the bar must be played down-bow (in France this was called the rule of *tiré et poussé*).

Tartini wrote that to play an *allegro sonabile* only a small part of the bow should be used.

Today it might seem that some of the things he taught are somewhat formal and outdated. They were due to the properties of

166

the old bow and the way in which it was held and partly also to ideas that were limited historically. This is true for instance of the fact that playing at the point and at the heel of the bow was insufficiently appreciated. Now Tartini's teaching also seems dogmatic when he stated that half-tone sequences must be played legato, or that a note differing in length from others tied to it should be separated from them in bowing.

On the whole, though, Tartini is far from being dogmatic in this manual that he wrote so laconically. He recommends the pupil to practice bowing in different directions and with different parts of the bow, in different kinds of change of position, "so that he is prepared for every situation that may arise."[90]

The most important thing is that one who uses the manual constantly senses the close connection between Tartini's advice on technique and his esthetic views, the expressive tasks that face the performer.

Very close to the *Rules for Bowing* is the equally laconically written *Letter to a Pupil*, which is of no less value for teaching purposes.

This letter was written by Tartini on March 5, 1760, in Padua in answer to the request of his pupil, Maddalena Lombardini, advising her how to practice the violin.[91] It must be said that at this time Maddalena Lombardini was already well known as an excellent violinist, harpsichord player, singer and composer.[92] Thus the advice given by Tartini in the *Letter* is not intended for a beginner.

Tartini puts bowing in the very first place, for it is necessary to have a complete mastery of bowing if one wants to use it equally well for *cantabile* and *sonabile*. He recommends starting the bow movement *(attaca)* very lightly and hardly audible, something like breathing. This technique depends on the lightness of the wrist, after which the sound (and consequently the pressure of the bow) can be increased at will. The purpose of this exercise is to avoid coarseness or harshness in starting the first note at the heel of the bow. Tartini recommends exercises with different parts of the bow, moving it in different directions (down and up).

Then he sets forth what is actually an exercise in *sons filés* (that is, in sustained notes on open strings), an exercise which is used in teaching the violin to this day; he recommends doing this with varying dynamic shades. Tartini considers this exercise to be the most difficult and most important and suggests that an hour should be devoted to it daily, part in the morning and part in the evening. In his opinion it gives the performer the needful mastery of the bow.

To develop lightness in the movement of the right wrist Tartini suggests that his pupil play, every day, a fast (fugal)[93] movement from Corelli's sonatas Op. 5, for instance the Sonata in D major. This fugue should be played staccato or martelé; though Tartini does not use these terms, he speaks of a short stroke, with a pause between the notes (see example 119).

All this should be played with the point of the bow, then between the point and the middle and finally with the middle of the bow. It must be practiced sometimes with a down-bow and sometimes with an up-bow.

Lastly, in order to acquire facility in bowing technique, Tartini recommends playing swift passages of semiquavers requiring a skip over a string or even over two strings, in different keys:

196

This brings the exercises for the right hand to an end. In spite of the laconism necessitated by the epistolary style, Tartini managed to cover all the main components of bowing technique: the *attacca* (striking of the string with the bow), "long bowings," exercises in the various dynamics of tone, in smooth and sharp bowings, in "leaps" across strings, exercises with various parts of the bow and exercises in moving the bow in different directions.[94]

His advice with respect to the technique of the left hand is still more laconic. In effect he gives one exercise for practice with the fingerboard. He recommends taking a violin (orchestral) part in a concerto, a mass, a psalm, etc., and playing it not in the first position, but upon the half shift (or in the second position), that is, with the first finger upon G on the first string. After this, begin in the next position (with the first finger on A), and so on to the end of the fingerboard. One must learn to play at sight in any position, which will give complete mastery of the fingerboard. Thus this exercise enables one to develop subtle muscular sensations based on the inner ear and the aural conceptions of the violinist.

Tartini's last piece of advice is on the trill, exercises in which simultaneously can help to strengthen the fingers of the left hand and to develop agility.

Of extreme importance is a remark made by Tartini, also to be found in his *Treatise on Ornaments*, as to the necessity for mastering the trill at different degrees of speed. He writes: "The same shake will not serve with equal propriety for a slow movement as for a quick one."[95]

Tartini recommends starting the trill slowly and gradually making it faster. He also speaks of trills made with the first finger, (upon an open string) and the fourth, or little, finger, which particularly needs to be developed.

In this letter, which might seem to be devoted to purely technical and methodological matters, we see Tartini as a fine musician reminding his pupil that each technical device, each habit in musical execution is developed to serve the purpose of carrying out some specific task of expression.

Such are the contents of the *Letter to a Pupil* which adds to our knowledge of Tartini's views on teaching and methods.

Let us now turn to another of Tartini's instructional works called *L'Arte del Arco, (The Art of Bowing)*, which comprises fifty variations on a Gavotte from the Violin Sonata in F major (Op. 6, No. 10) by Corelli.

In spite of the name by which this composition is generally known, it is by no means confined to bowing variations for it contains not a few difficulties for the left hand, too. Tartini displays exceptional inventiveness in these variations, using the most diverse combinations of technical devices which goes to show how profound was his understanding (for his time even exhaustive) of the modes of expression on the violin of which he himself had a perfect command.

These variations of Tartini's may be regarded as a kind of encyclopedic compendium—and a fairly complete one—of violin technique in the 18th century

The value of this work consists also in its combination of artistry and technique. Each variation on a successfully chosen simple and noble theme is in itself a small complete piece of music. In almost every one of them Tartini seeks to combine various devices in such a way as not to turn them into formal, monotonous studies and exercises. No wonder *The Art of Bowing* was adopted for use in concert programmes as well as in teaching, and many eminent violinists of the 19th and 20th centuries wrote arrangements for its performance.[96]

One of them, Joseph Szigeti, attributes more than historical importance to it. Citing an example from it in a book of his, he speaks of the forgotten original (meaning that Tartini's original *Art of Bowing* with its fifty variations has been almost completely supplanted by Kreisler's arrangement with three variations), telling violinists that in it "they will find guideposts for the performance of the great Italian master that will help them towards an approximation at least of an authentic performance of masterpieces of the Italian Baroque."[97]

The exceptional variety of bowing strokes in Tartini's variations is largely the product of his rhythmical wealth and his artistic inventiveness. Even without the autograph of *The Art of Bowing*, which has apparently been lost, it is quite possible to use the fabric of one or another of his variations to reconstruct his use of extremely different combinations of smooth, sharp (marked) and "bouncing" strokes.

True, the détaché is used more often than others in a number of variations as for instance in Nos. 4, 13, 15, 17, 21, 23, 31, 44, 46.[98] This stroke may be what is intended for Nos. 39 and 49. The declamatory portato stroke might have been used in Nos. 8 and 32.

Tartini uses the group of sharp strokes (martelé, staccato, marcato) and "bounding" strokes (spiccato, sautillé, saltato, jeté, flying staccato etc.) much more often; they are to be found in nearly all the variations.

Tartini often makes use of "leaps" of the bow across a string. This virtuoso device, which we also come across in the works of other Italian violinists of his time or earlier (Marini, Corelli, Vitali, Vivaldi, Veracini, Locatelli and others), was more or less typical of Italian musicians of the 17th and 18th centuries. Depending on the way it was used, it lent the music an energetic and determined character or one that was merry, graceful and dance-like. Sometimes it gave the illusion of being a kind of duet of a low voice and a high one. We must recall that Tartini included practice of this stroke in the series of basic exercises set forth in his *Letter to a Pupil*.

Tartini uses this note in its pure form (variation 7) and also in combination with other difficulties — ornaments, dynamic contrasts, "bounding strokes," chords, etc. (variations 26, 33, 46 and others):

Tartini constructs variation 8 with a dotted stroke:

170

There is an example of staccato in variation 45:

Examples of light bounding strokes can be found in variations 4, 11, 41:

In a number of variations bowing difficulties are complicated by rhythmical ones, as in No. 3 (syncopation), Nos. 4 and 41 (a combination of duplet and triplet patterns), No. 44 (the "Lombard style") etc. (examples 202, 205, 206):

As for the technique of the left hand, the devices are essentially connected with the devices in the technique of bowing. The various difficulties for the left hand can be found in almost all the variations.

Note the passage technique in variations 17, 31, 44, 46, requiring agility in fingering (examples 199, 206, 207, 208):

Close to these are the variations (of which there are a majority) in which we find an extensive use of the trill and other ornaments also requiring developed fingering technique in their execution:

Particular note should be taken of variations where doublestops are used in an interesting way—Nos. 11, 14, 22, 36, 40, 42, 43, 47 (examples 211, 212, 213):

In the following example from variation 48 Tartini uses double-stops, not moving parallel to each other, but as two independent voices, one of which serves as an accompaniment:

Variations 37 and 50 give examples of the use of chord technique:

In addition to everything else, Tartini's variations require perfect coordination of the movements of both hands.

The composition sets the performer complicated tasks of musical technique and it has to this day preserved its importance for teaching purposes. If these variations on a theme of Corelli's are not sufficiently used in our music teaching today, it can be explained by the fact that they have never been published in this country in the original and in full. The outstanding merits of Tartini's *Art of Bowing* make it extremely desirable that publishers should issue a complete edition of the work in a modern arrangement.

TARTINI'S SCHOOL

As we have said previously, Tartini founded the Paduan violin school, which he directed for over forty years. What did this school give to the world?

Musicians from different parts of the world came to learn from Tartini, to perfect their skill in playing the violin, and they called him the "maestro delle nazione." Antonio Capri, Tartini's Italian biographer, names over seventy of Tartini's pupils worthy of note in the history of violin playing. Among them were the Italians Paolo Alberghi, Pasqualino Bini, Giovanni Battista Carminati, Domenico Dall'Oglio, Maddalena Lombardini (Sirmen-Lombardini), Filippo Manfredi, Giulio Meneghini, Guglietto Tromba, Pietro Nardini, Giovanni Francesco Nicolai, Domenico Ferrari, Francesco Salieri and Giuseppe Antonio Capuzzi; the Germans Josef Holzbogen, Johann Gottlieb Graun, Karl Matthäus Lehneis, Johann Gottlieb Nauman and Friedrich Wilhelm Rust; the Dalmatian-born Michele Stratico; the Frenchmen Pierre Lahoussaye and André Noel Pagin; the Czech Antonin Kammel; the Spaniard Don-Paolo Gastarobbu; the Swede Anders Wesström and the Dutchman Pieter Hellendaal.

Tartini's principles of performing were also passed on by his pupils. Thus, the Czech violinist Frantisek Benda (1709-1786) learned them from Graun, and another Czech violinist, Vaclav Pichl (1741-1805), learned them from Nardini. The way the latter played delighted Leopold Mozart, who wrote: ". . . I have heard the famous Nardini . . . It is impossible to hear anything of greater beauty, purity, evenness of tone and melodiousness. And with all this he has nothing heavy in his playing."[99]

Many of Tartini's eminent contemporaries who were not directly pupils of his learned from him by listening to his performance and studying his works. A whole generation of violinists was brought up on the Paduan maestro's compositions.

But if we take his direct pupils alone, we can see by the marked artistic individuality of such of them as Pietro Nardini, Maddalena Lombardini, Domenico Ferrari, Pierre Lahoussaye, Filippo Manfredi or Domenico Dall'Oglio that Tartini was a sensitive, talented teacher. While instructing the young violinists in the general esthetic and pedagogical principles of his school, he gave each of them freedom to develop his own specific artistic talents. Yet Tartini's numerous pupils, as also his "musical grandchildren," who constituted his school, formed a single trend in the violin art, one might say in the bowing art, of the 18th and 19th centuries, a trend rich in offshoots.

A contemporary of Tartini's, Antonio Eximeno (1729-1808), spoke of him as the continuer of Corelli's famous school and wrote that "Tartini added elegance and mobility of the bow to the school. It was in this school, founded by Corelli and perfected by Tartini, that Costanzi, Boccherini, Bottesini, Pugnani, Nardini, Giardini, Manfredi, Lolli, Ferrari, Freddi and many other players of bow instruments, who delighted Europe, had matured their art."[100]

Giuseppe Tartini and his best pupils imbued the school with progressive features—humanity and democratism, uniformity of artistic principles in the arts of composition and execution, profundity and expression in execution, a high degree of cultivation in the tone, virtuoso skill that was not aimed at simply producing an outer impres-

Domenico Cimarosa

Niccolo Porpora with his pupils

sion, naturalness in the devices of violin technique.

The name of Tartini as the last outstanding figure in Italian violin art in the 18th century and as head of a school and author of many musical works that still retain their importance to a large extent, has always been profoundly honored, not only by his contemporaries but also by generations of violinists and music teachers since that time.[101]

Giuseppe Tartini's art, with its meaningfulness and humanity, comprises an important page in the history of the art of the violin. Many of his principles in methods of teaching are used to this day, and his best compositions still thrive both in music classes and on concert programmes.

Gaetano Pugnani

Chapter 5

Tartini in Russia

 Giuseppe Tartini is one of the leading figures of the Italian school of violin-playing in the 18th century, a school whose art is as meaningful today as it ever has been.

David Oistrakh

Tartini's name and his work came to be known in Russia in his lifetime. There were numerous Italian musicians who went to Russia at that time, eager to give concerts or to work in court or private chapels. There were also members of the Russian nobility who had been abroad, and all had tales to tell of Giuseppe Tartini, of his wonderful art, of his musical creations and of his teaching ability which had earned him wide recognition.

Among the Italian musicians who lived and worked in Russia in the 18th century were not only the composers and conductors Francesco Araya, Vincenzo Manfredini, Baltassare Galuppi, Tommaso Traetta, Giovanni Paisiello, Giuseppe Sarti and Domenico Cimarosa, but also a number of Italian violinists—Giovanni Verocai, Luigi Madonis, Pietro Mira (Pedrillo), Domenico Dall'Oglio, Giovanni Piantanida, Antonio Lolli, Carlo Cannobio[1] and others—who probably played not only their own works but compositions by the Paduan maestro too.[2]

In the course of nearly forty years (1735-1764) Tartini's school in Russia was well represented by his pupil Domenico Dall'Oglio, whose repertoire most certainly included works by his teacher in addition to his own compositions.[3]

Records exist according to which in the latter half of the 1760's Peter III, who played the violin himself, intended to invite Tartini to enter his service at court. Yakob Shtelin, who doubtless exaggerated the Russian monarch's interest in music, wrote: "He wants to bring old Tartini from Padua to Petersburg, for he considers that he belongs to his school."[4]

Tartini's fame as an outstanding musician spread throughout Russia while he was yet alive. It is in this light that one should view the unconfirmed assertion that the wonderful Russian natural-born violinist Ivan Khandoshkin (1747-1804) (who came of a family of serfs and was taught in his youth in St. Petersburg by the Italian violinist Tito Porta) reportedly later took lessons in violin-playing from Tartini in Padua.[5]

There can be no doubt, however, that the Russian violinist was familiar with Tartini's music and he probably played Tartini's compositions for the violin. For all Khandoshkin's originality and the specific Russian features in his art, his sonatas and even his variations on Russian songs reveal certain traits and techniques that show the closeness of these two violinist-composers.

That Khandoshkin was close to Tartini's school is also borne out by notes made by Vladimir Odoyevsky (1804-1869), the outstanding Russian musicologist in the thirties of the last century. In them he mentions the fact that Tartini's method was typical of Khandoshkin and that in his old age the Russian violinist played arpeggios with Tartini's bowing.[6]

In his lifetime Tartini's works must already have been included in the repertoire of talented serf musicians, most of whom remain unknown.

In 1784, some time after Tartini's death, his pupil, Maddalena Lombardini-Sirmen, made an exceptionally successful concert tour of St. Petersburg and Moscow that lasted several months. On February 13 of that year she gave a concert in Peter's Theater in Moscow; later, "the fine violin virtuoso," as the Russian papers called her, played at a concert in the Vospitatelny Dom (House of Education) and took part in other concerts in Moscow. On April 13 and May 7 Maddalena Lombardini gave concerts in St. Petersburg. Everywhere she went she performed her own compositions, not only as a violinist, but also as a vocalist and harpsichord player. She only left Russia in September, 1784.

It is of interest to note that a year later the catalogue of music which was on sale in Ivan Schokh's "Dutch Store" included violin duets by this pupil of Tartini's.

Three years before that the Italian violinist Gaetano Pugnani (1731-1798), also supposed by some authors (Eximeno, Fayolle, Dounias)[7] to have been a pupil of Tartini's, had been to Russia. Pugnani is known to have been a pupil of Somis and to have belonged to the Piedmont school of violin-playing, which does not rule out the possibility that he might, from time to time, have taken lessons from Tartini, although, according to F. Torrefranca, Tartini is a classicist and Pugnani is a romanticist.[8] It is very unlikely that the latter could have remained influenced by the style of the Paduan maestro.

Gaetano Pugnani arrived in St. Petersburg with his young pupil Giovanni Battista Viotti in the spring of 1781, and was a great success both at his public concerts and at court.[9]

Tartini's compositions were sold in Russia as early as the 18th century, as can be established from various publications of the time. For instance, the sales catalogue of Ivan Schokh's "Dutch Store" in Moscow for 1785 advertised Tartini's sonatas for the violin (*Twelve Sonatas* Op. 1 and *Six Sonatas* Op. 2).

In 1778, several years after Tartini's death, the Russian prince A.M. Byeloselsky, who had stayed in Italy in 1776, published a small book in the Hague called *De la Musique en Italie* in which he spoke of Tartini with great respect (p. 26). He wrote of the superiority of the Italians in the sphere of that "most splendid" of all instruments, the violin, "which was immortalized by Tartini, Nardini and Pugnani, just as Orpheus immortalized the lyre."[10]

Elsewhere in his book the same author wrote: "Those who study in Italy the art of combining sounds with interest often consult the treatises of Padre Martini, Tartini and Graun . . . ."[11]

Tartini is mentioned in a number of Russian publications of the early 19th century. In 1804 Leopold Mozart's *Method* for the violin (1756) was printed in St. Petersburg in a Russian translation by P. Torson (or Gorson) under the title of *Mr. Mozart's Thorough School for Violin.* Although Tartini is not mentioned in the book by name, his influence can be felt in much of it. For instance, even before the first edition of *The Devil's Trill* had come out, an example from the finale of that composition and one from the manuscript of a concerto of Tartini's were referred to by Leopold Mozart as having been written by "one of the most renowned composers of our times."[12] This Russian translation of 1804 (which is not always precise) puts it like this: "I here include two examples taken from a composition by a renowned composer of our times."[13] By that time the composer's name and his *Devil's Trill* sonata were already well-known to Russian music lovers.

On the first page of the Russian translation (1812) of *Méthode de Violon* by Baillot, Rode and Kreutzer (of the Paris Conservatoire, published there in 1804), it says that the violin, which "possesses different qualities, depending on the desire and disposition of the best musicians . . . is agreeable, touching and delightful under Tartini's bow."[14]

A year before the appearance of this publication, Tartini was mentioned in a newspaper called the *Moskovskiye Vedomosti.* It carried the oft-repeated story of the dream of "the renowned composer Tartini" that inspired him to write *The Devil's Trill,* which "all connoisseurs of music recognize as a masterpiece."[15]

It must be said that in the eighteen twenties both Tartini's sonatas and his *Variations on a Gavotte by Corelli* (*The Art of Bowing*) could be brought in Moscow and St. Petersburg shops; it was also possible to get them in lending libraries.[16] There can be no doubt that Tartini's works circulated in Russian musical circles.

Tartini, "the first and most excellent violinist," was one of a number of the world's most outstanding musicians to be featured in Kushenov-Dmitrievsky's *Lyrical Museum,* published in St. Petersburg in 1831. The eight-page article devoted to him contains the story of his life and work and concludes with this rather quaintly worded but true characterization: "His singing was full of life and feeling, while his harmony, though skillful, was effortless and pure. Among violinists he was always one of the first of those, who, having a perfect mastery of the bow, taught this art to others, too. The difficult passages in all his compositions for the violin, but above all the excellent musicians that he created, are unquestionable proof of his knowledge of *violin fingering.*"[17]

The author of this curious collection of articles names Nardini and Pugnani among the pupils and representatives of the "Tartini school."[18]

Tartini's popularity with the Russian intellectuals of the first half of the last century, or rather, the appeal that the musician's romantic image had for them, is borne out, among other things, by a *Fantasy-Intermezzo in Three Movements* entitled *Tartini* and devoted to the Italian violinist. Written in blank verse and signed N.K., it was printed in a St. Petersburg almanac called *Halcyon*, a collection of prose and poetry published in 1833.[19]

The play was written by the Russian poet and musician Nikolai Kukolnik (1809-1868), a friend of Michael Glinka's, who wrote music to his texts.[20]

The *Fantasy-Intermezzo* is about the love of young Tartini and Clarissa and how their love triumphed over Count Cornano. The scene is laid in Padua; there are a few other similarities to actual facts from Tartini's biography here and there, but the plot unfolds mainly according to the promptings of the author's romantic imagination.

Tartini's romantic image and his *Devil's Trill* sonata continued to capture the imagination of Russian writers. In 1851 one of them, N.D. Koshkaryov, adopted the pen name of Kapellmeister Kreisler (a character from E.T.A. Hoffman) and published a story in a St. Petersburg magazine, *Pantheon and Repertoire of the Russian Stage*, which he called "The Tartini Trill." He based it on facts from Tartini's life, but gave them a fantastic twist.[21]

A Russian dictionary of music from the middle of the last century called Tartini "the most renowned 18th century virtuoso and composer for the violin."[22] And on the eve of the centenary of Tartini's death a biographical essay on the composer appeared in the "Literary Supplement" of *Novelist.*[23]

Several pages were devoted to the Paduan violinist by Nikolai Kirilov in a book on violinists of the 17th-19th centuries that was printed in St. Petersburg in 1873.[24]

As early as the beginning of the last century the well-known Russian violinist Alexei Lvov (1798-1870), who was praised highly by Mikhail Glinka and Robert Schumann, studied Tartini's compositions to improve his playing. "From the age of 19," he recalled later, "I studied by myself, without teachers, and working constantly for three or four hours a day, I tried to form my style by making a careful study myself of such great violinists and musicians as Corelli, Tartini, Gaviniès, Viotti, Kreutzer, Baillot, Rode and others."[25]

Vladimir Odoyevsky, a contemporary of Alexei Lvov's, was perfectly familiar with Tartini's music and particularly valued his *Devil's Trill* sonata. In 1837 he made the subtle and penetrating remark that Tartini "had anticipated the romantic taste of our age" and that "a new epoch had begun for the violin" with *The Devil's Trill*.[26]

Vassili Bezekirsky (1835-1919), a well-known Russian violinist who often performed *The Devil's Trill*, placed Tartini together with Corelli and Veracini among the finest Italian violinists and composers, and he regarded the sonata as a work that merited inclusion in the repertoire of all violinists for a long, long time to come.[27]

Tartini's compositions for the violin were also in the repertoire of Henryk Wieniawski and Ferdinand Laub, the first professors of violin classes at the St. Petersburg and Moscow conservatories. There are accounts of an inspired performance of *The Devil's Trill* by Laub in Russia. This outstanding Czech violinist and artist, who found a second home in Russia, helped to create realistic traditions in the execution of Tartini's famous sonata and wrote his own cadenza for it.[28]

Leopold S. Auer (1845-1930), who was in charge of the violin class of the St. Petersburg conservatoire for nearly half a century (1868-1917), gave a prominent place to Tartini's sonatas both in his concert repertoire and in his teaching. An outstanding performer of *The Devil's Trill* and *Dido Deserted*, Auer paid special attention to these works in the books he wrote not long before he died: *Violin Playing as I Teach It* (London, 1921) and *Violin Master Works and their Interpretation* (New York, 1925)[29]

From the musical and artistic point of view, Leopold Auer places the two sonatas mentioned above on a par with Corelli's *Folia* and other outstanding works created by 17th and 18th century violinists. Auer writes: "In the works just mentioned we find, aside from musical invention, dramatic conception and perfection of form. They rank among the most significant compositions included in the entire range of violin literature. And their spontaneity is not merely a mental, an intellectual originality, an originality of clever calculation, as is the case with the majority of newly-discovered works by distinguished masters, whose very names are full of promise; but they have their origin in those deep founts from which genius alone draws inspiration."[30]

In another of his books, Auer says of Tartini's individual style that it corresponded to the esthetic needs of the time and, to a certain extent, of our times too. He wrote: "There is no doubt but that Tartini stood for the truest expression of the beauty of violin playing, for the best example of style, in the broadest sense of the word, of his epoch."[31]

Tartini's *Devil's Trill* sonata was in the repertoire of some of the most eminent Russian violinists, Vassili Bezerkirský, Karl Grigorovich, Konstantin Dumchev, Georgi Dulov, Miron Polyakin, Mikhail Erdenko and many others. The finest traditions of the Russian classical violin school in executing Tartini's music were continued and developed further in the Soviet art of violin-playing.

Tartini's works have found inspired interpreters among followers of the Soviet school of violin-playing. At the same time they have gained access in the Soviet Union to the greatest possible number of listeners who react sensitively and gratefully to the expressive music.

Tartini's compositions for the violin have been played at concerts given by David Oistrakh, Leonid Kogan, Vladimir Spivakov, Viktor Tretiakov and many other Soviet violinists. Tartini's concerto for the cello has been performed by Natalia Gutman and other cellists. Tartini's music for the violin is produced by the State Music Publishing House, it is recorded on discs and performed on the radio and TV. Among Soviet recordings of Tartini's music are those made by David Oistrakh, Igor Oistrakh, Galina Barinova, Marina Kozolupova, Yuli Sitkovetsky, Igor Bezrodny, Semen Snitkovsky, Ruben Agaronjan and other violinists.

Tartini's works are also in the curriculum of Soviet music schools, colleges of music and conservatoires. Examples from his music are widely used in instructional works by Soviet scholars, as, for instance, in Konstantin Mostras' works on methods of teaching violin.[32]

A collection of violin cadenzas compiled by Dmitri Tsyganov includes eleven cadenzas for *The Devil's Trill*, among them cadenzas by Leopold Auer, Mikhail Erdenko and Alexei Yanshinov. The collection also contains cadenzas for Tartini's Concerto in D minor, including cadenzas by Valentin Artemyev and Mikhail Khait.[33]

*   *   *   *

All that has been said in this book is evidence of the lively interest of Soviet musicians and audiences in Tartini's music. It is kept alive by its richness and expression, its simplicity and humanity, the clarity of its form, and the fact that it is in perfect harmony with the very nature of the violin.

The well-known composer, music critic and writer, Igor Glebov (B.V. Asafiev) concludes his vivid and interesting essay on *Dante and Music* with an expression of gratitude to Italian music of the 16th through 18th centuries "where much of the sun's energy still lies concealed, stimulating thought," a musical art that "radiates the joy of life and an untrammelled sense of its strength."[34] A measure of this gratitude is undoubtedly due to the shining, life-asserting work of the maestro from Padua, whose music is still capable of giving us joy and inspiration.

182

Notes

Introduction

[1]Maddalena Lombardini.

Chapter 1

[1]It is noteworthy that a similar reputation was enjoyed by Czech musicians, who were at that time compelled to seek employment beyond the confines of their own country, which had been occupied by the Hapsburgs.

[2]Suffice it to recall the Serbian "goosla," one of the forerunners of the violin, or the "Polish violin," an early form of instrument of the violin type which was described as early as the 16th century by M. Agricola: "Another kind of violin much used in Poland is tuned in fifths. They produce a fairly clearly sound . . . much more delicate, subtle and gracious than that of the Italian violins." [Martin Agricola. *Musica Instrumentalis Deutsch* (Vierte Ausgabe). Wittenberg, 1545, p. 42.]

[3]This is just what E. Peluzzi does in an article titled "Chi fu inventore del Violino" (*Rivista musicale Italiana*, 1941, Fasc.VII).

[4]The "resistance" of the tenor and the bass viol lasted longer than that of the others. As far back as the 18th century there were splendid performers and composers for the viol, among them Jean-Jacques Rousseau, M. Marais, Caix d'Hervelois and A. Forguerai in France or A. Kuhnel, J. Schenk and C.F. Abel in Germany. The great refinement of this instrument acted as both a brake and a stimulus to the development of the cello; however, by the turn of the century the cello had completely ousted the tenor viol. See L. Ginsburg. *The History of the Art of Cello Playing*. Book 1, Moscow, 1950, p. 148-166 and 266-273.

[5]The early development of violin-playing and the relatively limited use of the viol group of instruments in the Slavic countries (in Czechoslovakia, Poland and particularly in Russia) was largely caused by the complete inconsistency of the expressive potentials of the viol (or the viola da gamba) with the emotional, melodious qualities that are one of the main characteristics of the music of the Slavic peoples.

[6]History has preserved the name of one of the first eminent Italian violinists: Giambattista Giacomelli, called "Giambattista the Violinist." At the end of the 16th century he was known for softness yet breadth of tone.

[7]See M. Ivanov-Boretsky, *Reader in the History of Music*, Part 2, Moscow, 1936.

[8]See Monteverdi's preface to the work cited above. In the same composition he displays an early understanding of the dynamic possibilities of bow instruments by introducing the morendo effect of "making the bow die."

[9]In the score of *Orpheus* the bow group is represented by two small violins "alla francese," ten da braccio viols (viole da braccio), three da gamba viols and two double bass viols. As Boris Struve has convincingly proved (see his *Process of Formation of Viols and Violins*, Moscow, 1959, p. 198 ff.), by "da braccio viols" Monteverdi means instruments of the violin (and not the viol) family, including the violin proper;" *"violini piccoli alla francese"* would seem to mean the so-called quart-violins, which are tuned a fourth higher than the violin.

[10]In 1625 Carlo Farina entered the Dresden chapel, and ten years later he continued his career as a violinist in the chapel at Danzig (now Gdansk).

[11]The bass-part was usually given to the cello, which could be supported by the harpsichord or the organ playing from a figured bass.

[12]It is noteworthy that Monteverdi and Marini, who played such an imporant role in the history of the violin, both came from towns in the north of Italy (Cremona, Brescia) where perfected classical models of the violin were created by Gaspare da Salo, Maggini, Amati, Guarneri and Stradivari.

[13]It is the bow lyre (lira da tirar, lira da braccio) that is referred to here.

[14]Literally *Sonata for the Inventive Violin*. This sonata is part of Opus 8 (published in Venice in 1629), in which the technique of doublestops on the violin is used daringly.

[15]See Marc Pincherle: *Corelli*, Paris, 1933, p. 5.

[16]On music composed for the violin by masters of the Bologna school see H.G. Mishkin: "The Solo Violin Sonata of the Bologna School," *Musical Quarterly*, 1943. No. 1.

[17]According to other sources, he was also a pupil of Giovanni Benvenuti.

[18]This comparison by Geminiani is cited by John Hawkins, *General History of the Science and Practice of Music*, London (1766. Volume the Fourth, p. 310). According to him, Corelli's style of playing contained a combination of learning, elegance and emotion.

[19]See H. le Blanc. *Defense de la Basse de Viole* . . . Amsterdam, 1740.(The German translation: *Verteidigung da Viola de Gamba* . . . Kassel & Basel, 1951, p. 99.)

[20]The church style of the 17th and 18th centuries by no means implied that the music was clerical in character. The forms of church music at that time were often (especially in Italy) permeated with secular, democratic substance, and with their organs and splendid chapels the churches were often transformed into a kind of concert hall, accessible to large audiences made up of various sections of the population.

[21]The keyboard bass parts might be played by bow instruments as well (first the gamba, then the instruments that took its place: the cello and the double bass), also by plucked instruments (the lute and the theorbo). Not infrequently violin music would be accompanied by a bow bass (with no keyboard instruments).

[22]See Marc Pincherle, *Corelli*, p. 107. Some investigators rightly note elements of the sonata form in Corelli's *Folia* (see K. Kuznetsov and I. Yampolsky, *Arcangelo Corelli*, Moscow, 1953, p. 53).

[23]Vivaldi led the chapel in Manuta for several years; Vivaldi's absences from Venice were often connected with productions of his operas.

[24]In various papers of the conservatory Vivaldi is referred to as "Maestro de concerti," "Maestro di choro" (see M. Pincherle, *Antonio Vivaldi et la musique instrumentale*, Tome premier, Paris, 1948, p. 293).

[25]Vivaldi's concertos for the cello, for the viol d'amore and for wind instruments are second only to his violin concertos.

[26]For a thematic list of Vivaldi's published and unpublished works see the second volume of M. Pin-

cherle's monograph (M. Pincherle, *Antonio Vivaldi et la musique instrumentale*, Tome second, Paris, 1948).

[27] Later Bach rearranged some of the concertos from this opus for clavier and organ.

[28] Among these are concertos for two and for four violins.

[29] Program titles were given to other concertos of this opus as well: *Storm at Sea, Desire, The Hunt.*

[30] Tamara Livanova, *History of West European Music up to 1789,* Moscow-Leningrad, 1940, p. 344.

[31] The best of Vivaldi's immediate pupils were Johann Georg Pisendel, G. Fedele (Daniele Gottlob Treu), Giovanni Battista Samis, formerly a pupil of Corelli's.

[32] It was not for nothing that Tartini called Geminiani "furious" ("il furibondo Geminiani").

[33] See the published facsimile with a preface by David D. Boyden that was put out in London in 1952. Boyden disputes different dates of publication of this work by Geminiani as cited in some books. See also F. Geminiani, *A Treatise on Good Taste in the Art of Music,* London, 1749.

[34] F. Geminiani, *The Art of Playing on the Violin,* London, 1751, p. 1.

[35] "Easy to begin, difficult to end."

Chapter 2

[1] The Slavonic tribe (the Slovenes and the Croats) appeared in Istria as early as the beginning of the Middle Ages.

[2] Santo is the everyday name used by the Paduans to denote the Square and Basilica of St. Anthony.

[3] Marietta Shaginian, *Italiansky Dnevnik* (Italian Diary), Moscow, 1963, p. 23.

[4] Vernon Lee, *Italy: Musical Life in the 18th Century,* Moscow, 1915, p. 277-278.

[5] See F. Fanzago, *Elogi di Giuseppe Tartini,* Padua, 1770; Giorgio Benedetti, "Giuseppe Tartini." *Archeografo Triestino,* Trieste, 1896, p. 120; H. Mendel, *Musikalisches Conversations-Lexikon B.X.;* Charles Bouvet, *Une Lecon de Giuseppe Tartini,* Paris, 1918, p. 62; Paul Brainard, *Giuseppe Tartini,* "Die Musik in Geschichte und Gegenwart," *Lieferung* 120/121, p. 30.

[6] Quoted from Antonio Capri, *Giuseppe Tartini,* Milano, 1945, p. 18.

[7] At that period he fought several duels.

[8] Pierluigi Petrobelli, "Giuseppe Tartini," *Enciclopedia della Musica,* Volume Quarto, Milano, 1964, page 357.

[9] These features, which can already be traced in his sonatas of 1716, are much clearer in in the sonatas published in Dresden in 1721 and in London in 1744; in the latter the influence of Geminiani can be felt.

[10] According to the reminiscences of Tartini himelf, which are to be found in his *Treatises* (1754 and 1767), he had already been to Ancona in 1714, possibly even in 1713; however, Veracini stayed in London from January 23 until December 24, 1714. Therefore, if the violinists did not meet in 1716, as Minos Dounias claims (Tartini could have made a mistake in the date, after forty years), they could have done so early in 1714, before Veracini's departure for London. According to other authorities, Tartini met Veracini in both 1714 and 1716.

[11] Tartini's bow was six centimeters longer than Corelli's.

[12] Francesco Geminiani still held the bow at a palm's distance from the heel.

[13] Tartini later extended the fluting (longitudinal notches) that he introduced in the place where the bow is held to the entire stick. Today the firmness of the grip on the bow is achieved by a wire thread and a thin piece of leather on the stick where it is gripped.

[14] In 1722 in addition to the organists (there were four organs in the Church) it consisted of seven violinists, four viol players, two cellists, two double-bass players and one trumpeter. In 1744 there were eight violinists, three viol-players, three cellists, three double-bass players and one oboist. In 1770, when Charles Burney visited the Santo chapel, it consisted of eight violinists, four viol players, four cellists, four double-bass players and four performers on wind instruments. Tartini's pupils in the orchestra played too. On holidays other musicians were also invited, and then the musicians in the orchestra were often double in number.

[15] After being defeated in the battle of the White Mountain in 1627, Czechoslovakia came under the rule of the Hapsburgs.

[16] For details about A. Vandini, see L. Ginsburg's *History of Cello Playing,* Vol. I, Moscow 1950, pp. 102-103.

[17] Charles De Brosses, *Lettres familieres ecrites d'Italie en 1739 et 1740,* Deuxieme Edition, Tome I, Paris, p. 18.

[18] When Tartini's wife died, Vandini settled in his house to make him feel less lonely.

[19] Antonio Vandini survived his friend by only three years.

[20] Of the young Czech violinists of the twenties, Jan Krtitel Neruda (1705-1763) displayed the greatest talent.

[21] Igor Belza. *History of Czech Musical Culture,* Vol. I, Moscow, 1959, p. 202.

[22] A biographer of Tartini (see *Illustrazione del Prato della Valle.* Padova, 1807) goes so far as to claim that at that time the Italian violinist played in the Vienna court chapel as well.

[23] Tartini's concertos are here numbered in accordance with the thematic index compiled by M. Dounias and arranged according to tonality. See Minos Dounias, *Die Violinkonzerte Giuseppe Tartinis,* Berlin, 1935.

[24] In Prague gamba players enjoyed considerable popularity at that period. In Italy, however, the gamba had nearly everywhere been supplanted by the cello.

[25] From time to time Tartini visited his home town of Pirano when on holiday. It is known that occasionally he travelled to Parma, Camerino, Rome, Bergamo and other Italian cities.

[26] In the decades that followed, the Paduan chapel seems to have lost its former glory. In a letter from Italy dated October 10th, 1795, M.K. Oginsky (1765-1833), the well-known Polish composer, spoke of the mediocrity of the orchestras in Venice, Verona and Padua (see Igor Belza, *Mikhail Oginsky,* Moscow, 1965, p. 50).

[27] In recent times Tartini's *Trattato delle appogiature, Trattato di musica . . . .* and *De principi dell'armonia musicale . . . .* were re-issued in facsimile. We shall return to the *Trattato delle appogiature,* which was of great practical significance. As for the general theoretical system of Tartini's works and his system of musical theory, readers interested in these problems are referred to the following books: Antonio Capri, *Giuseppe Tartini,* (Capitoli VI), Milano, 1945; Alfred Rubelli, *Das musiktheoretische System Giuseppe Tartinis,* Winterthur, 1958.

Alfred Rubelli has published a German translation with his own commentary on Tartini's *Trattato di musica* (Giuseppe Tartini, *Traktat uber Music gemass der wahren Wissenschaft von der Harmonie*, Dusseldorf, 1966).

[28]Joseph-Jerome de Lalande, *Voyage d'un Francais en Italie, fait dans les annees 1765 et 1766, Tome hiutieme*, Paris, 1769, pp. 292-293.

[29]As the years went by Tartini suffered more and more from an arm injury which he had received in 1710.

[30]A gloom was cast over the last period of Tartini's life by the illness of his wife, who died in 1769.

[31]The Pythagoreans were the first to evolve the theory of harmony, which defined, as they believed, not only the structure, but also the content of everything existing. The naivete and historical limitations of the views of these ancient thinkers did not detract from the elements of spontaneous materialism and dialects in their theory, or from their desire to express harmony in numerical form. Proceeding from the assumption that everything cognizable has a number, without which nothing can be understood or cognized, the Pythagoreans made an attempt to apply this thesis to the cognizance of the laws of music and the science of music. (See A.F. Losev and V.P. Shestakov, *A History of Aesthetic Categories*, Moscow, 1965, pp. 36-84.)

[32]The Pythagorean understanding of music as a "harmonious combination of opposites" and "agreement of the diverse" (quoted from the above-mentioned book by A.F. Losev and V.P. Shestakov, p. 40) was further developed in the Renaissance, when it was complemented by the teaching of proportion (expressed numerically) as a major esthetic category. Rene Descartes (1596-1650) went further still. In his rationalistic esthetics he affirms as a key principle "unity in variety" which has a natural affinity with the Pythagorean "agreement of the diverse" that made such a distinct mark on the arts in the 17th and 18th centuries, as it did on the music of Giuseppe Tartini himself.

[33]Charles Burney, *The Present State of Music in France and Italy*, London, 1771, p. 124-126.

[34]"This city (Padua—L.G.) has been rendered no less famous, of late years, by the residence of Tartini, the celebrated composer and performer on the violin, than in ancient time, by having given birth to the great historian Livy," Charles Burney wrote in the year of Tartini's death (quoted from the same edition, p. 120).

Chapter 3

[1]The sonata referred to is the *Devil's Trill*—L.G.

[2]Among these exceptions are *Miserere,* which was first performed in the Sistine chapel in 1768, *Stabat Mater* and a few more vocal compositions. *Miserere* for a choir of five voices, in accordance with Tartini's manuscript in the library of the Paris Conservatory, was published as an appendix to a book called *Nel giorno della inaugurazione del monumento Giuseppe Tartini in Pirano*, Trieste, 1896. In Moscow this work was first performed in 1968 by the USSR State Academic Russian Choir conducted by A.V. Sveshnikov.

[3]Charles de Brosses, *Lettres familieres ecrites d'Italie en 1739 et 1740,* cited from the Russian translation in *Material and Documents on the History of Music*, Vol. II, edited by Prof. M.V. Ivanov-Boretsky, Moscow, 1934, p. 213.

[4]Academician B.V. Asafyev, *Collected Works*, Vol. V, Moscow, 1957, p. 244.

[5]Cited from a Russian translation in the book already referred to, compiled by M.V. Ivanov-Boretsky, p. 51.

[6]For the ancient sources of the imitation theory (which was not alien to Tartini) and the "affects" teaching that prevailed in esthetics in the 18th century, see S. Markus: *History of Musical Aesthetics*, Vol. I, Moscow, 1959, chap. 1.

[7]Romain Rolland: *Collected Works* (Russian translation), Vol. XVII, Leningrad, 1935, p. 206.

[8]S. Markus: *The History of Musical Aesthetics*, Vol. I, p. 47.

[9]From a letter from Luigi Boccherini to M.J. Cherier dated July 8, 1799. Cited by L. Picquot in *Boccherini. Notes et documents nouveaux par Georges de Saint-Foix*, Paris, 1930, p. 194.

[10]See *Denkmaler der Tonkunst in Osterreich*, B. XII, 2. This collection of Biber's work contains fifteen sonatas for violin and Passacaglia for solo violin, which to a certain degree was the prototype of Bach's *Chaconne*.

[11]It was not unusual for the fine arts to serve as an inspiration for musicians of later generations too. Suffice it to recall the pianoforte pieces from Liszt's *Years of Wandering* (1838-1839): *Sposalizio (The Betrothal),* which was written to accord with Raphael's picture of the same name, and *Il Pensieroso (The Thinker),* which resulted from the impression produced by the Michelangelo sculpture. Mussorgsky's *Pictures from an Exhibition* (1874) became widely known; in these the composer gave an artistic musical interpretation of his impressions at an exhibition by his friend, the artist V.A. Gartman. And Glazunov's one-act ballet, *Les Ruses d'amour* (1898), was created in consonance with the picture by Watteau.

[12]Some have it that this name was given to the sonata later.

[13]See Minos Dounias, *Die Violinkonzerte Giuseppe Tartinis, als Ausdruck einer Kunstlerpersonlichkeit und einer Kulturepoche*, Berlin, 1935, p. 91. In the thematic catalogue appended to this book Tartini's concertos are placed in order of tonality. The numbers of the concertos cited further are according to this catalogue by Minos Dounias.

[14]True, later, when a certain democratization of "ecclesiastical" practice came about, Tartini began to drop his ciphering.

[15]Giuseppe Tartini, *Trattato di Musica secondo la vera scienza dell'armonia*, Padua, 1754, p. 148 (cited here and further according to the facsimile published in New York, 1966).

[16]Music on subject matter and verses by Tasso has been written by Monteverdi, Lully, Gluck, Haydn, Salieri, Myslivecek, Rossini, Handel, Skokov, Dvorak and other composers.

[17]Here and further we refer to the thematic catalogue of Tartini's sonatas appended to P. Brainard's thesis (Paul Brainard, *Die Violinsonaten Giuseppe Tartinis*, Diss., Gottingen, 1959, p. 238-327); the sonatas are grouped according to their tonality in this catalogue. Also see a later edition of this catalogue by Accademia Tartiniana di Padova: Paul Brainard, *Le sonate per violino di Giuseppe Tartini. Catalogo tematico*, Milano, 1975.

[18]See Franz Xaver Kuhac, "Tartini und das kroatische Lied," *Prosojeta*, Agram, 1898, Nos. 1-3. S. Straznicky agrees with Kuhac (see Stanislav Straznicky, "Giuseppe Tartini und der kroatische Volksgesang," *Festschrift zu H. Riemanns 70. Geburtstag*). And the Czech investigator B. Studeny

finds a lot in common between Tartini's music and sonatas by the Czech composers W. Wodicka and J. Stamic (see Bruno Studney, *Beitrage zur Geschichte der Violinsonate im 18. Jahrhundert,* Munchen, 1911, p. 63).

[19] Giuseppe Tartini, *Trattato di Musica secondo la vera scienza dell-armonia,* p. 151.

[20] Giuseppe Tartini, *Trattato di Musica . . . .,* p. 158.

[21] A photocopy of the author's manuscript of both this Concerto and his concerto No. 124 in B minor that also belongs to his first period has kindly been placed at our disposal by the Music Archives of the San Antonio chapel in Padua. It is hard to read Tartini's manuscript with its tiny lettering and use of a number of signs, some used for the sake of speed, and others as the conventional signs of the period. For instance, Tartini designates the half-tone lowering of a sharp note by putting a flat sign instead of a natural. (This was sometimes still done by Beethoven. See the introductory remarks by N. Fishman in his *Deciphering Beethoven's Sketchbook for 1802-1803,* Moscow, 1962, p. 5.) It is a curious thing that more often than not Tartini concludes a movement with a tonic chord without a third (the so-called "empty" or "vuoto" chord). It is hard to tell whether Tartini relied in such cases on the mental completion of the chord by the inner ear, or whether the chord was in fact filled in by the organ if this instrument was used in the execution of the particular piece of music.

[22] *Trattato di Musica . . . .,* p. 129 and p. 148.

[23] *Ibid.,* p. 149.

[24] Boccherini was most likely familiar with Tartini's concerto and may have played the cello in performances of it; he might have remembered this concerto in particular because of the second movement, an Adagio, which begins with an expressive solo for the cello.

[25] Antonio Capri, *Giuseppe Tartini,* p. 197.

[26] Two four-movement concertos (Nos. 7 and 117) and two five-movement concertos (Nos. 14 and 23) are an exception; and even in these, additional movements written later might possibly have been played instead of the other movements.

[27] We shall return to the question of Tartini's understanding of the capriccio and the cadenza (he made a distinction between these two conceptions) when we take up his *Treatise on Ornaments.*

[28] The concerto was published in 1916 (Leipzig, E. Eulenburg) from a manuscript in the Mecklenburg Library in Schwerin.

[29] Published in Milan (Ricordi) in 1941.

[30] Tartini heard many an opera staged in Ancona, Venice and Padua (there were three opera houses in Padua); in those days operas by Leo, Porpora, Pergolesi, Vinci and other composers were shown.

[31] Gianrinaldo Carli. "Osservazioni sulla musica antica e moderna," *Opere,* t. XIV, p. 332 (cited according to M. Dounias, p. 146).

[32] Charles Henri de Blainville, *L'Esprit de l'Art Musical.* Geneve, 1754, p. 86.

[33] Cited from an article by Paul Brainard called "Giuseppe Tartini. 'Die Musik in Geschichte und Gegenwart'," *Lieferung* 120/121, p. 135.

[34] In accordance with the practice of the time, however, wind instruments (particularly the hautboys and the horns) were sometimes added to the bow quartet even when the original manuscript of the concerto had no such parts.

[35] The score was published by the Paduan publisher G. Zanibon in 1953.

[36] M. Dounias names three sources of manuscripts.

[37] A score with a pianoforte part by Friedrich Niggli was produced by Hug Co., Zurich, 1947.

[38] We must remember that this was the time of Gluck's reform of the opera.

[39] To this one may add that seventy-seven of the hundred and fifteen sonatas by Tartini mentioned by Dounias are in major keys, and one hundred and thirty-three of the hundred and eighty-seven given by Brainard. All the sonatas that we know by Boccherini, for violin and cello, are in major keys.

[40] Giuseppe Tartini, *Trattato di Musica . . . .,* p. 152. Tartini's ideas in this respect accord with those of his contemporary J.J. Quantz, who gave the major key the power to express "the merry, the audacious, the serious and the elevated," and the minor key the power to express "the languid, the sorrowful and the sweet." See J.J. Quantz, *Versuch einer Anweisung die Flote traversiere zu spielen,* Berlin, 1752. (Faksimile-Nachdruck der 3. Auflage, Berlin, 1780, herausgegeben von Hans-Peter Schmitz, Kassel und Basel, 1953, p. 108. Here and further, quotations will be from the latter publication of the facsimile.)

[41] Hamburg, Anton J. Benjamin (s.a.).

[42] New York, C. Fischer, 1943.

[43] The score and piano arrangement (E. Kaufmann) were published in Zurich (Hug) in 1958.

[44] In the USSR the Concerto in D minor was published (in an edition by G.W. Steiner) without any cadenzas, which limited its usefulness for concerto.

[45] New York, C. Fischer. M. Corti also produced an edition of the Concerto in D major (Milano, Ricordi).

[46] In the seventies the Carisch S.p.A. publishers in Milan began to produce some of Tartini's concertos from a manuscript in Padua. They have published to date his violin concertos Nos. 24, 67, 83, 96, 126 (edited by Edoardo Farina) and Nos. 12, 21, 56, 78, 115, 117 (edited by Claudio Scimone).

[47] This concerto was published in Hamburg (Sicorski) in Brinkman's edition. The Concerto in F major for the flute that remained in manuscript is also attributed to Tartini.

[48] It was about this time that the Czech gamba player Kozec achieved fame. His pupil for some time was Martin Berteau, who later headed the 18th century French cello school.

[49] Apart from this concerto of Tartini's, there is evidence only of a concerto for the gamba in G major of his that has not survived and a concerto for the same instrument by Graun.

[50] This concerto was first published in 1891 in Leipzig (Breitkopf) in an arrangement for the cello by Friedrich Grutzmacher; an edition by G. Salmon appeared in 1921 in Paris (Ricordi); and there is evidence of the existence of an edition by L. Delune in 1910. In 1929 it was published in Mainz by R. Hindemit (Schott) according to the original manuscript (the author's manuscript is in the *Gesellschaft fur Musikfreunde* archives in Vienna). Preference must be given to the last-mentioned edition. Here, unlike the Grutzmacher edition, the orchestral tutti are preserved in full, the cadenzas correspond more to the style of the composition and the original cadenza is given in the Finale.

[51] Leipzig—Wien, Musikwissenschaftlicher Verlag. A year later this concerto was published in Padua (Zanibon) in an edition by O. Ravanello and L. Silva with cadenzas by the latter.
The first edition of the concerto was undertaken by Orest Ravanello in 1903.

[52] Here mention must be made of Ettore Bonelli's free arrangement of Tartini's Concerto in F major

for bow instruments, two hautboys and two horns (Padova, Zanibon, 1957).

[53]P.L. Ginguene, *Concerto. Encyclopedie methodique. Musique.* Tome premier. Framery et Ginguene. Paris, 1791, p. 300.

[54]See P. Brainard, "Giuseppe Tartini," *Musik in Geschichte und Gegenwart* (Kassel), *Lieferung* 120/121, p. 131. In the thematic index of Tartini's sonatas in the same author's dissertation (Paul Brainard, *Die Violinsonaten Giuseppe Tartinis*, Diss., p. 238-327) in the main list alone there are one hundred and eight-seven sonatas, which with the additions add up to over two hundred. The thematic catalogue by Paul Brainard published in Milan in 1975 contains 190 violin sonatas and separate movements.

[55]Andreas Moser. *Geschichte des Violinspiels. Zweite verbesserte und erganzte Auflage von Hans-Joachim Nosselt.* Erster Band. *Das Violinspiel bis 1800* (Italien). Tutzing, 1966, p. 231.

[56]Tartini was already working on his *Twelve Sonatas,* ordered by a Dutch publisher, in 1731; then he dedicated them to his Venetian pupil G.A. Giustiniani. *VI Sonate a Violino, Violine o cimbalo,* Op. 1, published in 1732 (G. Witvogel), were reissued together with six others and an additional pastorale two years later by the Le Cene publishers. The same publishing house produced *VI Sonate a violino e violincello o cimbalo,* Op. 2, in 1745. A large number of sonatas were published in Tartini's lifetime by Le Clerc-Boivin, a publishing house in Paris.

[57]The fact that so much of Tartini's work was published during his lifetime is evidence of their early popularity at a time when most musicians mainly performed their own compositions.

[58]To date the Academia Tartiniana di Padova has published a facsimile edition of 26 sonatas for violin and bass arranged by Claudio Scimone and Edoardo Farina, with an introduction by Paul Brainard (Milano, Carische S.P.A., 1976). In the seventies the same publishers produced, in an arrangement by Edoardo Farina, *12 Sonate per Violino e Basso Continuo,* Op. 1 (Milano, 1972) and *Sei Sonate per Violino e Basso Continuo,* Op. 2 (Milano 1979); *Sonata Pastorale per Violino e Basso Continuo* (Milano, 1975); *Sei Sonate per Due Violini e Basso Continuo* (Milano, 1973).

[59]P. Brainard justly stresses the particular difficulty of classifying Tartini's sonatas according to periods. See Paul Brainard. *Die Violinsonaten Giuseppe Tartinis.* Diss.

[60]Minos Dounias, *Die Violinkonzerte Giuseppe Tartinis,* p. 53.

[61]Exceptions are some four, five and even seven movement sonatas (for example D5, D9, g8 according to Brainard).

[62]Quantz considered that in the transition from the old scheme of slow-fast-slow-fast to the more compact and effective scheme consisting of one slow movement and two fast ones, the influence of the taste of the widening circles of 18th century audiences was felt. They reacted more keenly to fast, lively music (J.J. Quantz: *Versuch einer Anweisung die Flote traversiere zu spielen,* 1752). In this connection Quantz contended that the Adagio should never be too long.

[63]While citing one more sonata with a sequence of fast-slow-fast (the 4th in D major), Brainard expresses his doubts as to whether it was composed by Tartini.

[64]It is interesting that Tartini should not have followed this rule in the three sonatas mentioned above that have the fast-slow-fast structure. The middle movement in them is in the minor tonality of the same name in the sonatas in the major key and in the parallel one in the sonata in the minor key.

[65]Charles Burney: *A General History of Music from the Earliest Ages to the Present Period,* Volume the Third, London, 1789, p. 563.

[66]Padova, G. Zanibon, 1951. E. Bonelli's arrangement is based on the first edition in Paris (L. Hue), which came out in 1745.

[67]G. Zanibon, the publisher, printed a free arrangement of this movement by E. Bonelli as an *Andante con Variazoni* (Padova, 1949).

[68]Among the latest numerous editions of Tartini's sonatas we would like to note eight published in a series called *I Classici della Musica Italiana Raccolta Nazionale diretta da Gabriele d'Annunzio.* N. 32. Milano, 1919 (Giuseppe Tartini. Sonate per Violino con Accompagnamento di Basso Alaborato per Pianoforte a Cura di G. Francesco Malipiero. Revisione Tecnica Violinistica di Mario Corti).

[69]The first to include it in his arrangement of the sonata (in 1862) was L.A. Zelner, who borrowed this movement from Sonata No. 5 of the same opus, transposing it from E minor into G minor and introducing several changes in the musical text (doublestops, chords, a dotted rhythm).

[70]Milano, Ricordi, 1921.

[71]Joseph Jerome de Lalande. *Voyage d'un Francois en Italie, fait dans les Annes 1765 et 1766. Tome huitieme,* Paris, 1760, p. 293-294.

[72]J.J. de Lalande is guilty of several inaccuracies in this book.

[73]According to Pavlov's theory, sleep is a braking of neural activity; but with nervous people the work of certain brain cells does not stop even in sleep. The braking occurs first in the cortex and then spreads downwards into the area beneath the cortex. When the breaking occurs, neural processes take place that are no longer subjected to analysis, and separate parts of the brain continue to work.

Meanwhile vestiges of former centers of irritation that have been strong centers (nidi) of excitement that Pavlov calls "sentry points" come into action. For instance, a violinist may sleep through a loud noise and yet be awakened by the faint sound of a violin; the heightened reaction to even soft strains from a violin may appear in a dream as the result of the reaction of this vigilant "sentry point."

In his "Lectures on the Work of the Great Cerebral Hemispheres" Pavlov says that "such an important act of the brain as synthesis may take place in parts of the hemispheres that are to a certain extent in a state of braking under the influence of some strong irritation that at that particular moment is predominant in the brain. This act may not even be conscious at the time, but it has occurred, and in favorable conditions it may be discovered in the consciousness ready (in a finished form) and seem to have arisen without any apparent cause." (I.P. Pavlov, *Complete Collection of Works,* 2nd edition, revised, Vol. IV, Moscow-Leningrad, 1951, p. 433).

[74]There are also other stories told by musicians of a kind of continuation of their creative work in dreams. Thus, Henrik Wieniawski asserted that his long search for a staccato bowing culminated in success after a dream he had had of it. Alexander Glazunov, who did not as a rule put his compositions on paper until they had matured in his mind (hence the small number of rough copies left by him), said that once he found in a dream the solution to a problem that had been tormenting him. "I recall one occasion," he wrote, "when there was a part of a composition that I just couldn't get right; it came to me in a dream, and when I awoke, the whole composition was complete." (A.K. Glazunov, *Letters, Articles, Reminiscences. Selection.* Moscow, 1958, p. 458.) These acts of creation

that took place "without any apparent cause" in the case of Tartini, Wieniawski and Glazunov may all be regarded in the light of Pavlov's teachings.

[75]K. Rosenschild: *History of Foreign Music to the Middle of the 18th Century,* Volume 1, Moscow, 1963, p. 195.

[76]In earlier editions this movement is called Tempo giusto della Scuola Tartinista, and in the most widespread arrangement by Fritz Kreisler, Allegro Energico

[77]In J.B. Cartier's *Methode* and in other early arrangements this movement is called Andante.

[78]Brainard writes that the motives of the movements in Tartini's sonatas in C major (No. 13), in G major (No. 30) and others are related to each other.

[79]No. 11 in the collection of sonatas arranged by E. Pente and M. Zanon (Moscow, 1937).

[80]The version published by J.B. Cartier and based on a manuscript placed at his disposal by Pierre Baillot coincides almost entirely with the manuscript copy in Padua.

[81]Henri Vieuxtemps is also the author of an arrangement of the sonata for a solo violin accompanied by a second violin, a viol and a cello.

[82]Georg Duburg (1799-1859) put some verses called "Tartini's Dream" in a book on the violin. See George Duburg, *The Violin,* Fifth Edition, London, 1878, p. 53-54. August Panseron (1796-1859), the well-known French composer, teacher and pupil of Francois Gossec, composed a ballad with the same name ("Le Sogne de Tartini") for the voice accompanied by violin obbligato and pianoforte. Among the performers of this piece were Jan Binder, who sang it in Vienna (1830) with the violinist Josef Slavik and the pianist Wilhelm Wurfel, and also Pauline Viardot.

In 1899 an opera by Stanislav Falehi (1851-1922) called *Tartini o il Trillo del Diavolo* was staged in Rome.

[83]Tartini's *Devil's Trill* with directions for performers, in an arrangement by J.J. Joachim and with his cadenzas, was included in the 3rd volume of J. Joachim and A. Moser's *Violinschule,* Berlin, 1905, B.III, p. 70-85.

[84]*Violin Cadenzas,* vol. 1, Cadenzas for Concertos and Sonatas by A. Corelli, G. Tartini and J. Viotti, edited by D. Tsyganov, Moscow-Leningrad, 1951.

[85]See the *Journal of the American Musicological Society,* 1961, No. 3, p. 383-393. The *26 Piccole Sonate per Violino e per Violino Solo* by Giuseppe Tartini was first published in Padua in 1970, arranged by Giovanni Guglielmo and with a foreword by the latter.

[86]Cited from A. Capri: *Giuseppe Tartini,* p.71.

[87]Brainard notes that the lower voice in the violin part in some of these sonatas forms octave sequences with the bass, and quite justly sees in this a confirmation of the possibility of performing these sonatas without a bass. He gives logical proof that some of the additions to the part of the violin, and also in the part of the bass voice itself, were made by Tartini later.

[85]Padova, Zanibon, 1935.

[89]These are movements in his sonatas.

[90]Sonata No. 2 in the collection arranged by E. Pente and M. Zanon (Moscow, 1937).

[91]One can judge how popular the melodic type of Corelli's theme was in the 18th century by several themes that are very close to it in Vivaldi's violin sonatas (Op. 1, No. 7, Op. 5, Nos. 5 and 13). See Walter Kolneder, *Antonio Vivaldi,* Wiesbaden, 1965, p. 58.

[92]See David D. Boyden, *The History of Violin Playing from its Origins to 1761 and its Relationship to the Violin and Violin Music,* London, 1965, p. 271.

[93]Around 1745 there appeared in Paris an edition called *Nouvelle Etude . . . par Mr. P. Pinelli. Augmentee d'une gavotte de Corelli, travailles et doubles par Mr. G. Tartini.* 1758 saw the publication in Paris of *L'Arte del Arco ou l'Art de l'Archet contenant 38 variations composees sur la plus belle gavotte de Corelli.*

[94]Cartier also included in his *Methode* an "Adagio de Mr. Tartini varie de plusieurs facons differentes, tres utiles aux personnes qui veulent apprendre a faire des traitssous chaque notte de l'Harmonie . . ." for violin with bass. There are all kinds of variations by Tartini in it (seventeen "diminutions") of the Grave from his own sonata in F major (Op. 2, No. 5) that are purely sketches (etudes) and exercises of considerable difficulty, mainly for developing ornamentation techniques (finger techniques), which, as Andreas Moser has grounds to believe, were written by Tartini for his own private practice and not intended for publication. Later they went through new editions in Vienna and Paris, but were not very much used in the teaching of music.

[95]There are also transcriptions of this composition for the viola (C. Meyer, 1894), for the cello (P. Bazelair, 1920; J. Stutschewsky, 1923; K. Vapordjiev, 1967) and for double-bass (A. Gouffe).

[97]Trio-sonatas by Tartini have been published time and again in arrangements by E. Pente, H. Riman, H. Damek, Q. Maganini, E. Schenk and others. One of the sonatas has been published in a transcription by P. Bazelair for two cellos and pianoforte. In 1973 the Carisch S.P.A. publishers (Milan) and the Academia Tartiniana jointly printed an arrangement by Edoardo Farina of Tartini's *Sei Sonate per Due Violini e Basso Continuo,* the manuscript of which is in Padua (in the Basilica of St. Anthony, MS 1906).

[98]Michelangelo Abbado, "Giuseppe Tartini," *Enciclopedia della Musica,* Volume Quatro, Milan, 1964, p. 356-357.

[99]B. Paumgartner, *Mozart,* Zurich, 1945. p. 170.

[100]Several of Tartini's quartets have been published as "Symphonies" (E. Pente, M. Aggado, H. Erdmann). Modern publications of this genre of interest are the Andante and the Presto from Tartini's Quartet in D major, published in a transcription for a bow orchestra by E. Bonelli (Padua, G. Zanibon, 1948).

Chapter 4

[1]See *Trattato di Musica,* p. 149.

[2]Jean-Jacques Rousseau, *Collection Complete des Oeuvres,* Tome dix-huitieme, contenant le premier Volume du Dictionnaire de Musique, Bruxelles, 1804, p. 422.

[3]"He does not play, he sings on the violin." J. Mainwaring, *Memoirs of the life of Handel,* London, 1760. (Cited according to an article by E. Heron-Allen on Giuseppe Tartini in *Grove. Dictionary of Music and Musicians,* Vol. VIII, fifth edition, London, 1954.)

[4]Hubert le Blanc sees the peak of Somis' mastery of the violin in the fact that his was the best bowing in Europe, in his skill in holding a sound so long that the very "recollection of it took one's breath

away" (Hubert le Blanc, *Defense de la Basse de Viole contre les Entreprises du Violon et les Pretentions du Violoncel)*. Quoted from the German edition *Verteidigung der Viola da Gamba . . .* Kassel und Basel, 1951, p. 99).

[5]This manuscript was found by P. Petrobelli in Venice and contains the Italian text of Tartini's *Treatise on Ornaments (i.e.,* the original text). It has been appended in facsimile to a modern edition of the *Treatise* prepared by E.R. Jacobi (Celle—New York, 1961), and quotations from Tartini in the present book have been taken from this edition. As for G.F. Nicolai, according to Charles Burney he was one of the best violinists to be found in Rome in 1770 (see Charles Burney, *Present State of Music in France and Italy . . . .*, London, 1771, p. 287).

[6]These words were cited in 1823 in his *Methode* by B. Campagnoli, who was a pupil of Nardini's, hence the musical "grandchild" of Tartini (see B. Campagnoli, *Nouvelle Methode de la Mecanique Progressive du Jeu de Violon*, Leipsic, Cinquieme Partie, p. 17).

[7]Johann Joachim Quantz, *Selbstbiographie,* F.W. Marpurg, Historisch-kritische Beytrage sur Aufnahme der Musik, Band I, III Stuck, Berlin, 1755. (Quoted in Andreas Moser's *Geschichte des Violinspiels,* Berlin, 1923, p. 252.)

[8]True, Moser immediately remarks that "his moving and noble manner of execution was soon to become the most powerful side of his playing." (Andreas Moser, *Geschichte des Violinspiels, Zweite verbesserte und erganzte Auflage von Hans-Joachim Nosselt,* Erster Band, p. 227.)

[9]Johann Joachim Quantz, *Versuch einer Anweisung die Flote traversiere zu spielen,* Berlin, 1752 (Faksimile-Nachdruck der 3 Auflage, 1789, herausgegeben von Hans-Peter Schmitz, Kassel und Basel, 1953).

[10]J.J. Quantz, *Versuch einer Anweisung die Flote traversiere zu spielen,* p. 310. Quantz finds practically nothing in Tartini's compositions "but dry, naive and quite commonplace ideas that might at any rate apply to comic rather than to serious music."

[11]*Ibid.,* p. 323.

[12]*Ibid.,* p. 311

[13]Minos Dounias, *Die Violinkonzerte Giuseppe Tartinis,* p. 41.

[14]See the article, already mentioned, by Michelangelo Abbado in *Enciclopedia della Musica,* Volume Quarto, p. 353-354.

[15]N.G. Chernyshevsky (1828-1889) valued the violin highly for its quality of "being closer than all the other instruments to the human voice," and considered that a musician was deserving of special praise if "the human voice could be heard in the sound of his instrument." The great publicist must have meant not so much the closeness of the sonic characteristics of voice and instrument as the skill of the instrumentalist in using the idiom of his instrument to express human feelings and experiences as strongly as a singer expresses them with his voice (see N.G. Chernyshevsky, "The Aesthetic Relationship of Art to Reality," in a collection entitled *Of Art,* Moscow, 1950, p. 58).

[16]See L. Gerber, *Historisch-Biographisches Lexicon der Tonkunstler,* Leipzig, 1790, p. 621-622.

[17]Charles de Brosses, *Lettres familieres,* Paris, 1860, p. 220.

[18]Charles Burney, *The Present State of Music in Germany,* Vol. I, London, 1773, p. 173.

[19]Charles Burney, *The Present State of Music in France and Italy,* London, 1771, pp. 249-250.

[20]*Ibid.,* p. 43.

[21]See Charles Burney, *The Present State of Music in Germany,* Vol. I, p. 173.

[22]Michael Corrette, *Ecole d'Orphee,* Paris, 1738.

[23]See Wilhelm Josef von Wasielewski, *Die Violine und ihre Meister,* Funfte Auflage, Leipzig, 1910, p. 150.

[24]It is this instructional composition of Tartini's that opens the Italian version of his *Treatise on Ornaments* (mentioned earlier) that has come down to us in a handwritten copy by G.F. Nikolai. See Giuseppe Tartini, *Regole per le arcate (Traite des Agrements de la Musique. Mit dem Faksimile des italienischen Original textes herausgegeben von Erwin R. Jacobi),* Celle—New York, 1961.

[25]The *Treatise* (as we will call the *Treatise on Ornaments* by Tartini in further references), p. 57(3). Here and further page numbers will be given according to the edition of E.R. Jacobi (1961); the page numbers of Nicolai's manuscript will be given in brackets.

[26]Giuseppe Tartini, *Trattato di Musica . . .,* Padua, 1754, pp. 148-149.

[27]From Francois Fayolle, *Paganini et Beriot,* Paris, 1881, p. 26, here cited from Wilhelm Josef von Wasielewski, *Die Violine und ihre Meister,* Funfte Auflage, Leipzig, 1910, p. 141.

[28]This letter is partly cited in Antonio Capri's book *Giuseppe Tartini,* pp. 17-18. The full text of the letter was kindly placed at our disposal by Professor Cesare Barison of the Giuseppe Tartini Conservatoire in Trieste.

[29]In the letter to Tartini (1744) already cited, Gianrinaldo Carli wrote: "Studying, like Pythagoras, the relationships between sounds, you recognized the necessity to make the violin strings thicker and lengthen the bow, to make the vibrations more even and the sound softer and more susceptible to variation" (A. Capri, *op. cit.,* p. 18).

[30]Stefano Arteaga, *Le Revoluzioni del Teatro Musicale Italiano . . .,* Vol. I, Bologna, 1783, p. 294.

[31]See A. Capri, *Giuseppe Tartini,* p. 362.

[32]"A Letter from the late Signor Tartini to Signora Maddalena Lombardini," translated by Dr. Charles Burney and quoted according to the *Treatise on Ornaments in Music,* edited by Erwin R. Jacobi, p. 133.

   Whereas the term "cantabile" (from the Italian "cantare," to sing) that we come across so often in Tartini's works has become the word now regularly used in music to designate a "singing" quality, a tunefulness in music and in its execution, the term "sonabile" (from the Italian "sonare," to play), meaning "instrumental liveliness" in music and in its execution, has long gone out of use. (More of these terms later.)

[33]Evidence of this is given by Wilhelm Josef von Wasielewski in his *Die Violine und ihre Meister,* Funfte Auflage, p. 140.

[34]Cited according to Alberto Bachmann, *Les Grands Violinistes du Passe,* Paris, 1913, p. 357.

[35]*Treatise,* p. 120 (39). Here sciolto is opposed to legato. But sciolto can also be translated as swiftly, adroitly. The first movement of the Sonata in G major (No. 1 in Brainard's catalog), the Andante, has the heading "Sciolto" in the manuscript, and the next movement, Allegro cantabile. It is symptomatic of esthetical theories of Tartini and his period that an allegro need not necessarily be swift, or an andante, cantabile—it is all a question of which affect the music expresses.

[36]See Vincent Duckles and Minnie Elmer with the assistance of Pierluigi Petrobelli, *Thematic Catalog*

of a Manuscript Collection of Eighteenth-Century Italian Instrumental Music in the University of California, Berkeley Music Library, Berkeley and Los Angeles, 1963, p. 327.

[37]See Paul Brainard, Die Violinsonaten Giuseppe Tartinis, Diss., p. 301.

[38]F.J. Fetis. Biographie Universelle des Musiciens et Bibliographie Generale de la Musique, Tome Sixieme, Bruxelles, 1840, p. 21.

[39]Pablo Casals called intonation the most important part of phrasing (see A. Borisyak, Essays on the School of Pablo Casals, Moscow, 1929, p. 55).

[40]Treatise, p. 85 (16).

[41]See N.A. Garbuzov, The Zone Nature of Hearing Sounds of Different Heights, Moscow, 1948.

[42]In our days Pablo Casals declared that this difference belonged to so-called expressive accuracy of intonation ("justesse expressive"). He said, "I can prove with my system that there is a greater distance between a D flat and a C sharp than there is in a semitone like C—D flat or C sharp—D natural." (J.M. Corredor, Conversations with Casals, London, 1956, p. 197.)

[43]P. 85 of the treatise in question.

[44]F.M. Fayolle, Notices sur Corelli, Tartini, Gavinies, Pugnani et Viotti, Paris, 1810, p. 15. Though the "third sound" was used after Tartini for the purpose of verifying intonation in a number of violin Methods (L. Mozart, 1756; B. Campagnoli, 1797 and others), we should note the limitations in the practical significance of the device, since if it is true that a given acoustic phenomenon is formed only when there is the right correlation between the two upper tones, it cannot yet be considered an absolute criterion for the purity of intonation in that particular key. While admitting that Tartini's "third sound" could serve to check the accuracy of the interval, C. Flesch does not see much practical use in this phenomenon (see C. Flesch, The Art of Playing the Violin, Vol. I, edited by K.A. Fortunatov, Moscow, 1964, pp. 30-31). H. Becker attributes a certain significance to "the Tartini combinational tones" for work on the pure intoning of doublestops (see Hugo Becker and Dago Ryner, Mechanik und Aesthetik des Violoncellspiels, Wien, 1929, p. 146).

[45]His daring mastery of shifts of position, the leaps and the developed bowing technique gives us reason to suppose that Tartini held his violin against his collar-bone and pressed it with his chin; his violin technique already required that the instrument be held firmly.

[46]Meyer-Raubinek constructed a special etude on a development of this device, using a motive from the Devil's Trill (see Hans Meyer-Raubinek, Moderne Etuden fur Violine unter Berucksichtigung technischer Motive aus Meisterwerken der Violinliteratur, Vol. I, Berlin, 1929, p. 21, No. 10).

[47]Andreas Moser, Geschichte des Violinspiels, Zweite verbesserte un erganzte Auflage von Hans-Joachim Nosselt, Tutzing, 1966, p. 230.

[48]This is according to the well-grounded opinion of Dounias; L. de la Laurencie and A. Moser regard this work as having appeared before 1750; A. Capri considers that it came out around 1730; E.R. Jacobi puts it between 1752 (the year when Quantz' Method appeared, without any references to Tartini's Treatise) and 1756 (the year of publication of Leopold Mozart's Method for Violin, in which much was borrowed from Tartini's Treatise).

[49]Giuseppe Tartini, Traite des Agremens de la Musique . . ., Paris (1771).

[50]In the original it was entitled Trattato della appogiature si ascendenti che discendenti per violino come pure il trillo, tremolo, mordente ed altro con dichiarazione delle cadenze naturali e composte (Treatise for violin on appoggiatura both rising and falling, and also on the trill, the tremolo, the mordent and other ornaments with explanations of natural and composite cadenzas).

[51]Among other things, Tartini brings a certain light to bear on the most controversial question of all: how to play grace notes in the music of his time. "No other ornament has given rise to so many confused theories as the grace notes," writes Beyschlag; "no other has been the source of such endless difficulty for anybody going in for old-world music" (Adolf Beyschlag, Die Ornamentik der Musik, 2. Auflage, Leipzig, 1953, p. 103).

[52]Sometimes even violinists in an orchestra would improvise in their own way in playing their parts.

[53]See "Adagio de Mr. Tartini, varie de plusieurs facons differentes . . ." in J.B. Cartier's L'Art du Violon (Paris, 1798), containing 17 variations on the first movement of a Sonata in F major (F5 in Brainard's catalog).

[54]The dates in brackets are those of the publication of the works of the musicians in questions.

[55]See Joseph Joachim and Andreas Moser, Violinschule, Band III, Leipzig, 1905, p. 18.

[56]Francesco Geminiani, The Art of Playing on the Violin, London, 1751, pp. 7-8 (Facsimile edition, edited with an introduction by David D. Boyden, London).

[57]Giuseppe Tartini, Trattato di Musica, p. 149-150.

[58]Regole per arrivare a saper ben suonar il Violino col vero fondamento di saper sicura mente tutto quello, chesi foi; buono ancora a tutti quelli, ch'esercitano la Musica siano Cantanti, o Suonatori date in luce dal celebre Signor Giuseppe Tartini per uso di chi avva .volonta di stiadiare. Copiate da Giovanni Francesco Nicolai suo Scolaro.

[59]The value of E.R. Jacobi's publication (Celle-New York, 1961), according to which (since it also contains a facsimile of Nicolai's manuscript) we shall from now on quote from the Treatise, is enhanced by the fact that it has the first publication of this hitherto unknown work of Tartini's appended to it, and also by the fact that likewise appended (in Italian, German, French and English) is the full text of his Letter to a Pupil, which we shall also consider further. Thus, in quoting in all these works of Tartini's, we have been able to check with the Italian original in all cases of doubt. We will give just one example, which, unfortunately, remained uncorrected in E.R. Jacobi's publication (though in his preface he displays a perfect understanding of the matter). The Italian term "messa di voce," which means a certain manner of singing, is incorrectly translated into all three languages as "semitone" (intervals of half a tone), which completely distorts the sense.

　　Nicolai's manuscript, we may also note, contains an appendix in the form of a collection of Tartini's cadenzas (and some of his own) entitled Raccolta di diversi altri modi naturali di Cadenze Naturali e di Cadenze fatte ad arbitrio del medesimo Signor Giuseppe Tartini fatte di Giovanni Francesco Nicolai suo Scolare (A collection of various other natural figures for natural cadenzas and free cadenzas composed by the same Signor Giuseppe Tartini, collected by his pupil Giovanni Francesco Nicolai). This appendix was not included in the above-mentioned publication by E.R. Jacobi.

[60]Libro de regole, ed Esempi necesari ben Suonare dal Signor Giuseppe Tartini (see a description of this manuscript in an article by D. Boyden, "The Missing Italian Manuscript of Tartini's Des Agremens," published in the Musical Quarterly, 1960, No. 3).

[61]The division into two parts is found in the published editions of the Treatise, but not in Nicolai's manuscript.

[62]The *Treatise*, p. 68(6). In citing this principle of Tartini's Flesch stresses that it is true for us today, too, and should still be followed (especially in controversial cases). See Carl Flesch, *Die Kunst des Violinspiels*, II Band, Berlin, 1928, p. 21.

[63]The *Treatise*, p. 70(8).

[64]The *Treatise*, p.74(10). A comparison between musical ornaments and salt in food can be found as early as the 17th century in the *Traite de la Viole* . . . by J.-J. Rousseau (Paris, 1687, p. 75.)

[65]The *Treatise*, pp. 10-11 in Nicolai's manuscript.

[66]The *Treatise*, p. 89(17).

[67]*Ibid.*, p. 91(19).

[68]Tartini does not say that vibration has a dynamic effect as well.

[69]See the *Treatise*, p. 84(15).

[70]Leopold Mozart, *Grundliche Violinschule*, Augsburg, 1756 (Faksimile-Ausgabe, Leipzig, 1956, pp. 243-244).

[71]L. Spohr, who lived in the epoch of romanticism, restricted the use of vibrato in his *Violin School* (1831) and made a wavy line over the notes to be vibrated.

[72]The *Treatise*, p. 86(16).

[73]The *Treatise*, p. 94(20).

[74]In a footnote E.R. Jacobi particularly stresses the role of the singing that Tartini had heard in Pirano and Venice, where Tartini had many pupils, friends and admirers.

[75]The *Treatise*, p. 105(28).

[76]The *Treatise*, p. 106(29).

[77]*Ibid.*, p. 106(29).

[78]*Ibid.*, p. 109(30).

[79]The *Treatise*, p. 117(37).

[80]*Ibid.*, p. 117(37).

[81]See Minos Dounias, *Die Violinkonzerte Giuseppe Tartinis*, p. 105.

[82]An improvised cadenza would sometimes be added to the capriccio.

[83]An excerpt from Tartini's *Trattato di Musica* containing this statement is cited in the above book by Dounias, p. 104.

[84]The *Treatise*, p. 118(37).

[85]The *Treatise*, p. 119(38).

[86]The *Treatise*, p. 55(2).

[87]The *Treatise*, p. 57-58(3).

[88]*Ibid.*, p. 57(3).

[89]The *Treatise*, p. 56(2).

[90]*Ibid.*, p. 56(2).

[91]The manuscript of this *Letter* is in the Urban Museum Pomorski Muzej "Sergej Masera" of Piran (Yugoslavia), the composer's birthplace. Some authors (including M. Dounias) consider it to be an autograph, while others (including E.R. Jacobi) think it is a copy belonging to a contemporary of Tartini's. The *Letter* has been published again and again in different languages. The first Italian edition appeared in the year of Tartini's death, in Venice, in *L'Europa Letteraria*, 1770, t.V.

[92]Maddalena Lombardini was born in 1735 in Venice, lost her parents early and was brought up in the "dei Mendicanti" conservatory. After leaving it she spent some time improving her play under Tartini's guidance and then started giving concerts. She is known to have given successful concerts beyond the borders of Italy as well, in Paris, London, Dresden, Petersburg and Moscow.

[93]When Tartini wrote "fuga del Corelli," he did not specificially mean a composition in the form of a fugue, but one that was written in equal lengths (in this case, in sixteenths), or, as the author of the French translation remarked, "une fugue de notes" ("a running of notes"). This was the way that several other musicians of the time used the word "fugue."

[94]In going through Tartini's instructions on working on bowing strokes and their execution, the reader of today must keep in mind the peculiarities of Tartini's bow and his way of holding it. See an article by Sol Babitz called "Differences between 18th century and modern violin bowing" in *The Score and IMA Magazine*, 1957, March.

[95]The *Treatise*, p. 136.

[96]In a commentary to the Soviet edition (which we have already mentioned) of Flesch's *Art of Violin Playing*, K.A. Fortunatov rightly calls Tartini's *Art of Bowing* a classical work, the importance of which "lies in his generalization of the experience of 18th century bowing technique" (p. 259).

[97]Joseph Szigeti, *A Violinist's Notebook*, London, 1964, p. 140.

[98]The numbers of the variations are given according to F. David's arrangement. The examples are cited according to the *Methode* of Cartier, who had the original manuscript at his disposal.

[99]In a letter of July 11, 1763. *Mozart, Briefe und Aufzeichnungen, Gesamtausgabe* (Herausgegeben von W. Bauer und O.E. Deutsch), Band I, Kassel, 1962, p. 75.

[100]D. Antonio Eximeno, *Dell' Origine e delle Regole della Musica colla Storia del suo Progresso, decadenza e rinnovazione*, Roma, 1774, p. 437.

[101]It is said that the great and famous virtuoso and romanticist Niccolo Paganini, whose importance goes far beyond the borders of his native land, would bare his head as a sign of extreme respect for his famous compatriot whenever Tartini's name was pronounced. And the outstanding Polish violinist, Karol Lipinski, who was already very well-known, strove to study the traditions of Tartini's school whenever he met his pupils. (See V. Grigoryev, *Karol Lipinski*, Moscow, 1977, pp. 19-21.)

Chapter 5

[1]On the activities of all these violinists in Russia see R. Aloys Mooser, *Violinistes-compositeurs italiens en Russie au XVII-e Siecle*, Milano, 1938-1948.

[2]Tartini's compositions were played in Russia by the brothers Johann and Andreas Hubner, German violinists who served at court. See Yakob Shtelin, *Muzyka i balet v Rossii XVIII veka*, Leningrad, 1935 (Jacob Stahlin, *Music and Ballet in Russia in the 18th Century*, Leningrad, 1935), p. 78.

[3]Among the works that he wrote in Russia are symphonies "in the Russian style" and two collections of sonatas for violin and bass (one of which was composed in 1738 and published in Amsterdam in the same year). For D. Dall'Oglio see R. Aloys Mooser, *Annales de la Musique et des Musiciens en Russie au XVIII-e Siecle*, I, Geneve, 1948, pp. 131-136.

[4]Stahlin's notes on the Russian Tsar, Peter III, *Chtenia v obshestve istorii i drevnostei Rossiiskikh (Lectures in the Society of the History and Relics of Russia's Past)*, 1866, Book 4, p. 101. See also T. Livanova, *Russkaya muzykalnaya kultura XVIII veka (Russian Musical Culture of the 18th Century)*, Vol. II, Moscow, 1953, p. 401.

[5]See, among others, Z. Durov, *Ocherk istorii muzyki v Rossii (Essay on the History of Music in Russia)*, an appendix to A. Dommer's *Rukovodsto k izucheniyu istorii muzyki (Guide to a Study of the History of Music)*, Moscow, 1894, p. 586. G. Fesechko, who earlier asserted that Khandoshkin had been to Italy (see *Sovyetskaya Muzyka—Soviet Music*—1950, No. 12, p. 67), wrote in a book published later (*Ivan Yevstafyevich Khandoshkin*, Leningrad, 1972, p. 27), that the fact had not been definitely established due to absence of documentary evidence. This lack of evidence of Khandoshkin's having studied music in Italy raises legitimate doubts as to the probability of this version, which was supported by A. Mooser and I. Yampolsky.

[6]These notes are now in Pushkin House in Leningrad (the USSR Academy of Sciences Institute of Russian Literature); they have been reproduced in facsimile in Yampolsky's *Russkoye skripichnoye iskusstvo (Russian Art of Violin-Playing)*, I, Moscow-Leningrad, 1951, pp. 354-358.

[7]See Antonio Eximeno, *Dell' Origine e delle Regole della Musica*, Rome, 1772; F. Fayolle, *Notices sur Corelli, Tartini, Gavinies, Pugnani et Viotti*, Paris, 1810; Minos Dounias, *Die Violinkonzerte Giuseppe Tartinis*, Berlin, 1935.

[8]F. Torrefranca, *Le Origini italiane del Romantismo musicale*, Torino, 1930, p. 565.

[9]In the same year, while travelling in Italy, N.A. Lvov (1751-1803), a well-known figure in Russian cultural life and author of a book called *O russkom narodnom penii (Russian Folk Singing)* and opera librettos, was delighted by the performance of P. Nardini, Tartini's best pupil, whom he heard in Florence.

[10]The quotation is taken from the Russian translation by M.D. Shtern of A.M. Byeloselsky's book, published as an appendix to section 3 of the first volume of T. Livanova's *Russkaya muzykalnaya kultura XVIII veka (Russian Musical Culture of the 18th Century)*, Moscow, 1952, p. 446.

[11]*Ibid.*, p. 443.

[12]Leopold Mozart, *Grundliche Violinschule*, Dritte vermehrte Auflage, 1787 (Faksimile-Ausgabe), p. 240. One also feels the "presence" of Tartini in this *Method* in the part devoted to fingering and other sections.

[13]*Osnovatelnoye skripichnoye uchilishche g. Mozarta (Mr. Mozart's Thorough School for Violin)*, St. Petersburg, 1804, p. 184.

[14]*Skripichnaya shkola Rode, Baillot i Kreitzera (Methode de Violon de Rode, Baillot et Kreutzer)*, St. Petersburg, 1812; second edition, St. Petersburg, 1829, p. 1.

[15]*Moskovskiye Vedomosti*, 1803, Nov. 18, No. 92.

[16]See, for instance, the *Katalog raznym notam, prodayushchimsa u Karla Pavlovicha Lengolda v Moskve, v muzykalnoi yevo lavke, sostoyashchei na Ilyinke v dome Plotnikova (Catalogue of Music Sold at Karl Pavlovich Lengold's in Moscow, in his music shop on Ilyinka St. in Plotnikov's house)*, Moscow, 1820;

[17]*Liricheskii museum, soderzhashchii v sebe kratkoye nachertanye istorii muzyki s prisovokup- leniem zhizneopisanii nekotorykh znamenitykh artistov i virtuosov onoi (Lyrical Museum, containing a brief outline of the history of music together with the life stories of some famous musicians and virtuosos)*, published by Kushenov-Dmitriyevsky, St. Petersburg, 1831, p. 51.

[18]*Ibid.*, pp. 74 and 178.

[19]*Altsiona (Halcyon)* was issued in 1831, 1832 and 1833. A.S. Pushkin, V.F. Odoyevsky, P.A. Vyazernsky, E.A. Baratynsky and other eminent writers and poets collaborated in producing it.

[20]Among these is the cycle called *Proshchanie s Peterburgom (Farewell to St. Petersburg)*, the romance *Somnenie (Doubt)*, the music to the tragedy *Knyaz Kholmsky (Prince Kholmsky)* and other compositions.

[21]See Kapellmeister Kreisler, *Rasskazy starovo muzykanta. Tartinieva trel. Sonata dlya skripki (Tales of an Old Musician, The Tartini Trill, Sonata for Violin)*, 1720, in *Panteon i repertuar russkoi stseny (Pantheon and Repertoire for the Russian Stage)*, edited by F. Koni, Vol. V, September, Book 9, St. Petersburg, 1851, *Istoria iskusstva (History of Art)*, pp. 1-52.

[22]See Adolph Garras, *Ruchnoi muzykalny slovar s pribavleniem biografii izvestnykh kompositorov, artistov i diletantov (A Handy Dictionary of Music with Biographies of Well-Known Composers, Performers and Dilettantes)*, Moscow, 1894, pp. 199-203.

[23]See the *Literaturnoye pribavlenie k 'Nuvellistu' ('Novelist' Literary Supplement)*, February, 1869, p. 13.

[24]See Nikolai Kirilov, *Skripachi XVII, XVIII i XIX stoletii (Violinists of the 17th, 18th, and 19th Centuries)*, St. Petersburg, 1873, pp. 13-19. There is also an essay on Tartini in A. Mikhel's *Kratkaya entsiklopedia smychkovykh instrumentov (Short Encyclopaedia of Bow Instruments)*, Moscow, 1894, pp. 199-203.

[25]A.F. Lvov, *Soviety nachinayushchemu igrat na skripke (Advice to the Beginner on the Violin)* (1859), fourth edition, Moscow, 1912, p. IV.

[26]V.F. Odoyevsky, *Muzykalno-literaturnoye nasledie (Musical and Literary Heritage)*, edited by G.B. Bernandt, Moscow, 1956, p. 142.

[27]See V.V. Bezekirsky, *Kratkii istoricheskii obzor muzykalnoskripichnovo iskusstva s XVII po XX v (A Short Historical Survey of Violin Art from the 17th to the 20th Centuries)*, Kiev-Warsaw, 1913, p. 4.

[28]See Bohuslav Sich, *Ferdinand Laub*, Prague, 1951, p. 130.

[29]The first of these books was edited by S.L. Ginsburg and reprinted in Leningrad in 1929, and a second edition came out in 1933. It was published once again in Moscow in 1965 together with Auer's second book, this new book being edited by I. Yampolsky.

[30]L. Auer, *Violin Master Works and their Interpretation*, New York, 1925, p. 2 (p. 124, Russian edition).

[31]L. Auer, *Violin Playing as I Teach It*, London, 1921, p. 142 (p. 94, Russian edition).

[32]See K. Mostras, *Intonatsia na skripke (Intonation on the Violin)*, Moscow, 1948; *Dinamika v skripichnom iskusstve (Dynamics in Violin-playing)*, Moscow, 1956, and particularly *Ritmicheskaya distsiplina skripacha (The Violinist's Rhythmic Discipline)*, Moscow, 1951.

[33]See *Skripichnye kadentsii. Vypusk I. Kadentsii k kontsertam i sonatam A. Corelli, G. Tartini i G. Viotti (Violin Cadenzas, Issue One, Cadenzas and Sonatas for Concertos and Sonatas by A. Corelli, G. Tartini and G. Viotti)*, edited by D. Tsyganov, Moscow-Leningrad, 1951.

[34]Igor Glebov (B.V. Asafyev), *Dante i muzyka (Dante and Music)*, Petrograd, 1921, p. 50.

Appendices

Giuseppe Tartini wrote twenty-six *Little Sonatas for Violin and Cello, and for Solo Violin,* probably between 1745 and 1770.

Tartini sent a group of these sonatas to his friend Count Algarotti, Court Chamberlain to Frederick the Great, to be performed, and in his letter dated February 24, 1750, he wrote: "My little sonatas for solo violin have the bass part for 'ceremony,' a detail I neglected to write you. I play them without the bass and this is my true intention." Consequently, not all the twenty-six sonatas have the cello part. The first fourteen do have cello parts, but only some movements of No. 17 and No. 19 have the bass. In the rest the bass staff has either been left blank or omitted altogether. It is interesting to note that Tartini preferred the cello to the harpsichord. The *Little Sonatas* have an important place in Tartini's total output, not only for their form but also for the degree of pedagogical advancement. It was around 1744 that Tartini changed his style of extreme difficulty to graceful and expressive melody.

In 1970 Giovanni Guglielmo of Padua edited the original autograph manuscript housed in the Musical Archives of St. Anthony's Basilica at Padua. Published by Zanibon, this edition is based on the indications that Tartini left in the margins of the pages. Maestro Guglielmo writes in his preface that his work applied to the interpretations of the original text, which is sometimes fragmentary and inexact. He corrected mistakes of rhythmic, harmonic and ornamental character due evidently to the composer's hurry, and he also added some dynamic signs that reflect the taste of the times.

The following pages are some of the *Little Sonatas* as edited by Maestro Guglielmo, plus all the original autographs in Tartini's own hand, integrated as much as possible. Following these is a reproduction of the original Ferdinand David edition of Tartini's *Art of Bowing.*

GIOVANNI GUGLIELMO'S RECOMMENDATIONS FOR
TARTINI'S MUSIC

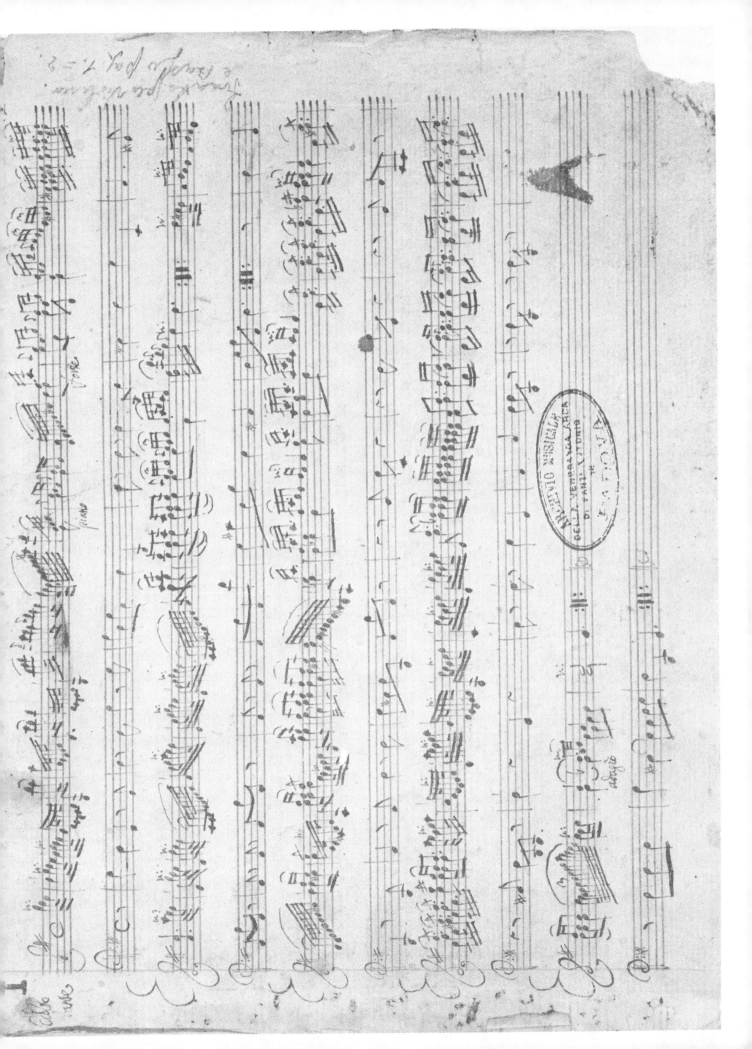

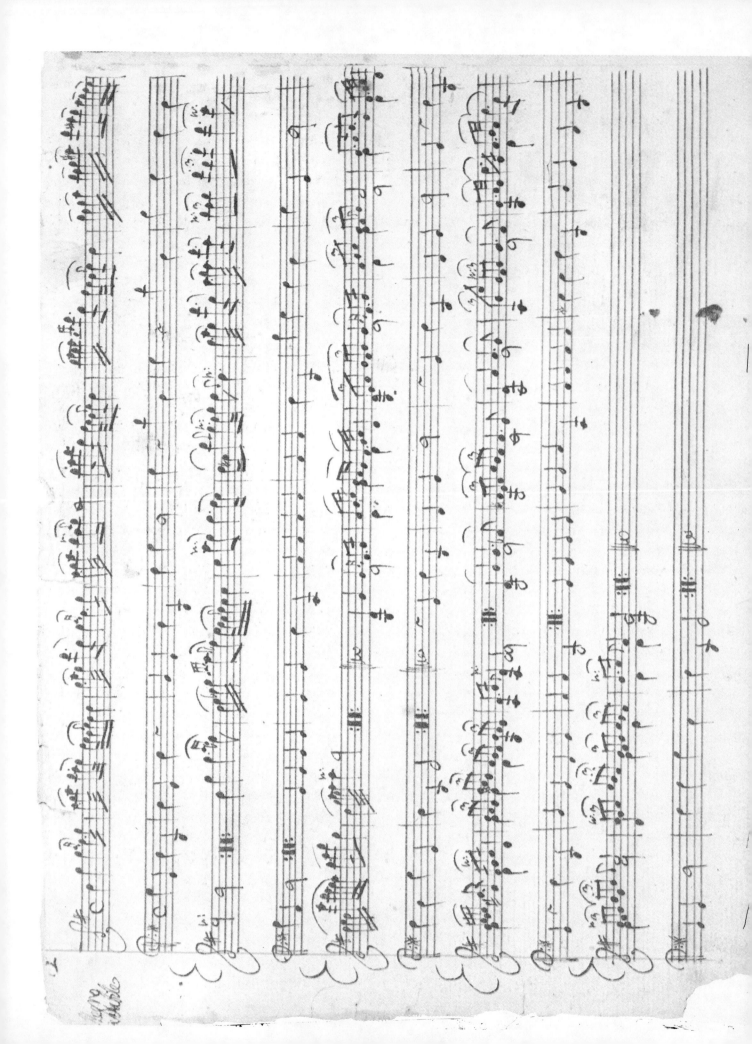

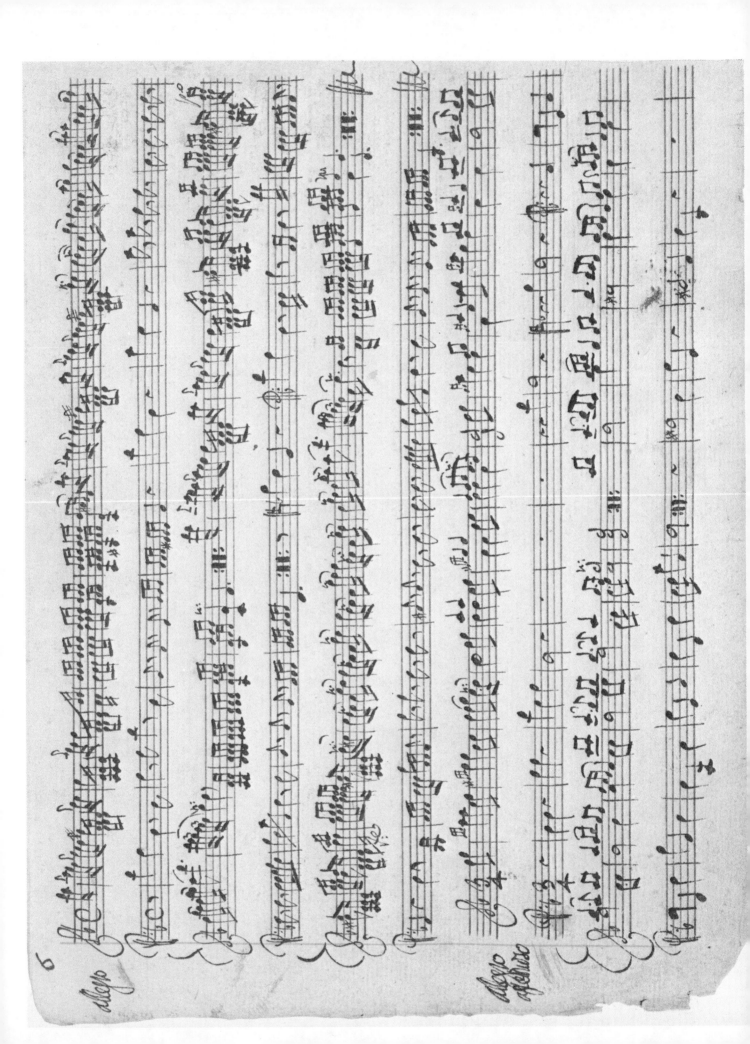

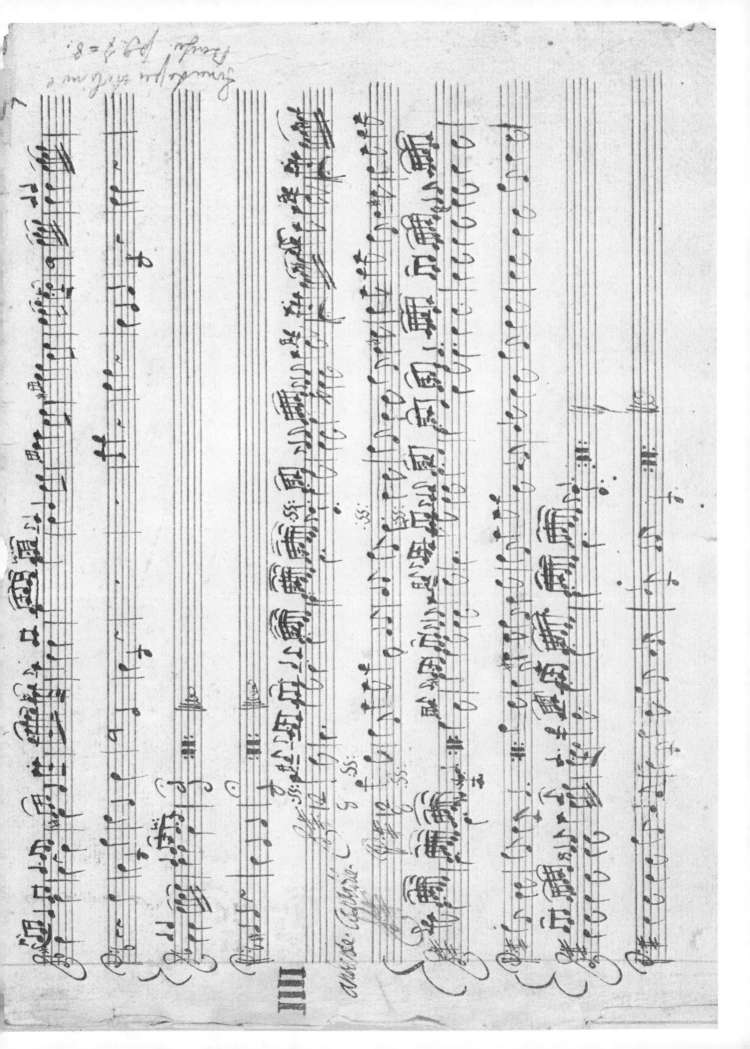

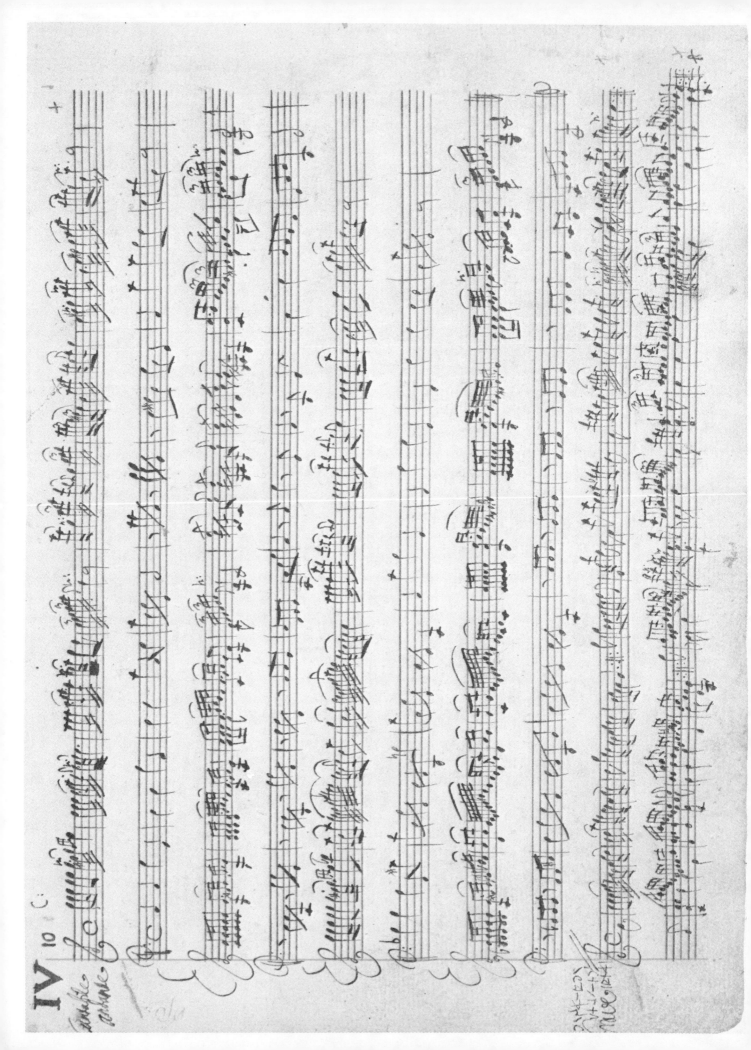

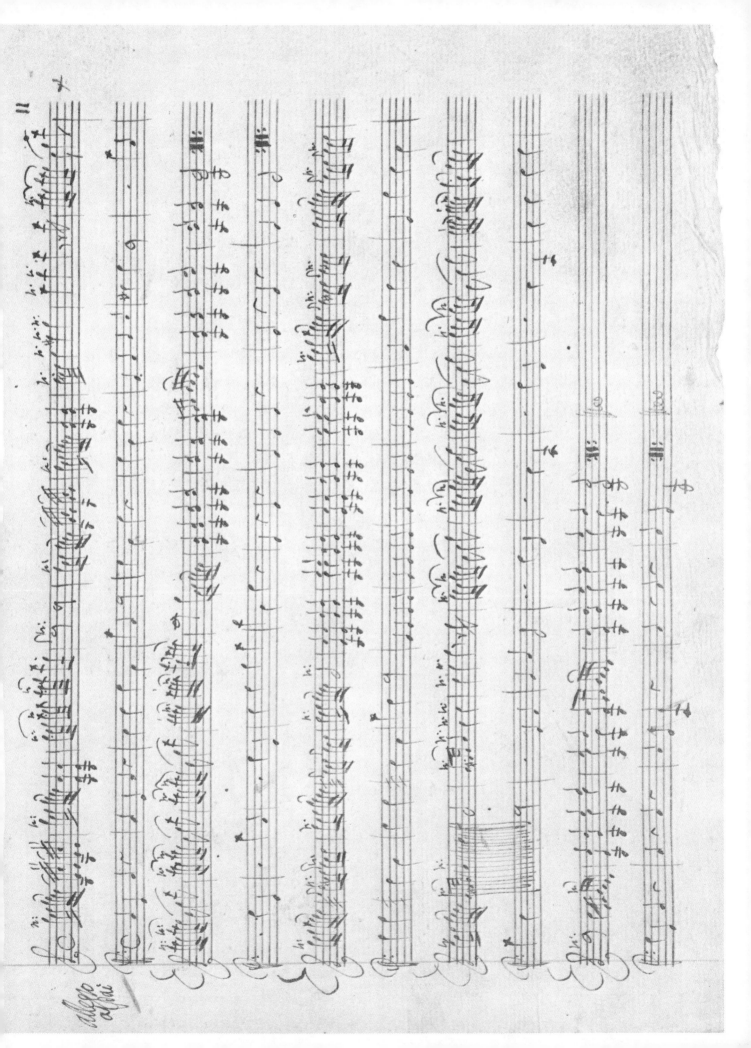

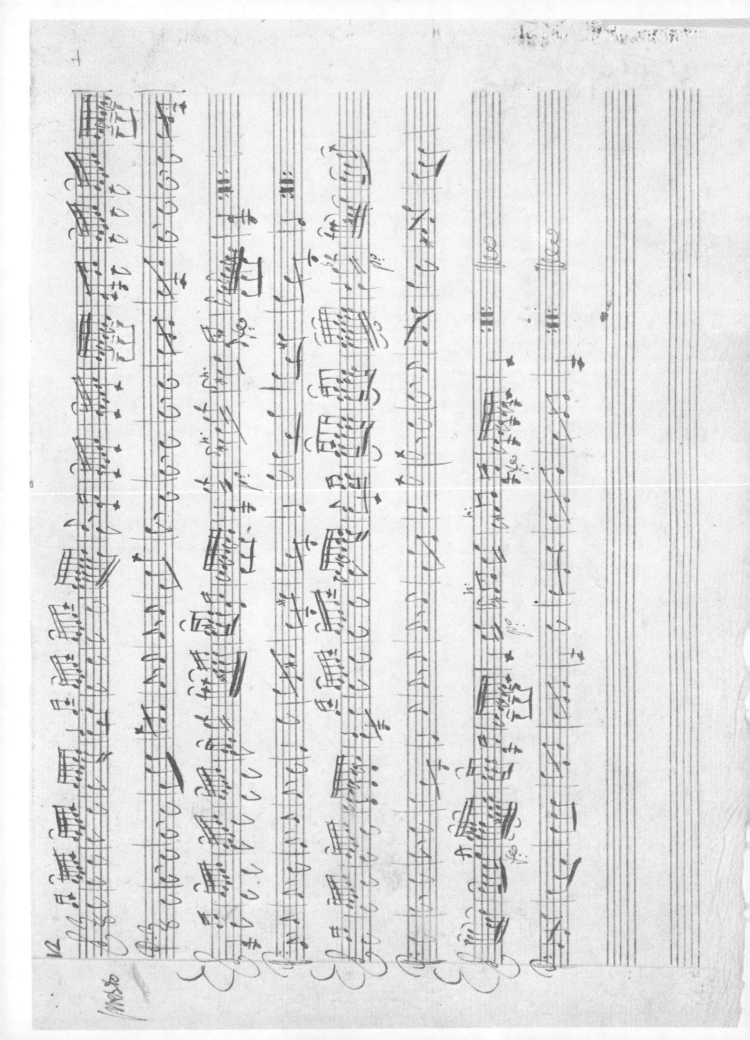

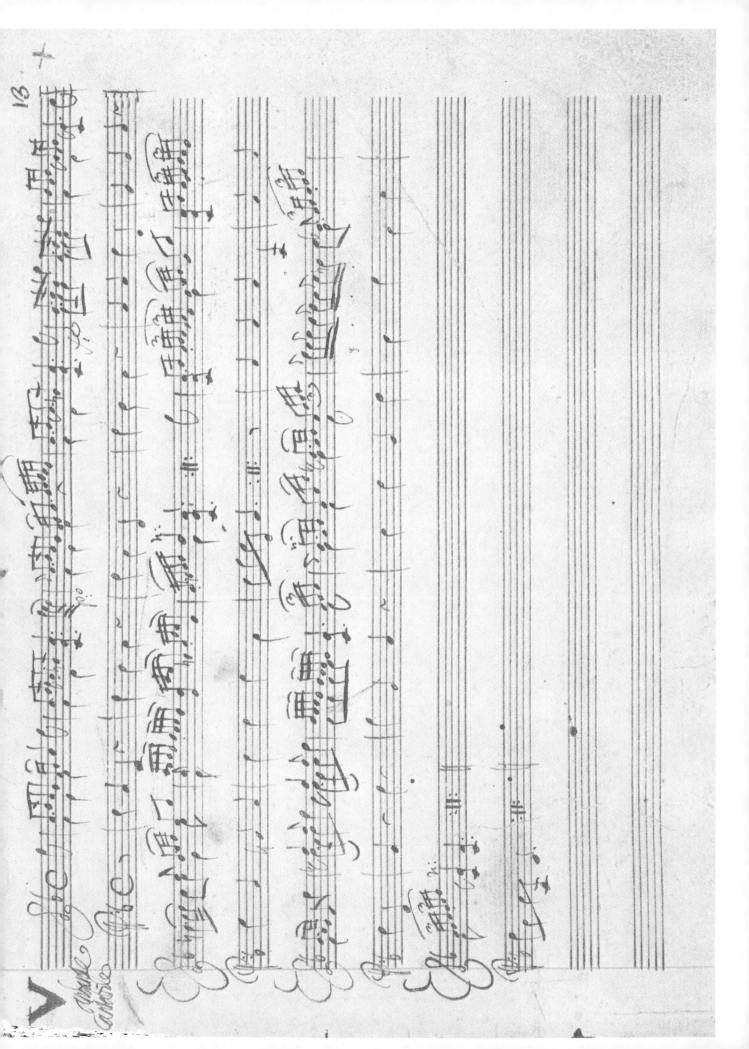

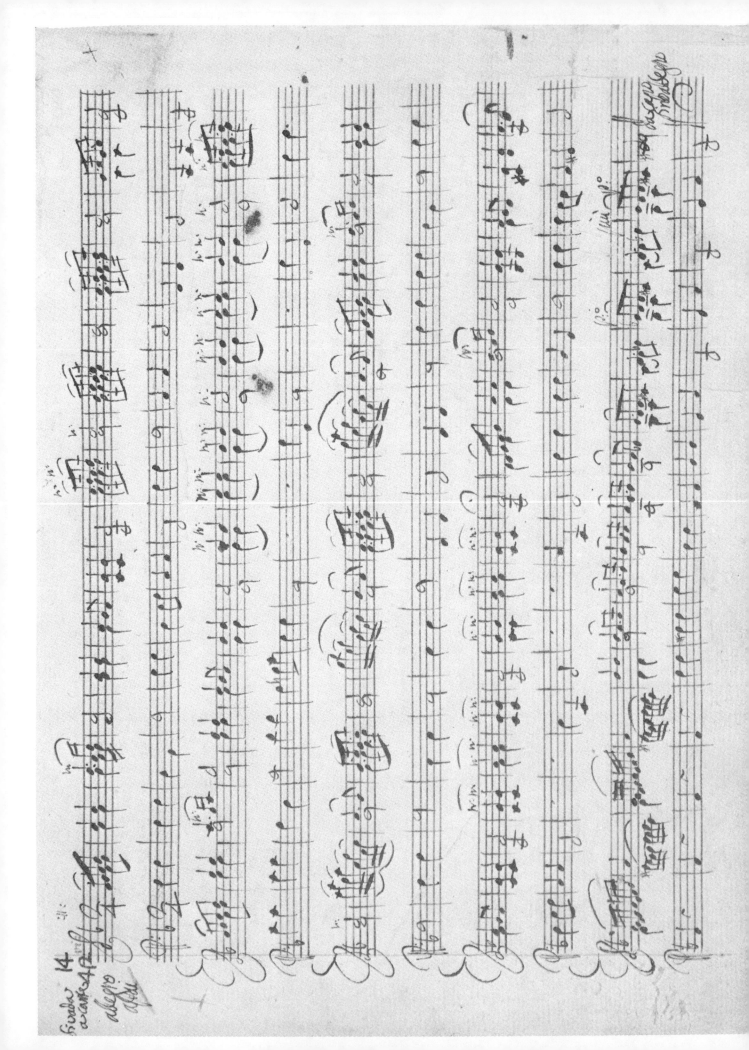

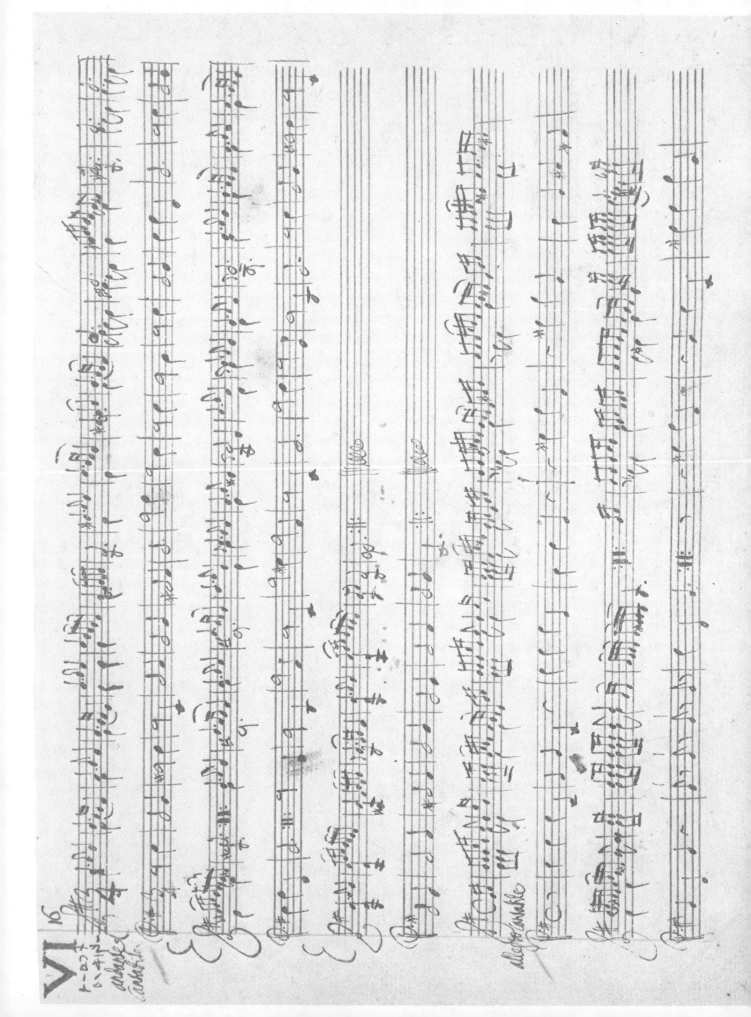

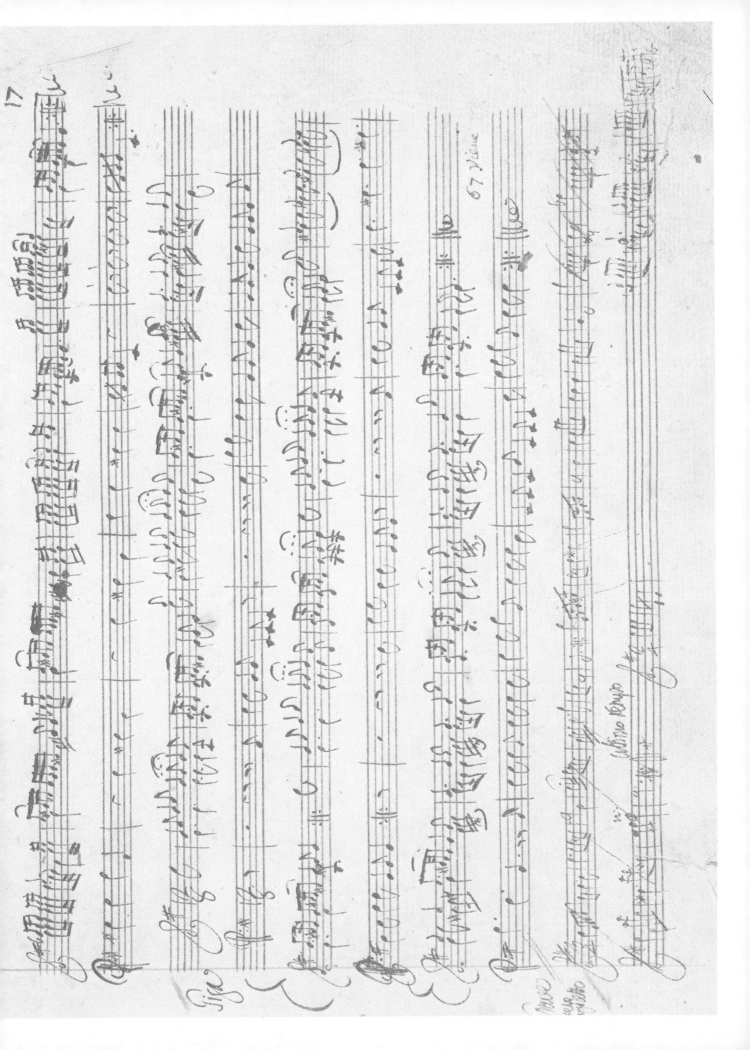

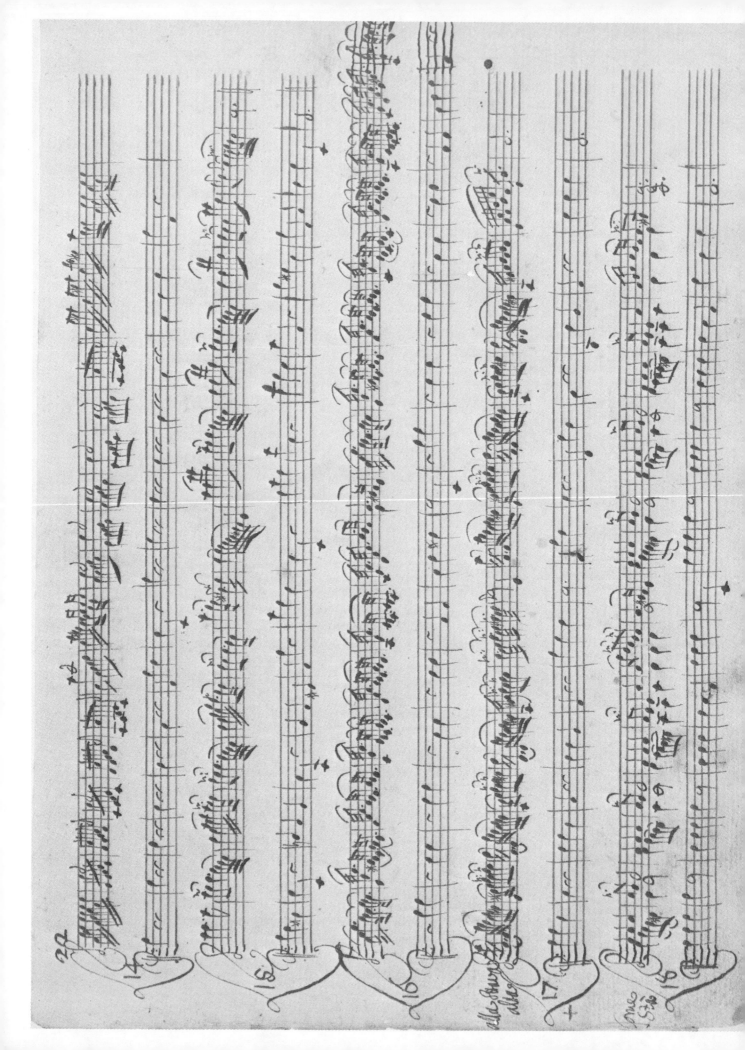

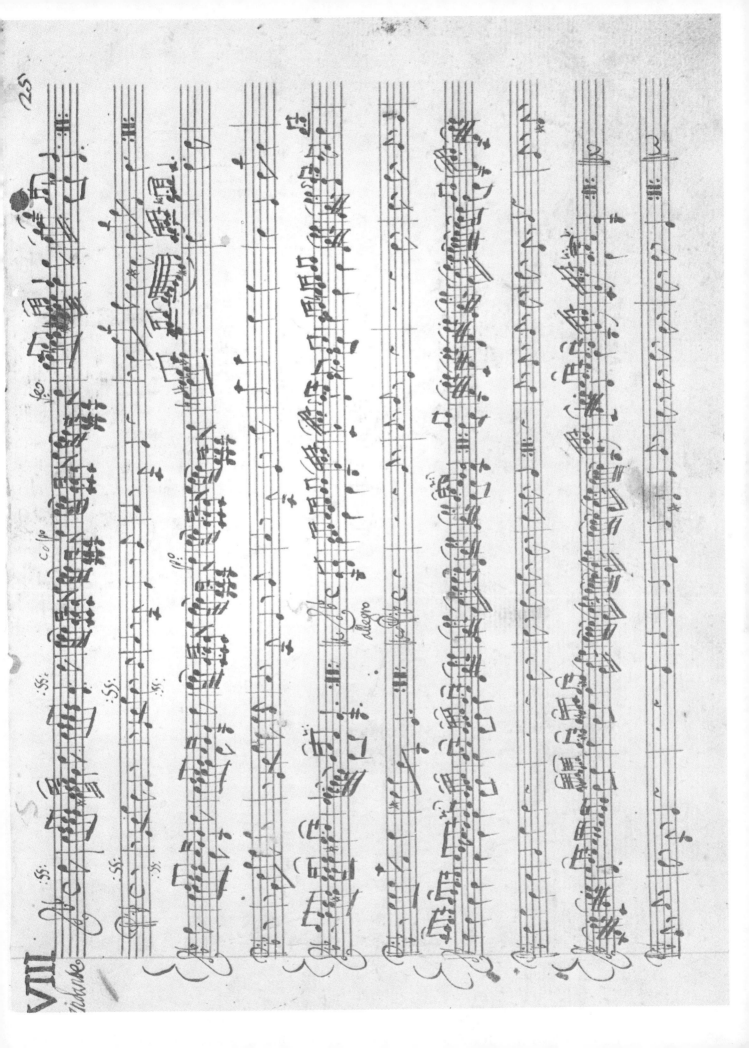

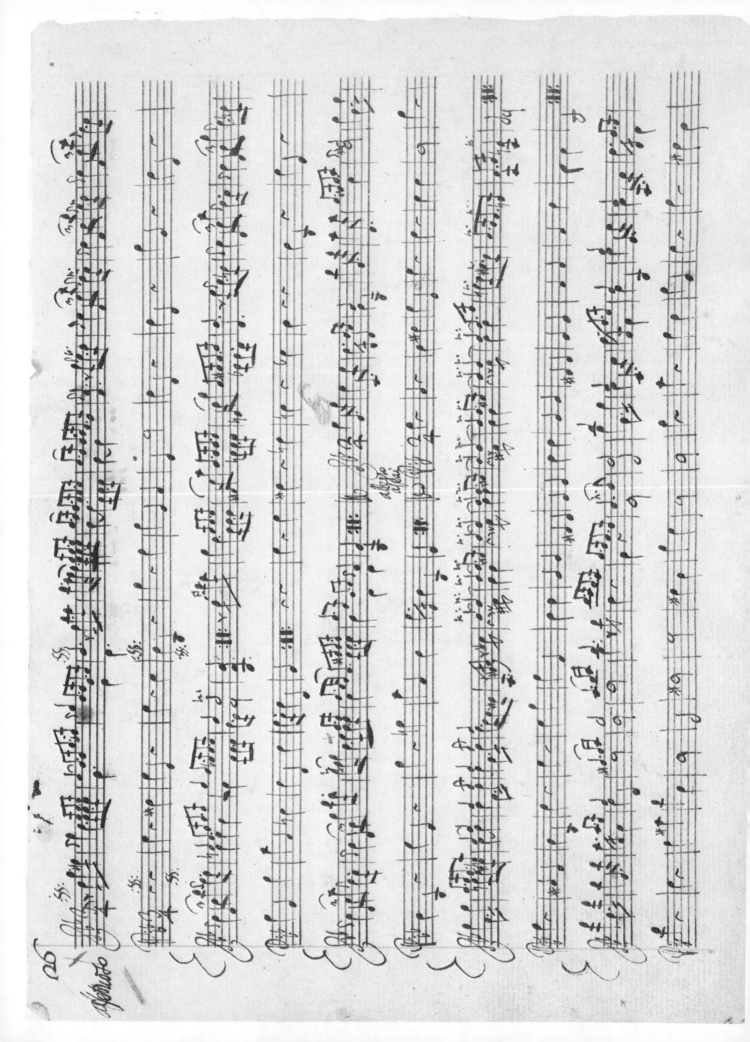

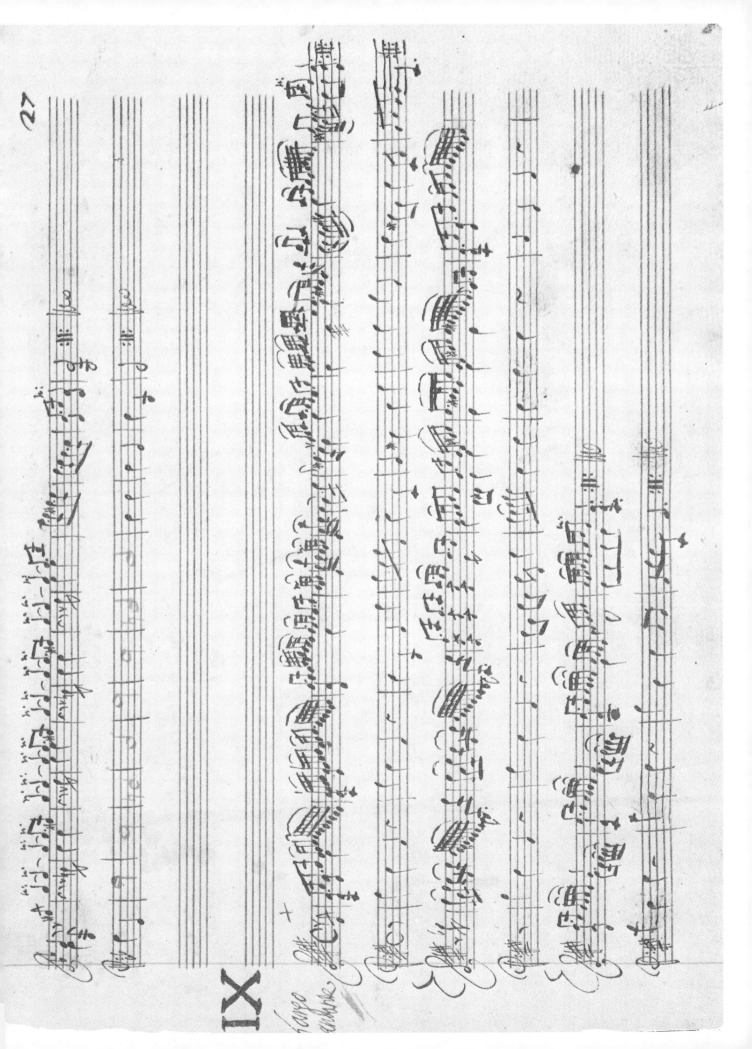

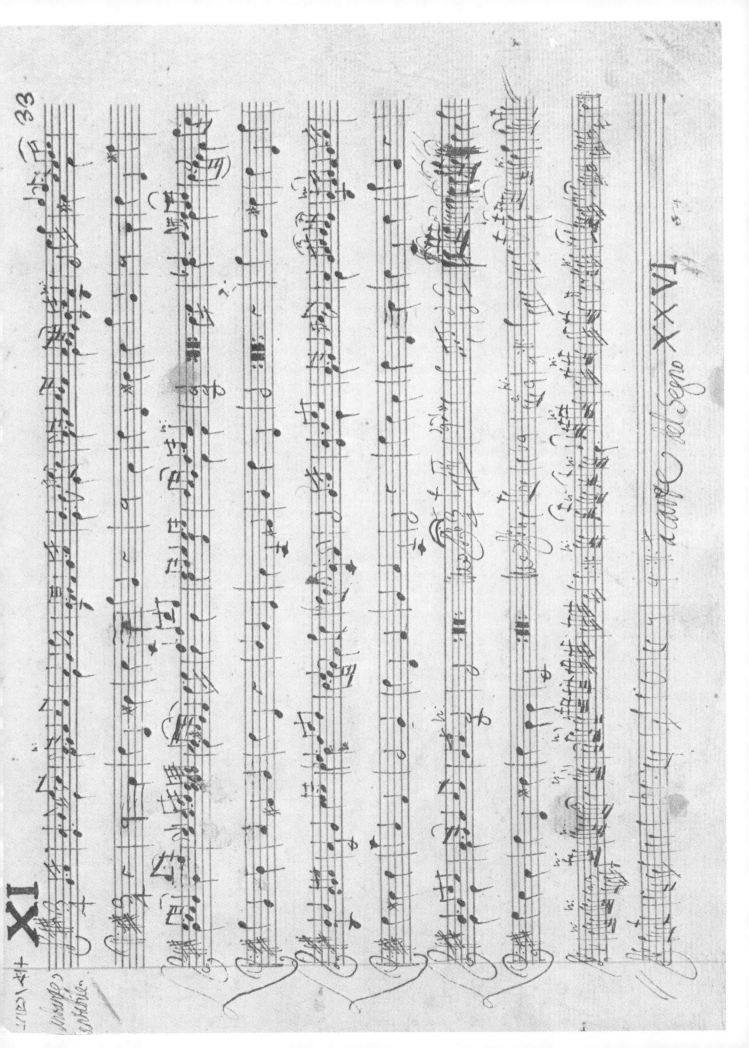

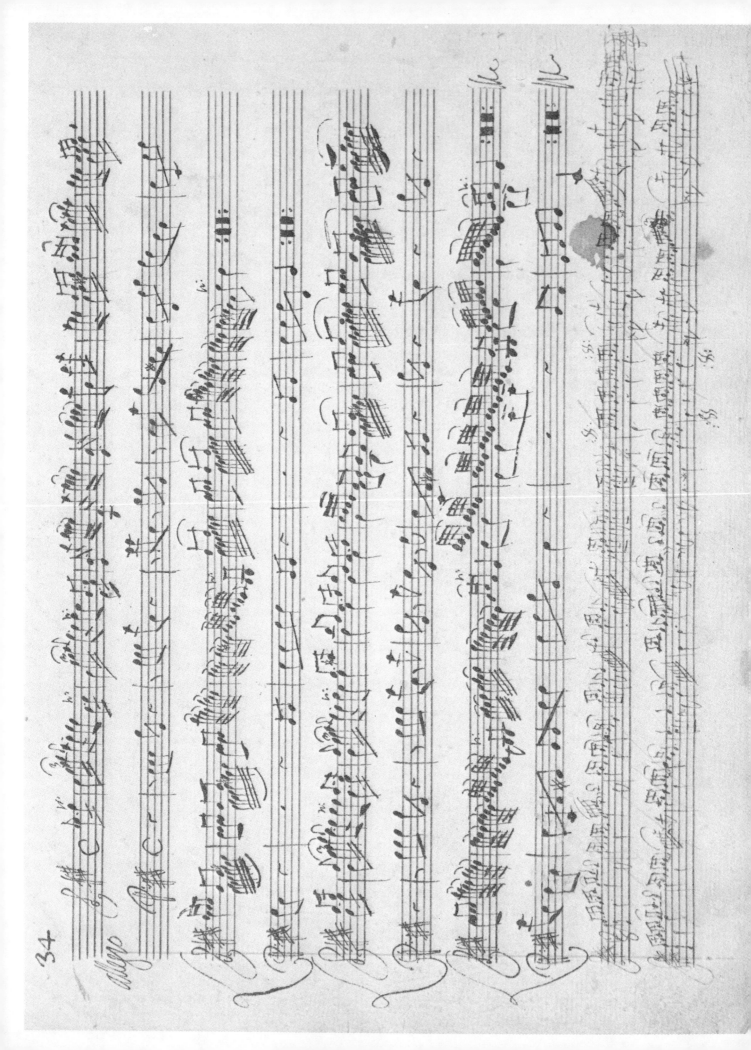

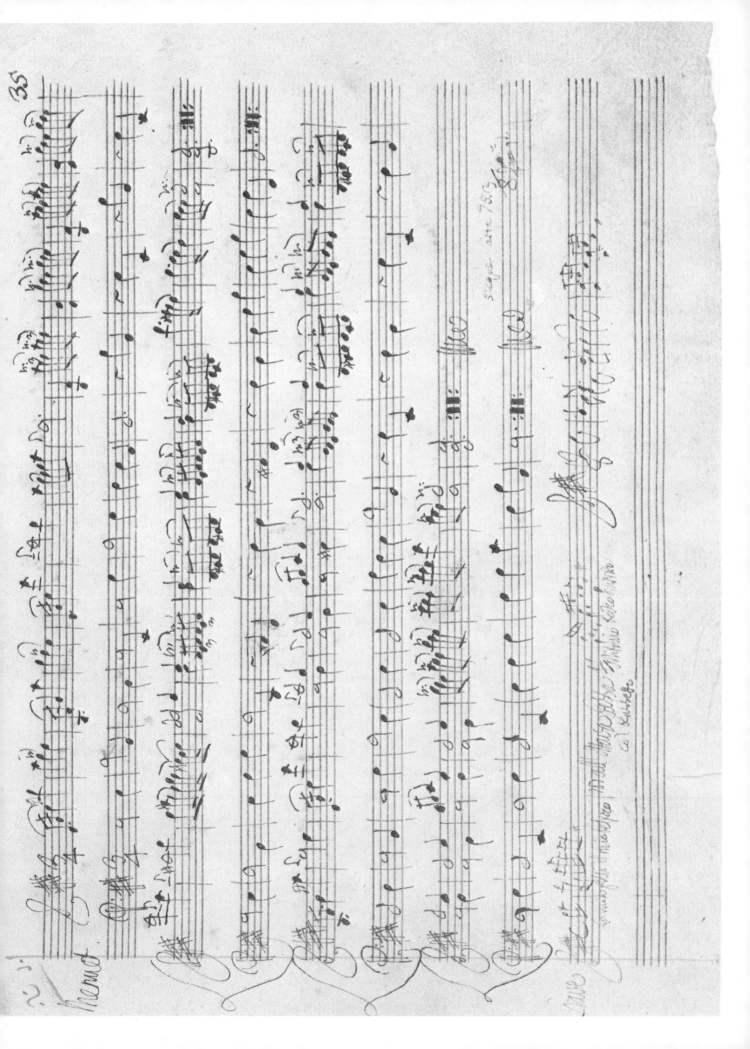

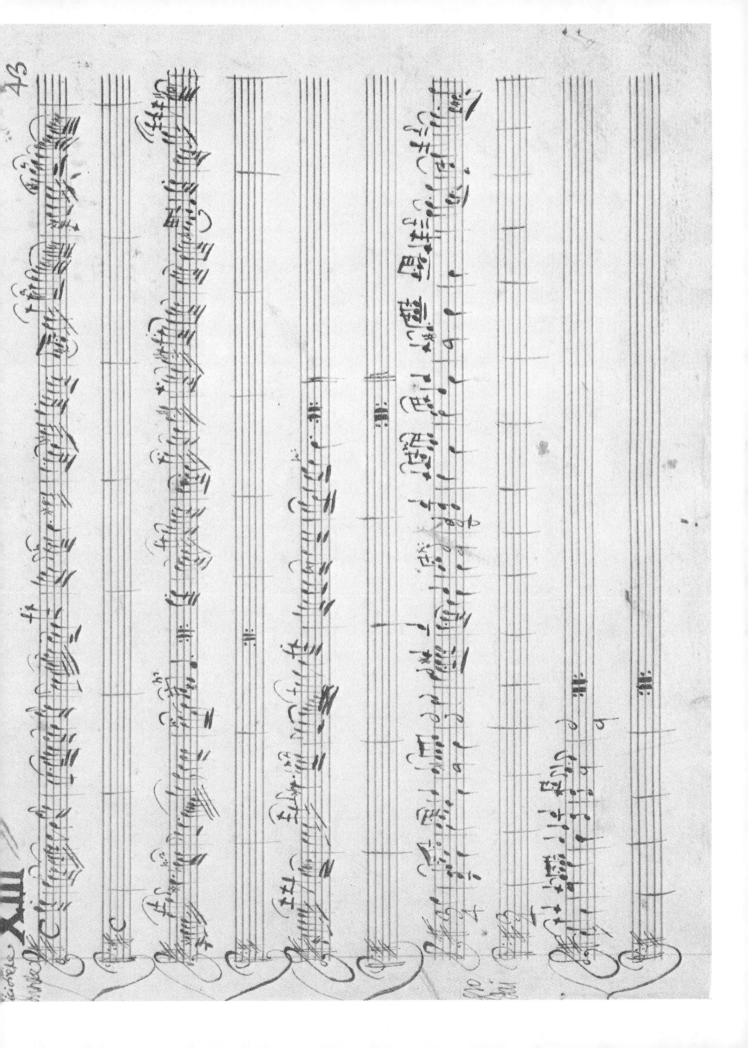

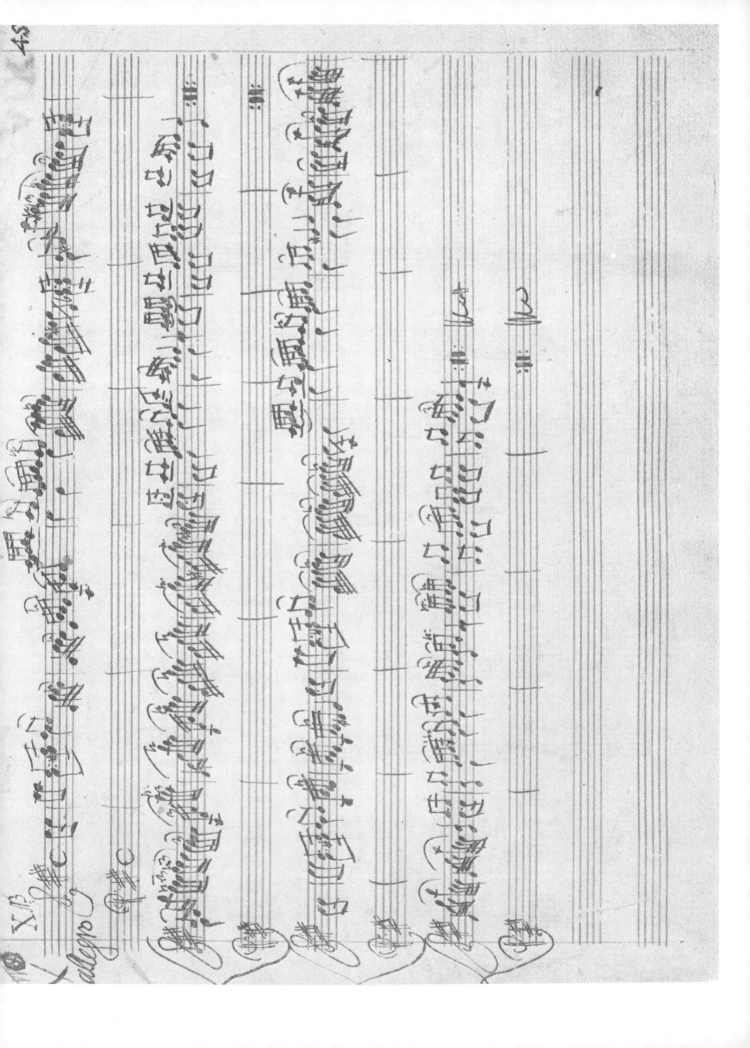

SONATA XIII

(in Re magg. - B. h 1)

per Violino solo

G. TARTINI
(G. GUGLIELMO)

DURATA: MIN. 10

VIOLINO

(in battere)

GIGA, allegro affettuoso

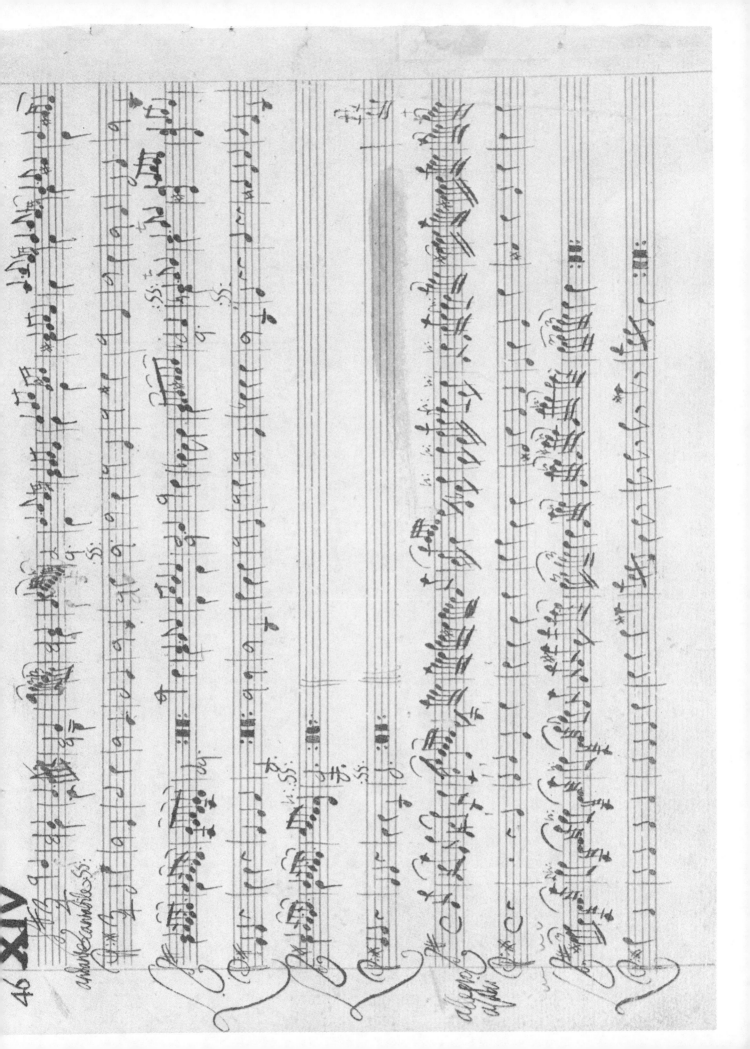

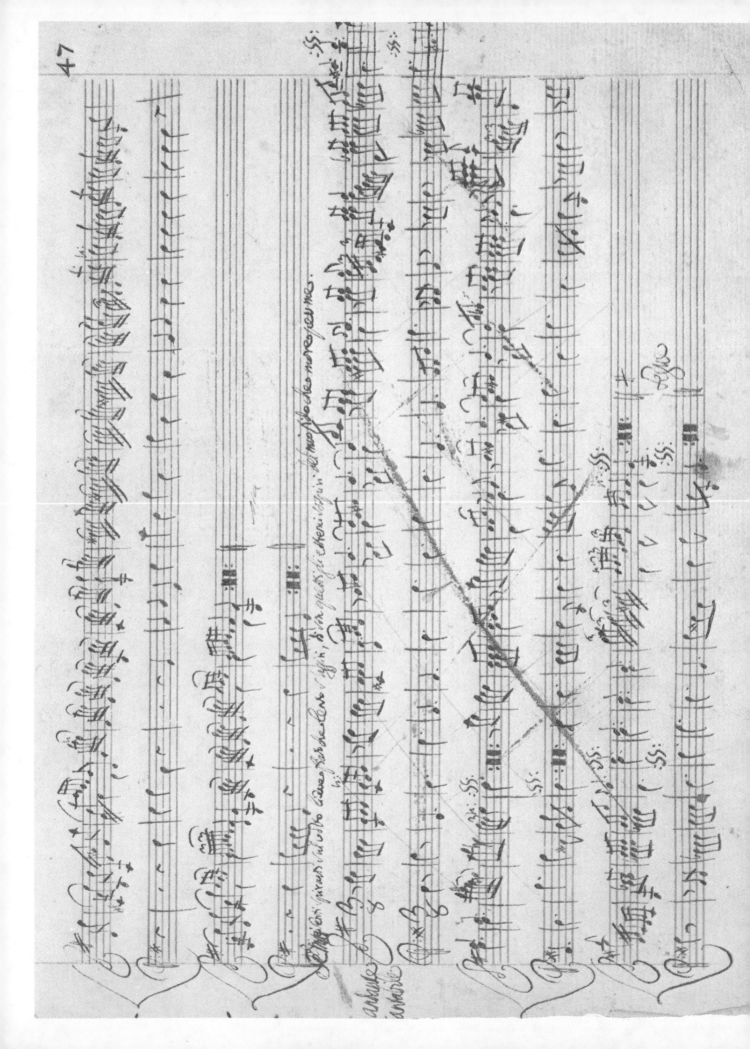

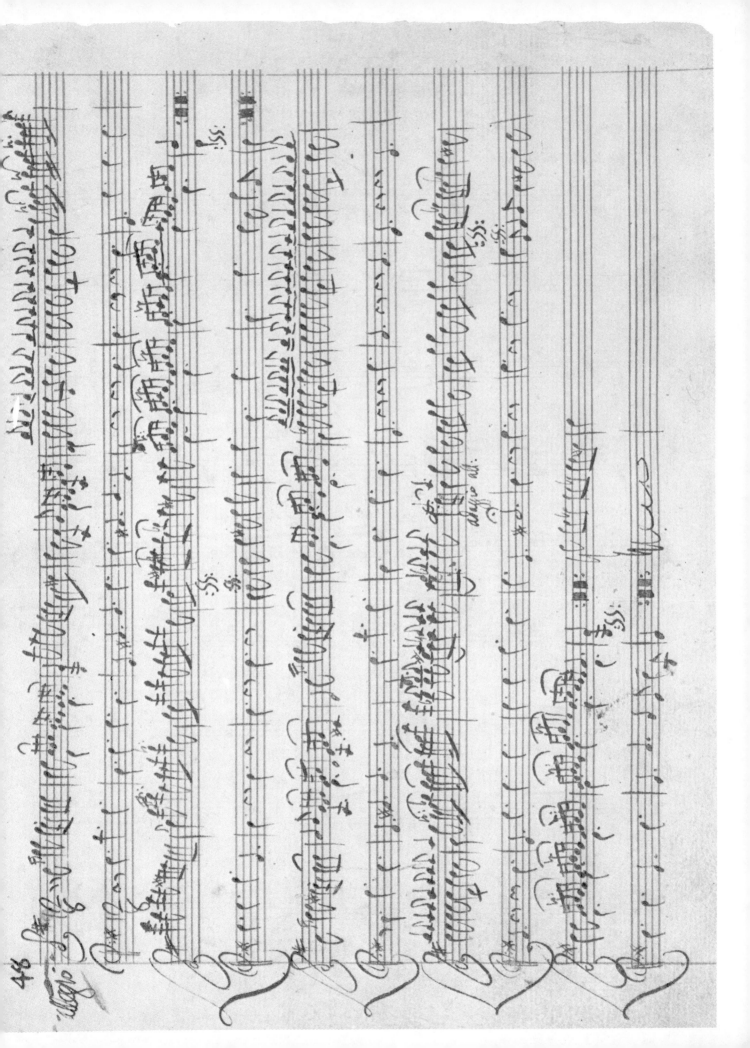

SONATA XIV
(in Sol magg. - B. G 4)
per Violino e Violoncello

G. TARTINI
(G. GUGLIELMO)

DURATA: MIN. 8

Andante cantabile

VIOLINO

VIOLINO

✿ Sopra il primo pentagramma c'è il seguente versetto:
  "Se senti spirarti sul volto lieve fiato che lento s'aggiri,
  dì son questi gli alterni sospiri del mio fido che muore per me.

VIOLINO

SONATA XIV

(in Sol magg. - B. G 4)

G. TARTINI
(G. GUGLIELMO)

Andante cantabile

Allegro assai

VIOLONCELLO

✿ Eseguire come le battute 1 e 2.

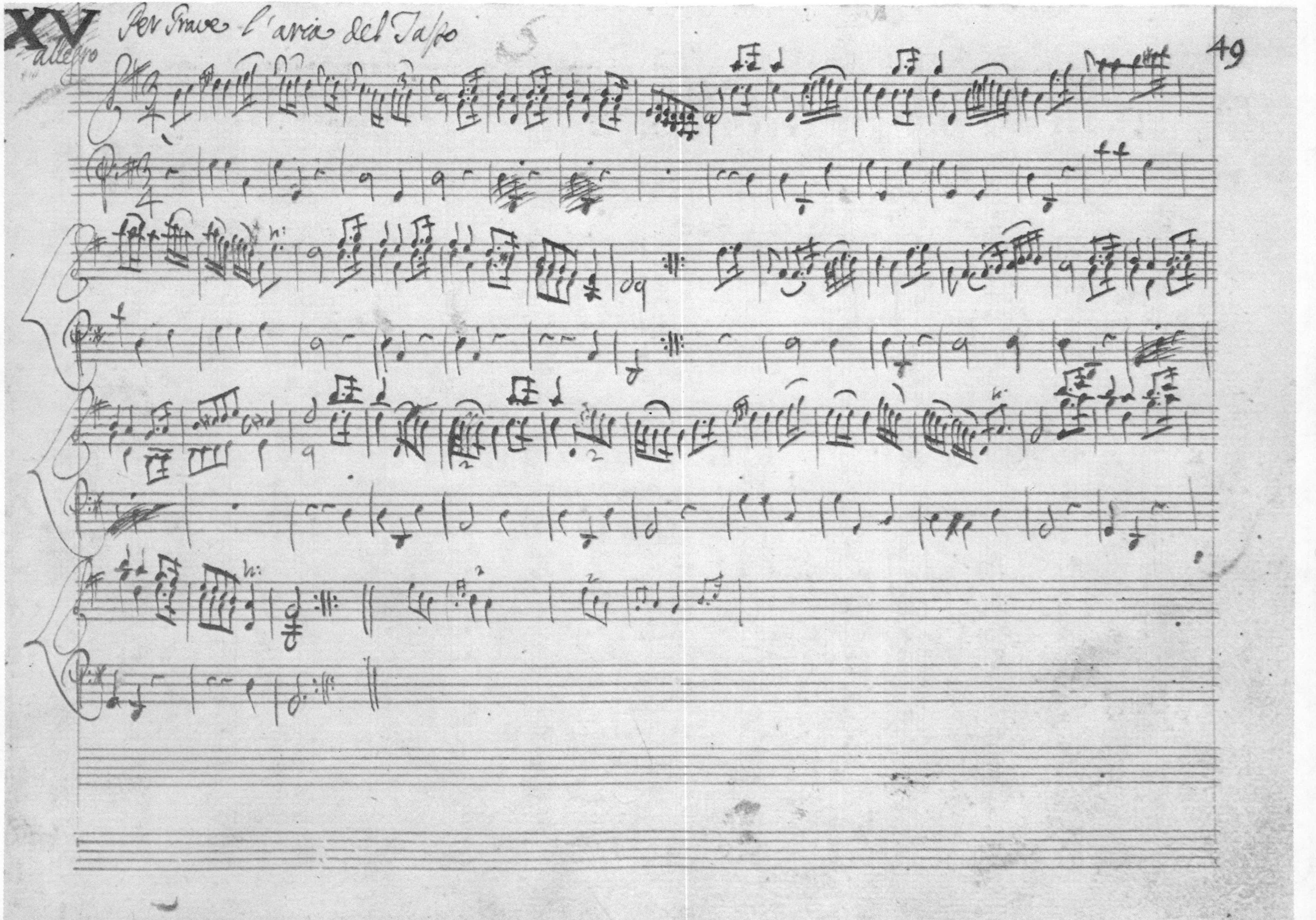
XV
Per Grave l'aria del Tasso
allegro
49

SONATA XV

(in Sol magg.-B. G 3)

per Violino e Violoncello

DURATA: MIN. 6, 30"

G. TARTINI
(G. GUGLIELMO)

ARIA DEL TASSO (Violino solo)(✱)

lie - to ti prendo e poi la not - te quan - do tut-te in al - to si - len - zio

e - ran le co - se, vi - di in so-gno un guer - ri - er che mi - nac -

cian - do a me sul vol - to il fer - ro nu - do po - se

✱ Questo Tempo appartiene alla Sonata XII. - In calce alla Sonata XV Tartini ha scritto "Per Grave l'Aria del Tasso„

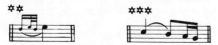

Allegro

VIOLINO

Allegro

✩ opp. come nella Iᵃ parte

SONATA XV

(in Sol magg. - B. G 3)

G. TARTINI
(G. GUGLIELMO)

GRAVE - ARIA del TASSO - (per Violino solo) - Cello tacet

✿ Eseguire come la battuta 1

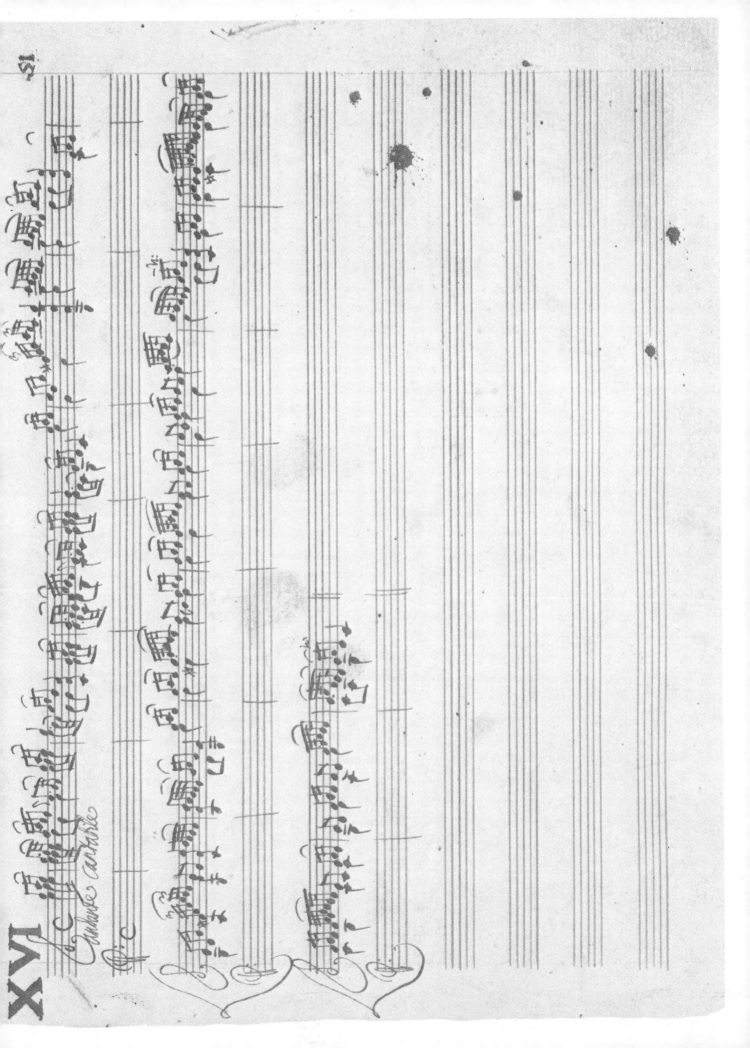

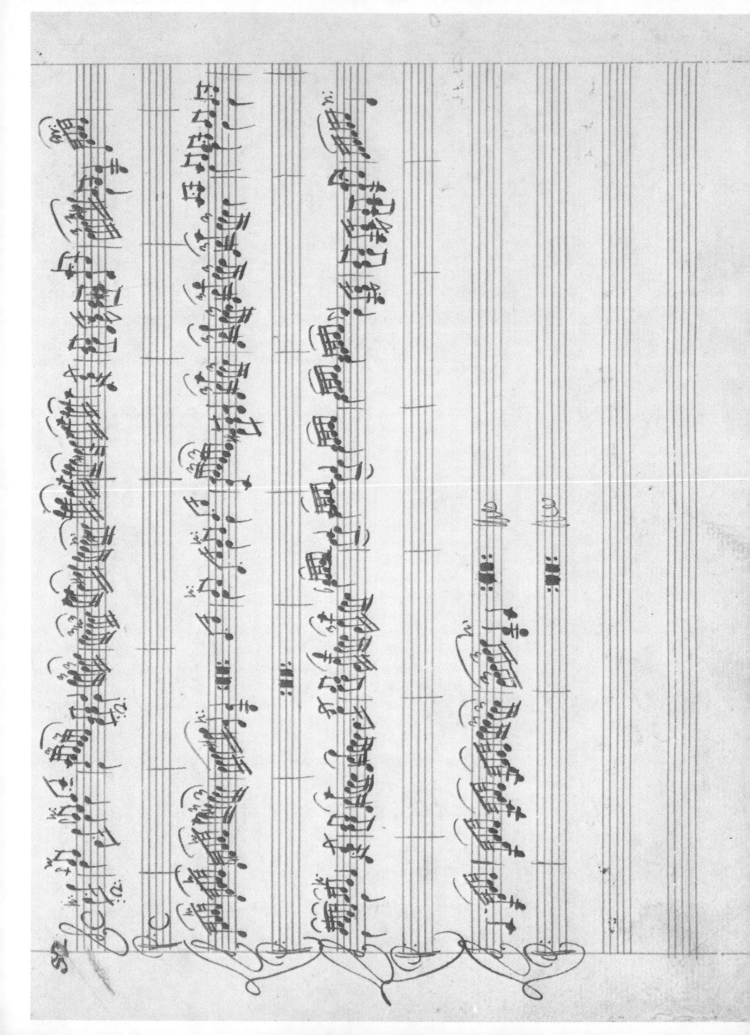

SONATA XVI

(in Do magg. - B.C 2)

per Violino solo

DURATA: MIN. 7

G. TARTINI
(G. GUGLIELMO)

Andante cantabile

VIOLINO

✭ Non c'è indicazione di Tempo nell'originale

VIOLINO

✿ Non c'è nessuna indicazione di Tempo nell'originale

Menuet

VIOLINO

SONATA XVII

(in Re magg.-B.D 2)

VIOLINO

per Violino solo

G. TARTINI
(G. GUGLIELMO)

DURATA: MIN. 9

✿ Sotto il pentagramma del Violino c'è il versetto "dì se senti"

VIOLINO

✿ Non v'è indicazione di tempo nell'originale.
Sotto l'intero brano vi sono i versi di un'Aria del Tasso appartenenti alle Sonate XII e XV

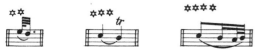

VIOLINO

FURLANA (per Violino e Violoncello) ✶

✶ Questo Tempo potrà essere sostituito dal Minuetto II della Sonata XIX che Tartini ha trascritto per Violino solo sotto l'Andante cantabile.

In alcune Sonate per Violino solo vi sono dei tempi col Violoncello

Dalla SONATA XVII in Re magg.

G. TARTINI
(G. GUGLIELMO)

Furlana

Dalla SONATA XIX in Re magg.

Allegro assai

Minuetto II

ARIA – Allegro assai ✿

✿ Ripetere altre 4 volte con i Ritornelli

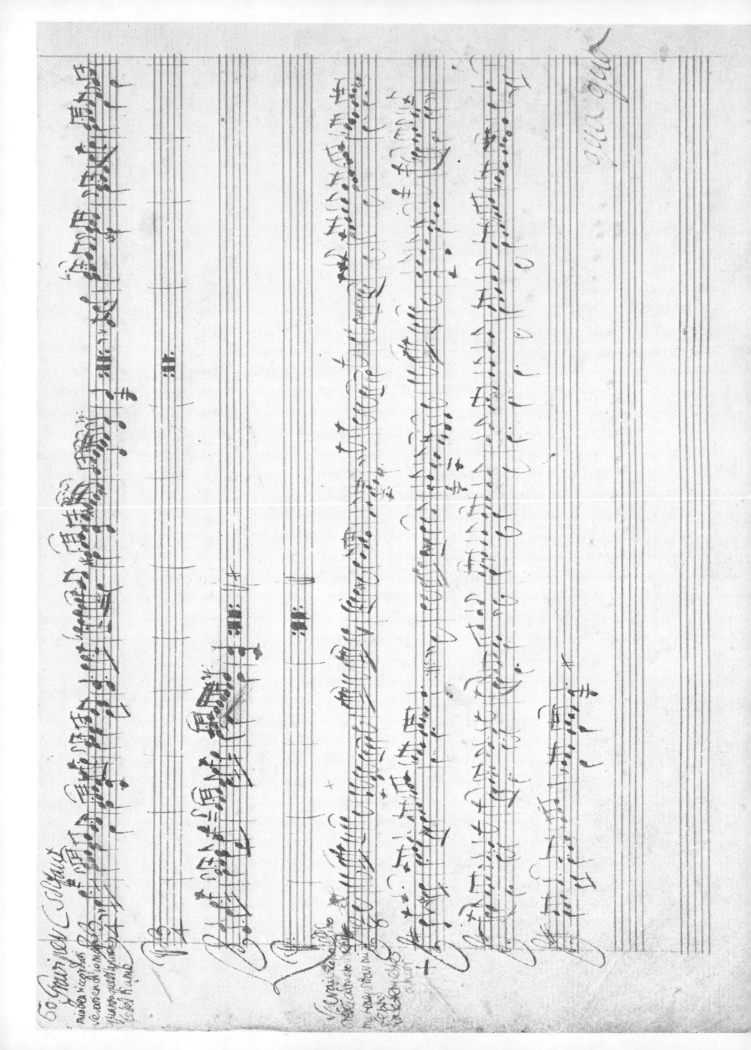

SONATA XVIII

(in Do magg. - B. C 3)

per Violino solo

G. TARTINI
(G. GUGLIELMO)

DURATA: MIN. 6

✿ Sotto l'indicazione del Tempo è scritto "amatissimo"

VIOLINO

✿ Indicazione originale.
  Modo di eseguire indicato dall'Autore:

VIOLINO

Allegro assai

GRAVI (per CSolfaut) ✿

✿ P. Brainard cataloga questo Tempo con C 14.
✿✿ c'è il versetto "mio ben ......"

VIOLINO

GIGA ✷

✷ Non c'è nessuna indicazione di Tempo nell'originale su questo brano composto in epoca posteriore e che, probabil-mente, in considerazione anche delle diverse tonalità, non appartiene a questa Sonata.

SONATA XIX

(in Re magg. - B. D 3)
per Violino solo

VIOLINO

G. TARTINI
(G. GUGLIELMO)

DURATA: MIN. 7

Andante cantabile ✿

✿ ci sono 2 versetti:
  a) "sciogli le mie......,,
  b) "lascia ch'io dica addio,,.

✿✿ legatura originale

✿✿✿ come le battute 1 e 2

✿✿✿✿

VIOLINO

Allegro assai (per Violino e Violoncello)

✿ Nell'originale é indicato $\frac{2}{8}$.

SICILIANA - Andante

VIOLINO

* Indicazione originale

MINUETTO II (per Violino e Violoncello) ✿

✿ Questo Minuetto è stato ricopiato dall'A. nella versione per Violino solo sotto l'Andante cantabile della Sonata XVII.

oppure simili alla battuta 10

ARIA - Allegro assai (per Violino e Violoncello)

✿ ✿✿ Nell'originale sta scritto così:

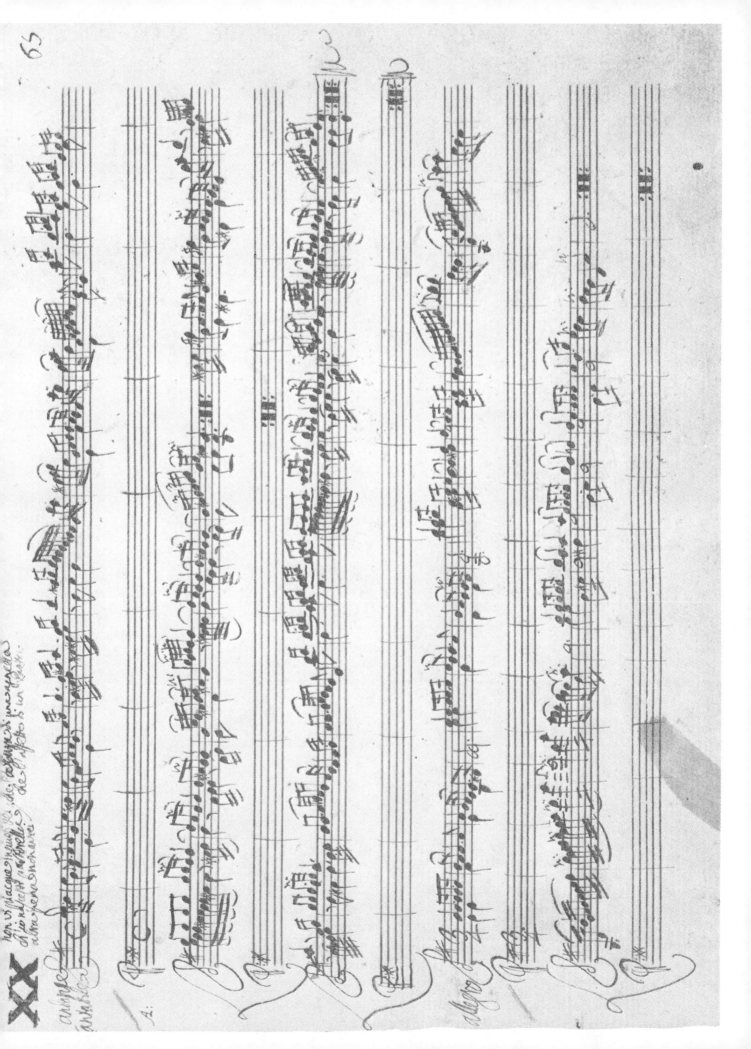

L'onda che mormora tra sponda e sponda; l'aura che tremola tra fronda e fronda, è meno instabile del vostro cuor.

SONATA XX

(in Mi min. - B. e 2)

per Violino solo

VIOLINO

G. TARTINI
(G. GUGLIELMO)

DURATA: MIN. 6 circa

✿ In calce c'è il versetto "Non ti piacque......"

VIOLINO

VIOLINO

VIOLINO

* In calce c'è un versetto: "L'onda che ...."

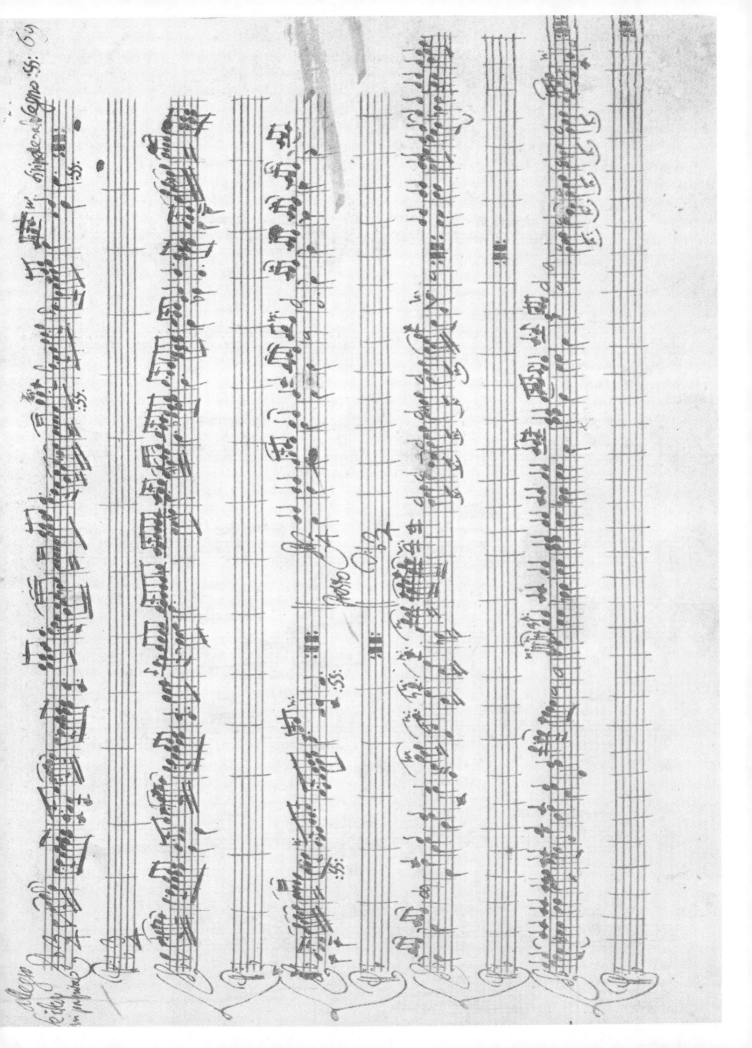

SONATA XXI

VIOLINO

(in Fa magg. - B. F 2)

per Violino solo

G. TARTINI
(G. GUGLIELMO)

DURATA: MIN. 6' 30"

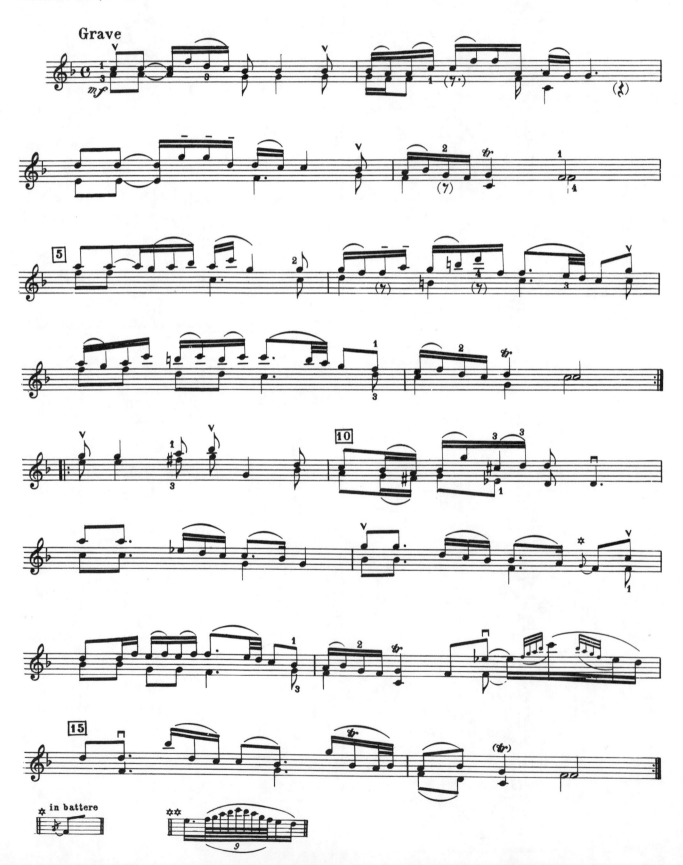

VIOLINO

Allegro non presto✼

✼ Sotto l'indicazione di tempo c'è il versetto : „ ombra cara che qui d'intorno „

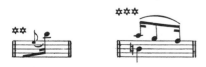

VIOLINO

✿ C'è il seguente versetto: Se il cor mi palpita,,

VIOLINO

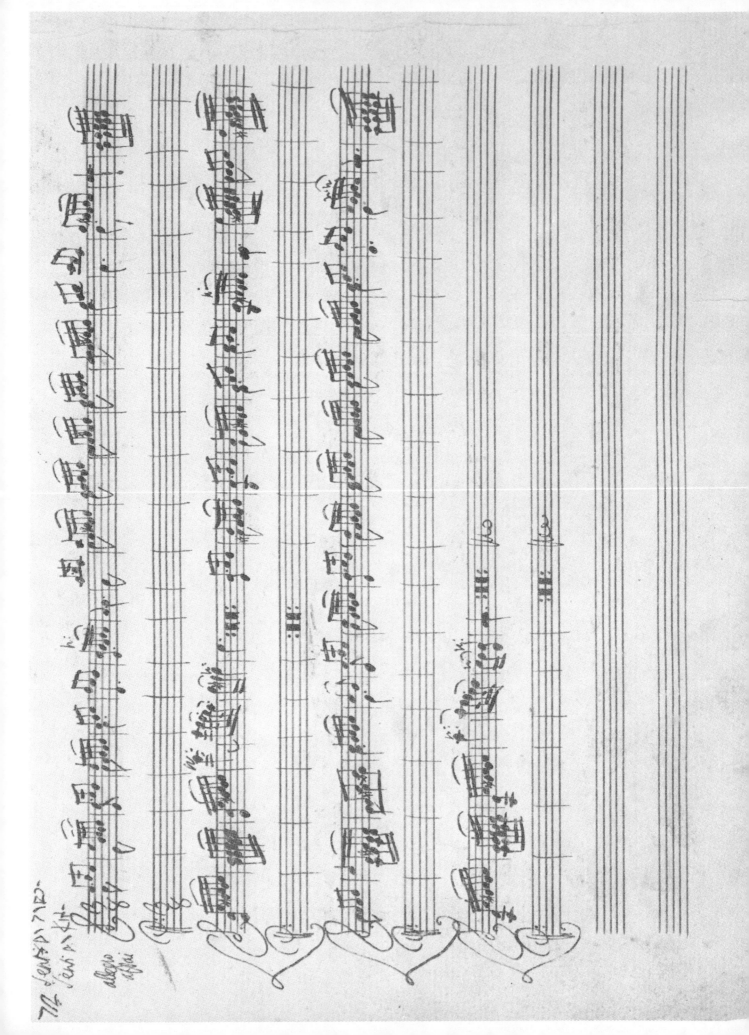

SONATA XXII

VIOLINO

(in La min. - B. a 2)
per Violino solo

G. TARTINI
(G. GUGLIELMO)

DURATA: MIN. 8' 30''

✳ In calce c'è il versetto: "Deh serbate Amici ...,,

✳ In calce c'è il versetto: "Tra l'orror della tempesta,,

VIOLINO

VIOLINO

✿ In criptografia c'è il versetto: "Senti la fonte — Senti lo mare,,
✿✿ legature originali

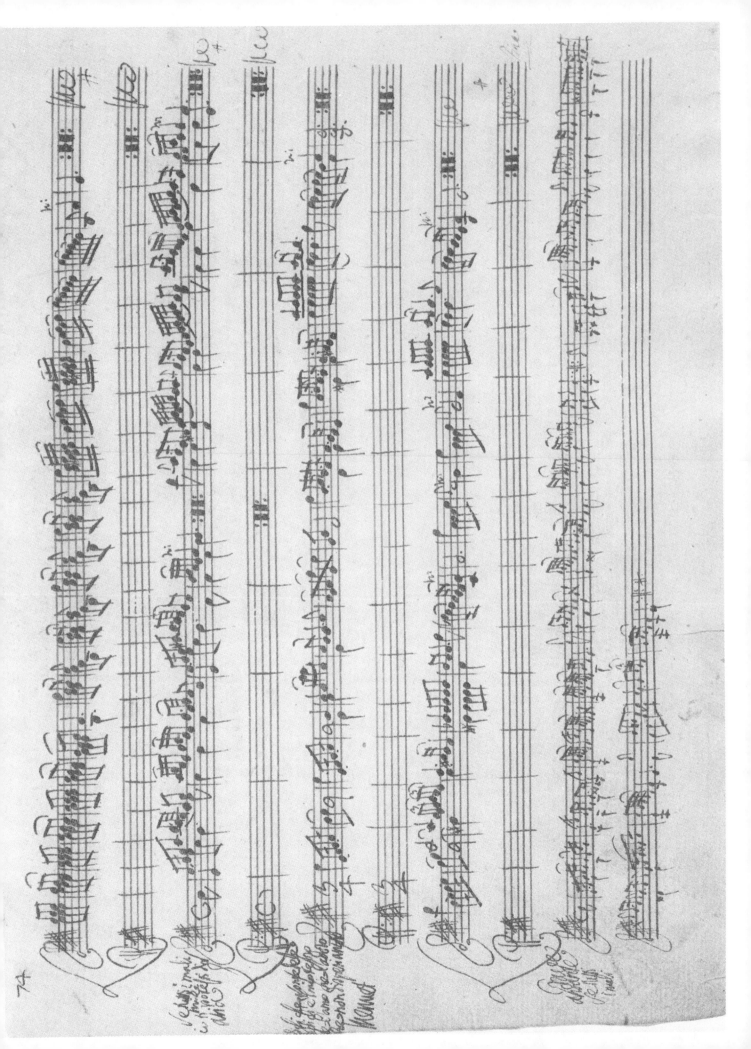

74

SONATA XXIII

(in Mi magg. - B. E 2)

per Violino solo

G. TARTINI
(G. GUGLIELMO)

DURATA: MIN. 8

✿ In calce il seguente versetto: "Lascia ch'io dica addio al caro albergo mio al praticello,,

VIOLINO

VIOLINO

VIOLINO

✿ In calce il seguente versetto: "Se tutti i mali„

✿ Non c'è indicazione di tempo nell'originale.

VIOLINO

✿ Questo tempo composto in epoca posteriore probabilmente non appartiene a questa Sonata essendo di tonalità diversa.

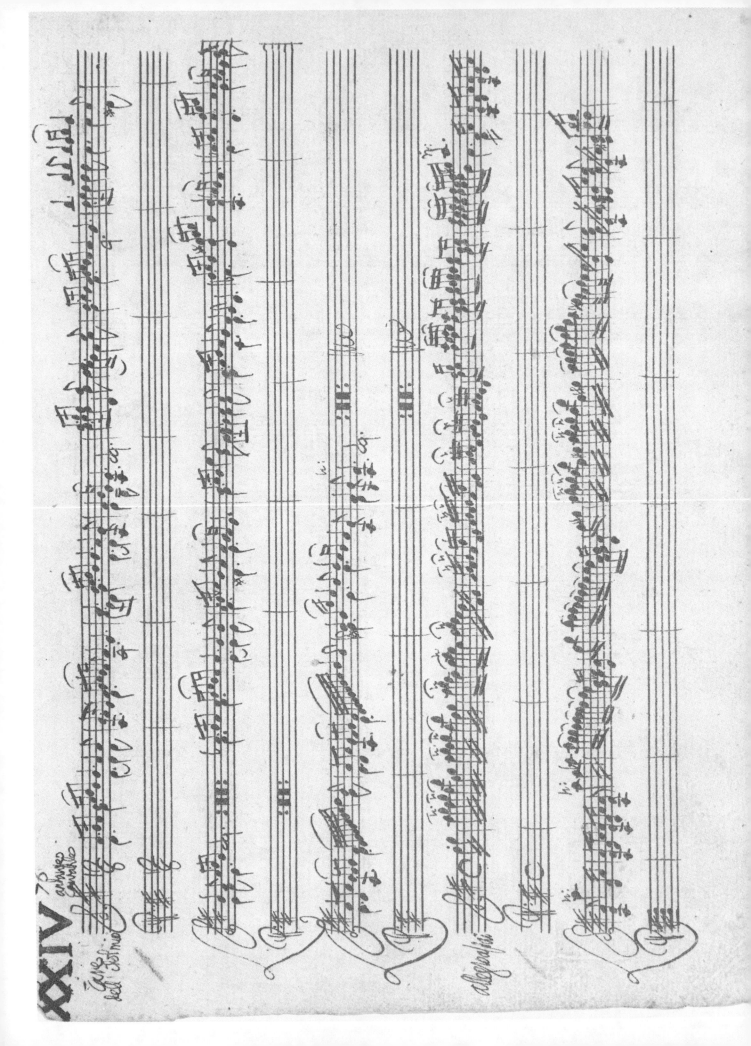

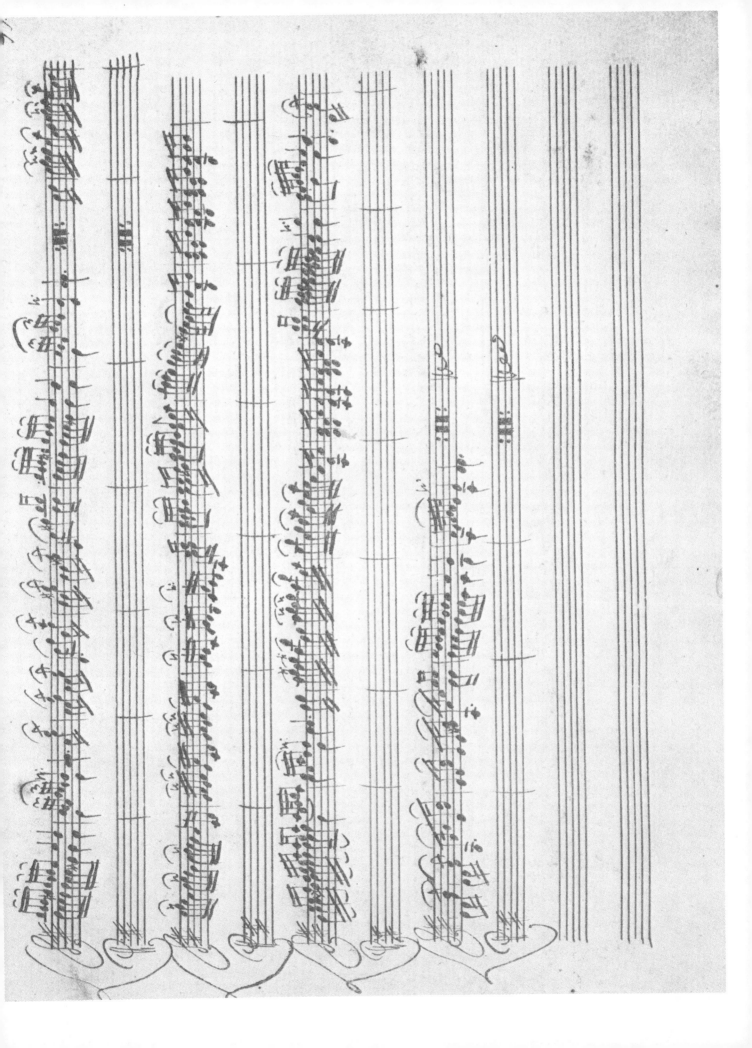

SONATA XXIV

(in Re magg.- B. D. 4)

per Violino solo

G. TARTINI
(G. GUGLIELMO)

DURATA: MIN. 8

✽ In calce il versetto: "Care dell'idol mio,,

VIOLINO

Allegro assai

VIOLINO

ARIA Cantabile ✻

✻ In calce il versetto: "Alla stagion novella fin dall'opposto lido
torna la rondinella il nido a riveder "

VIOLINO

✿ Non c'è nessuna indicazione di tempo nell'originale.
  In calce c'è il versetto seguente: "Amico fato guidami in porto nè un cor fedele lascia perir„

VIOLINO

✿ Non c'è nessuna indicazione di tempo nell'originale.

✿✿ Sotto le prime 6 battute c'è il seguente versetto: "Amico il fato mi guida.....,,

✿✿✿ Le note tra parentesi sono state aggiunte in epoca posteriore.

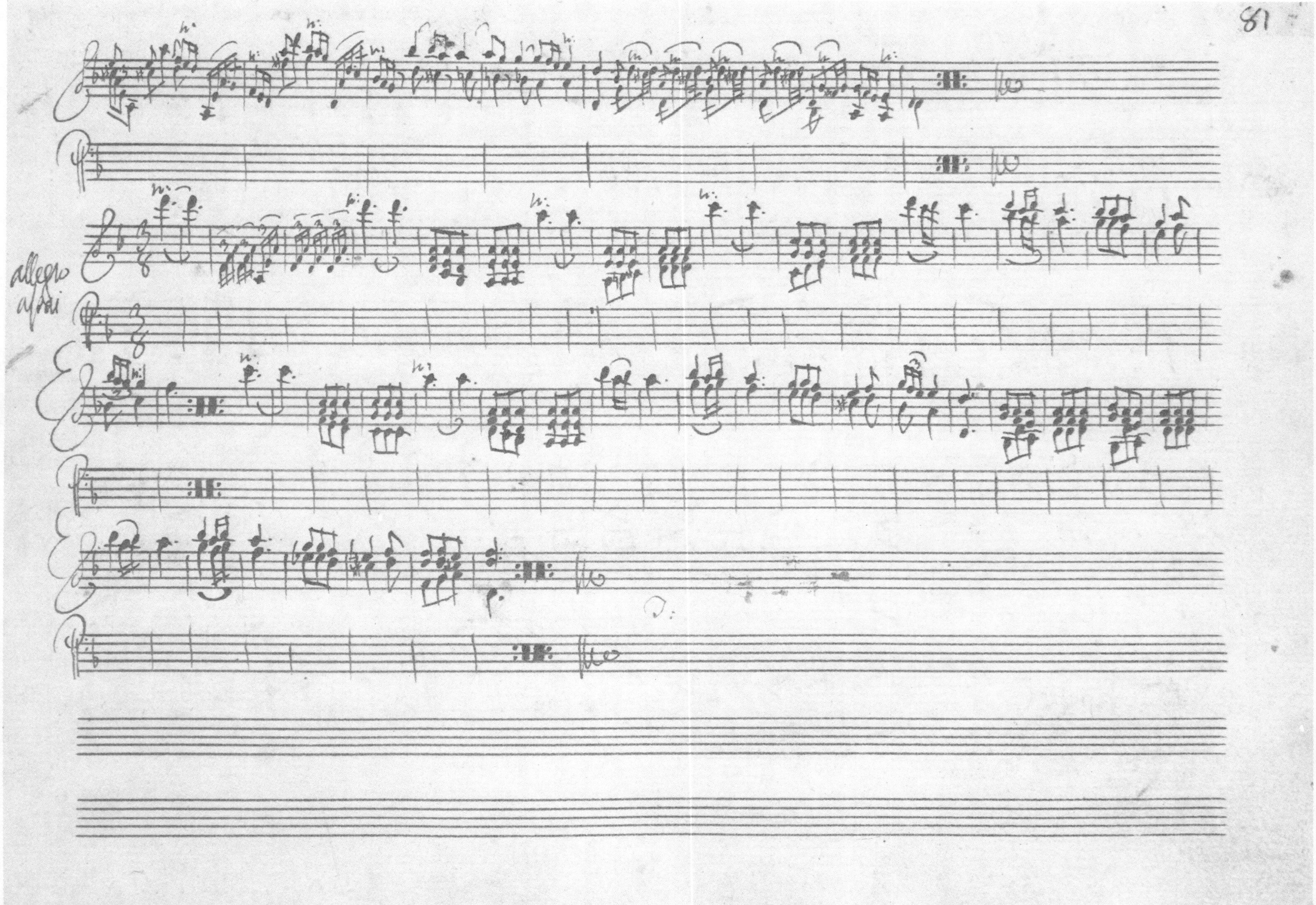
allegro assai

SONATA XXV

VIOLINO

(in La min. - B. d **2**)

per Violino solo

G. TARTINI
(G. GUGLIELMO)

DURATA: MIN. 6

VIOLINO

Allegro assai

Tempo deis' mia cara no' che no' putto restar la pensè d'amore desmitofa l'elira.

SONATA XXVI

(in Sol magg. - B. G 5)

per Violino solo

G. TARTINI
(G. GUGLIELMO)

DURATA: MIN. 8

(SICILIANA) ✱

✱ Non c'è nessuna indicazione di tempo nell'originale.
  In calce c'è il versetto: "Senza de ti mia cara nò che nò posso star, la pena è così amara che mi fa delirar,,.

MENUET

VIOLINO

✿ Non c'è nessuna indicazione di tempo nell'originale.

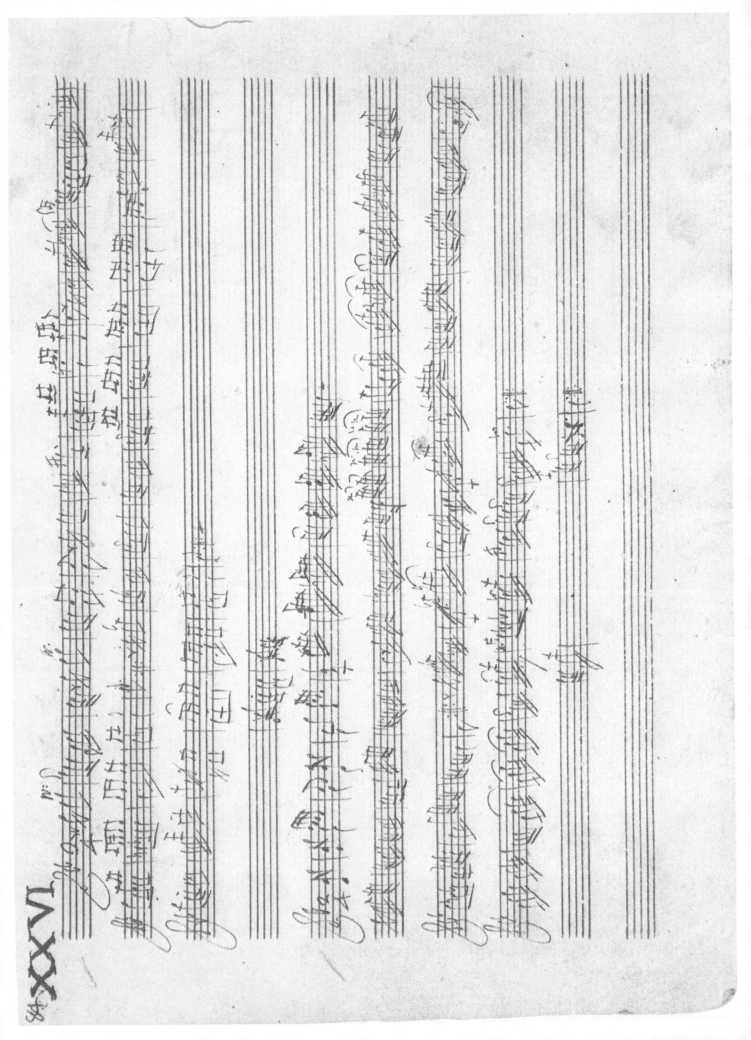

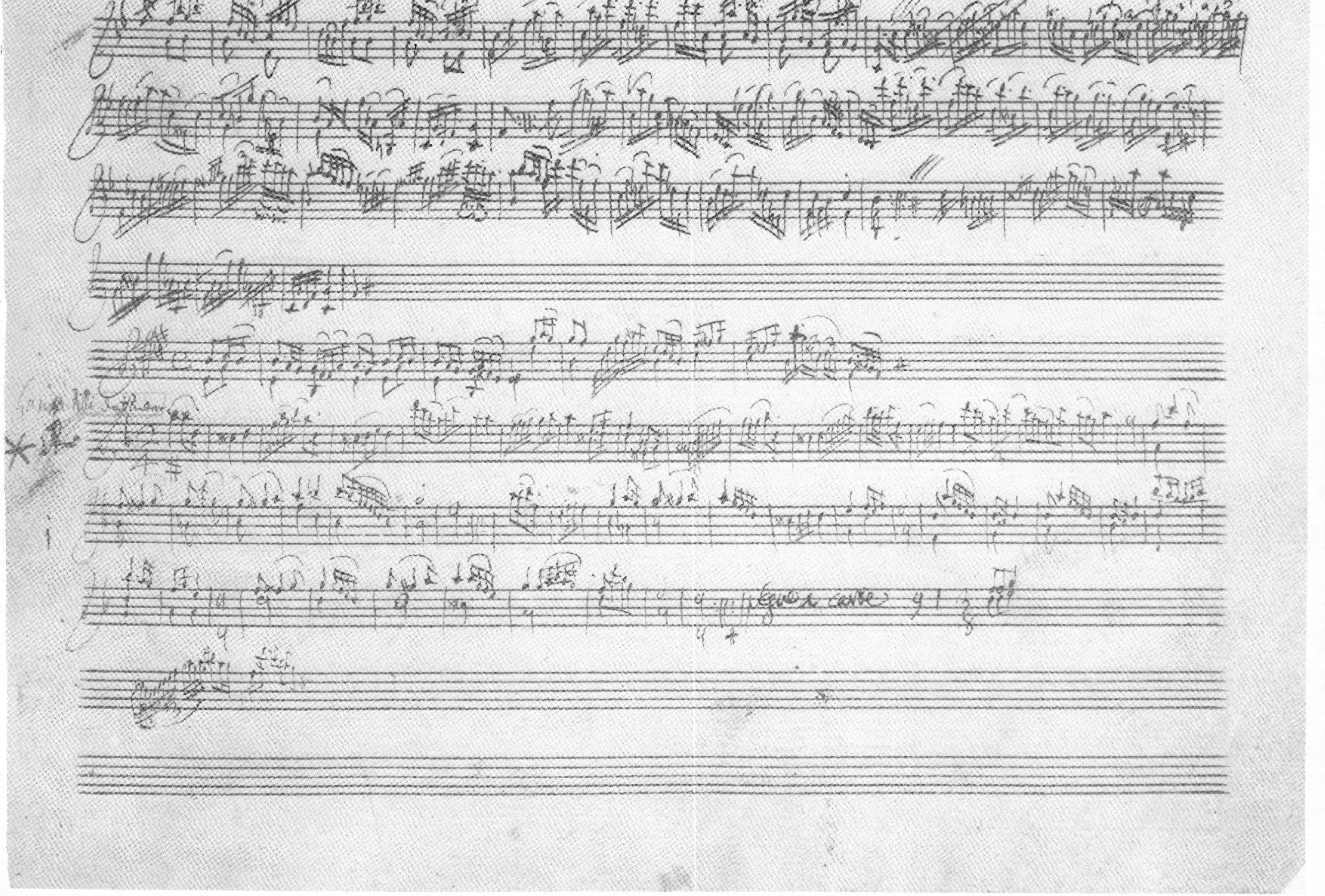
segue a carte

86
Grave Rui
vi è un principio di Grave qui dietro a carte 85
meglio qui sotto
partita mutata a carte 92

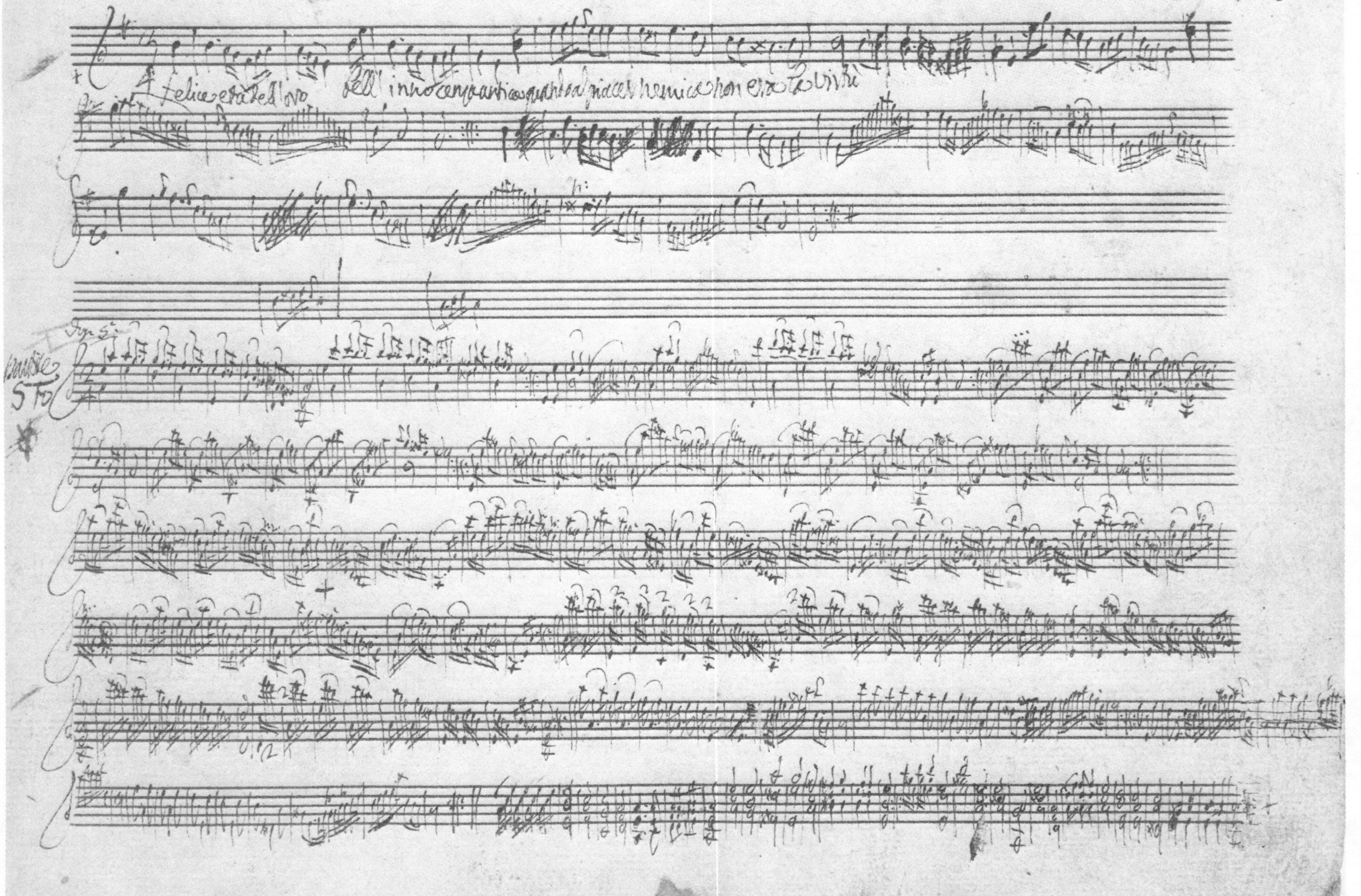
felice era dell'oro

3
Dite almeno amiche fronde
se il mio ben più rivedrò;
Ah che l'Eco mi risponde
e mi par che dica no.
Sento un dolce mormorio
un sospir forse sarà
un sospir dell'idol mio,
che mi dice tornerà.
4
Ah ch'è il suon del rio che frange
tra que' sassi il fresco umor.
E non mormora, ma piange
per pietà del mio dolor.
Ma se torna, fia pur tardo
il ritorno, e la pietà
che pietoso in van lo sguardo
sul mio cener volgerà.

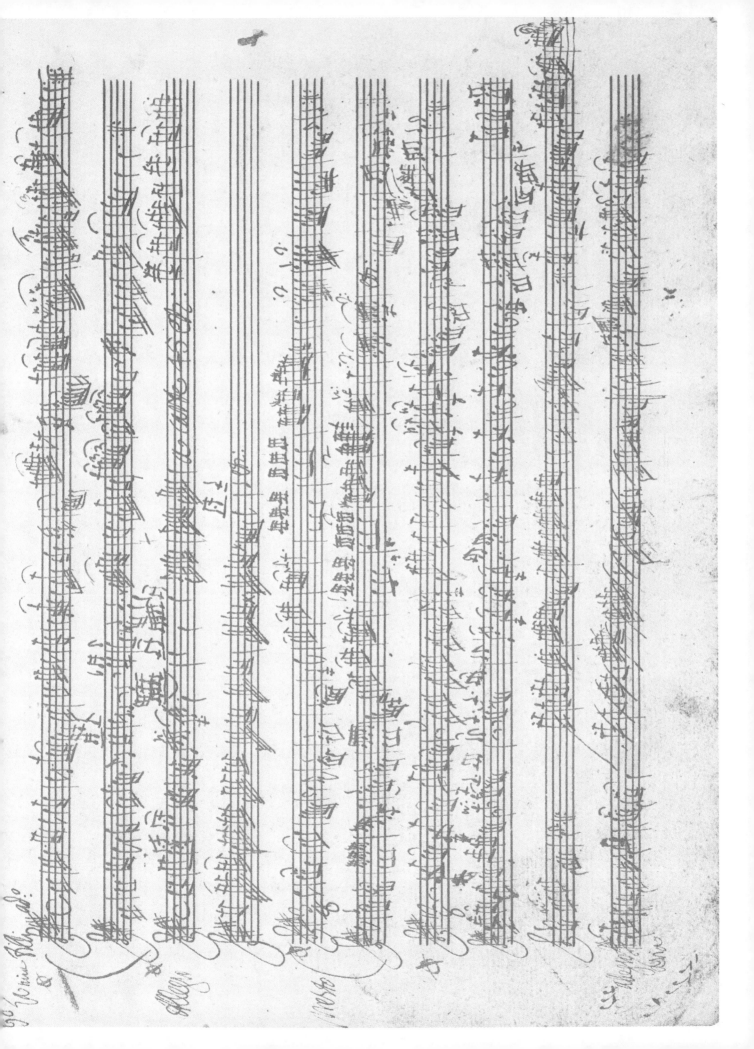

Per il primo Allegro cantabile tirato a arte 95

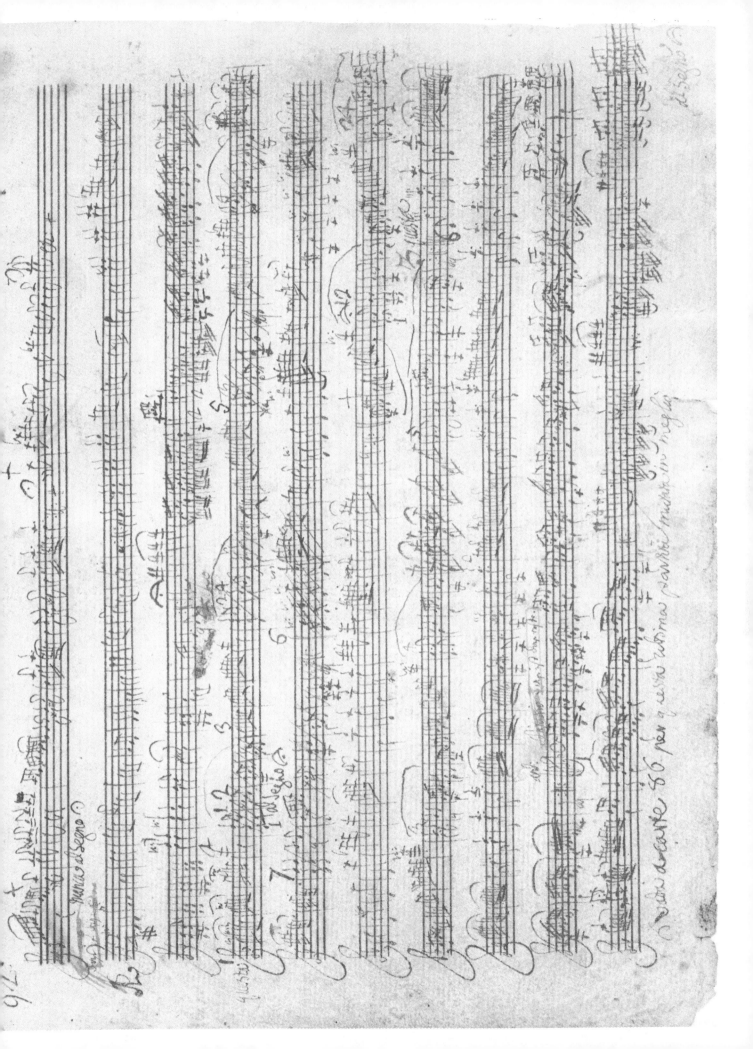

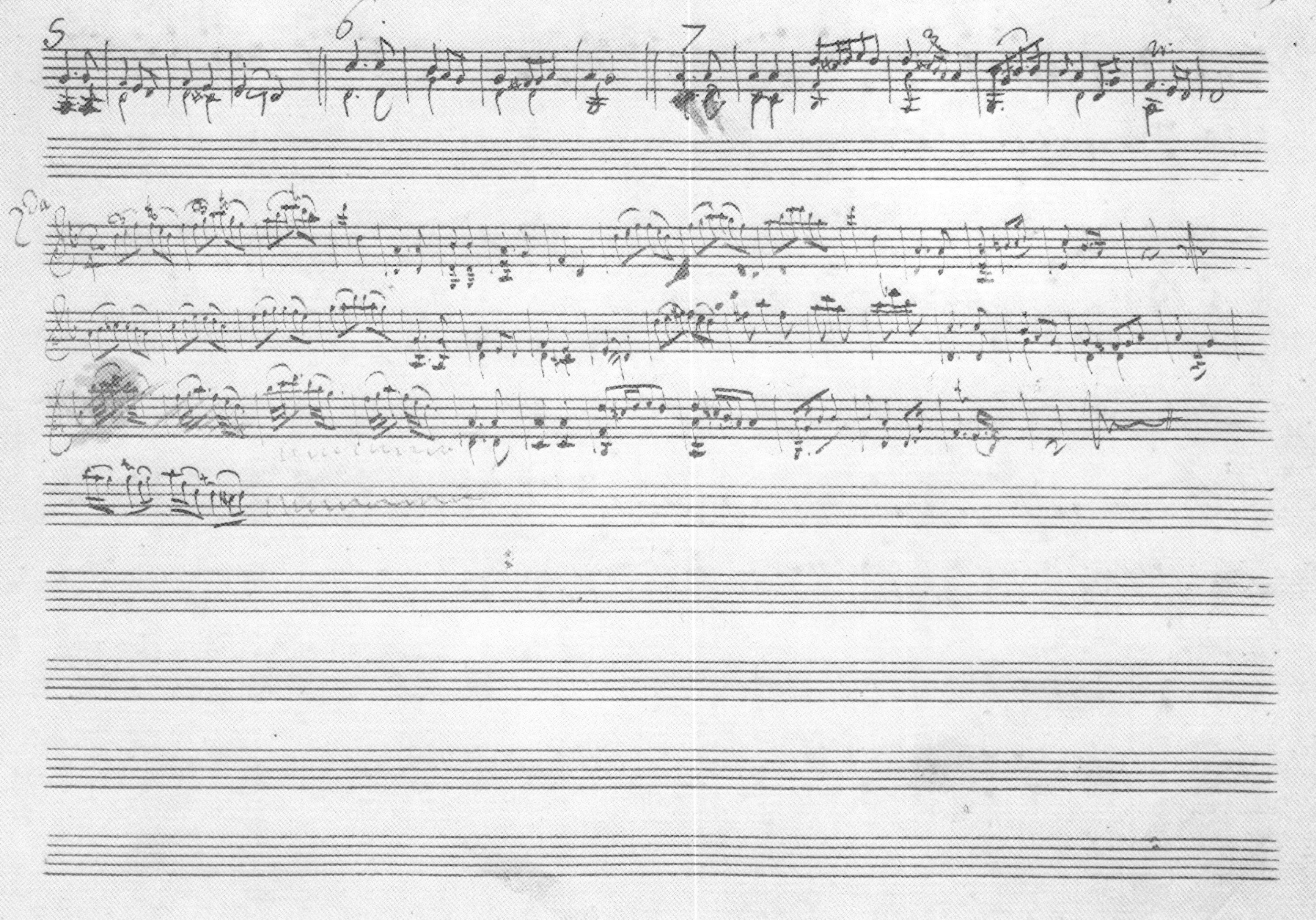

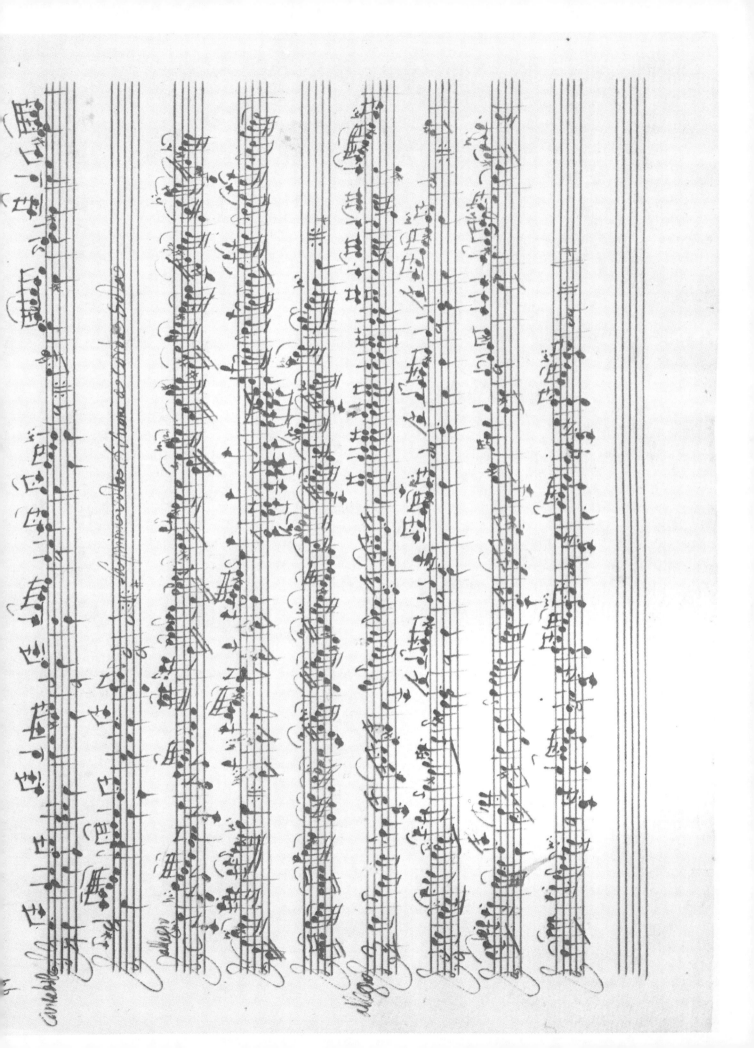

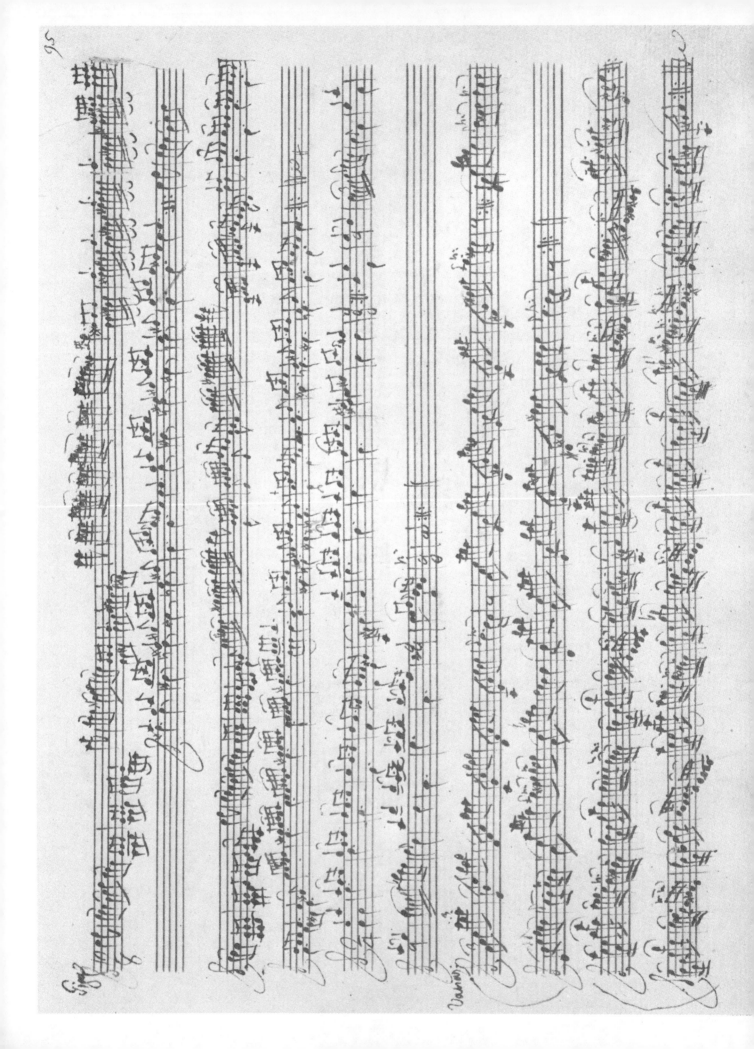

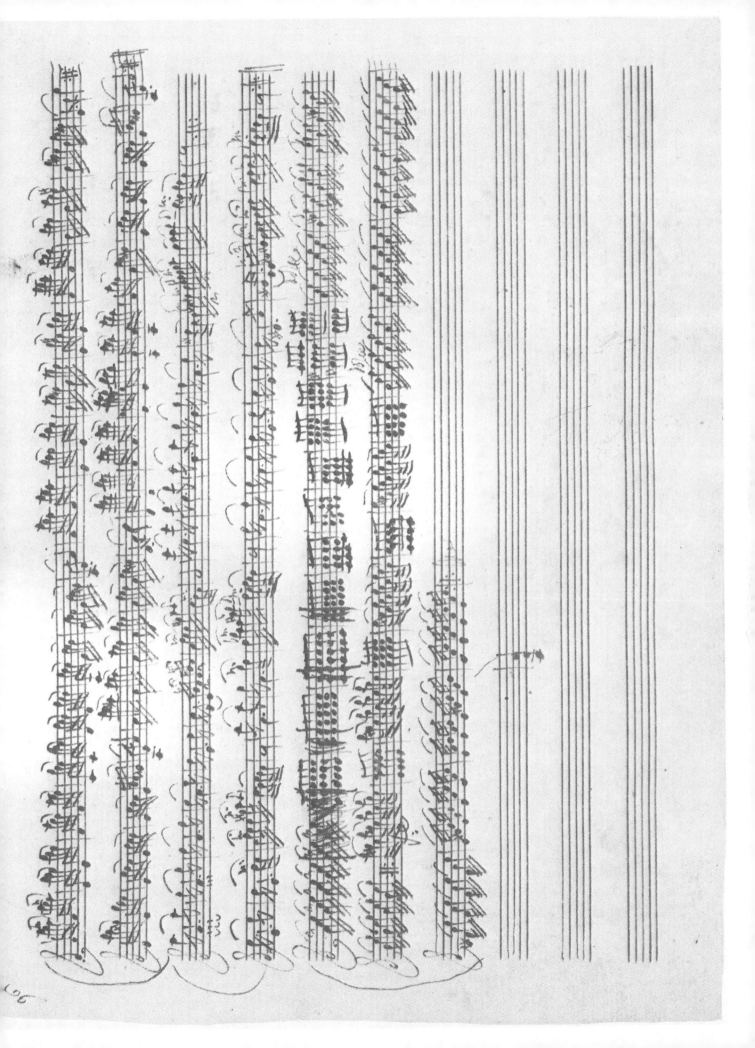

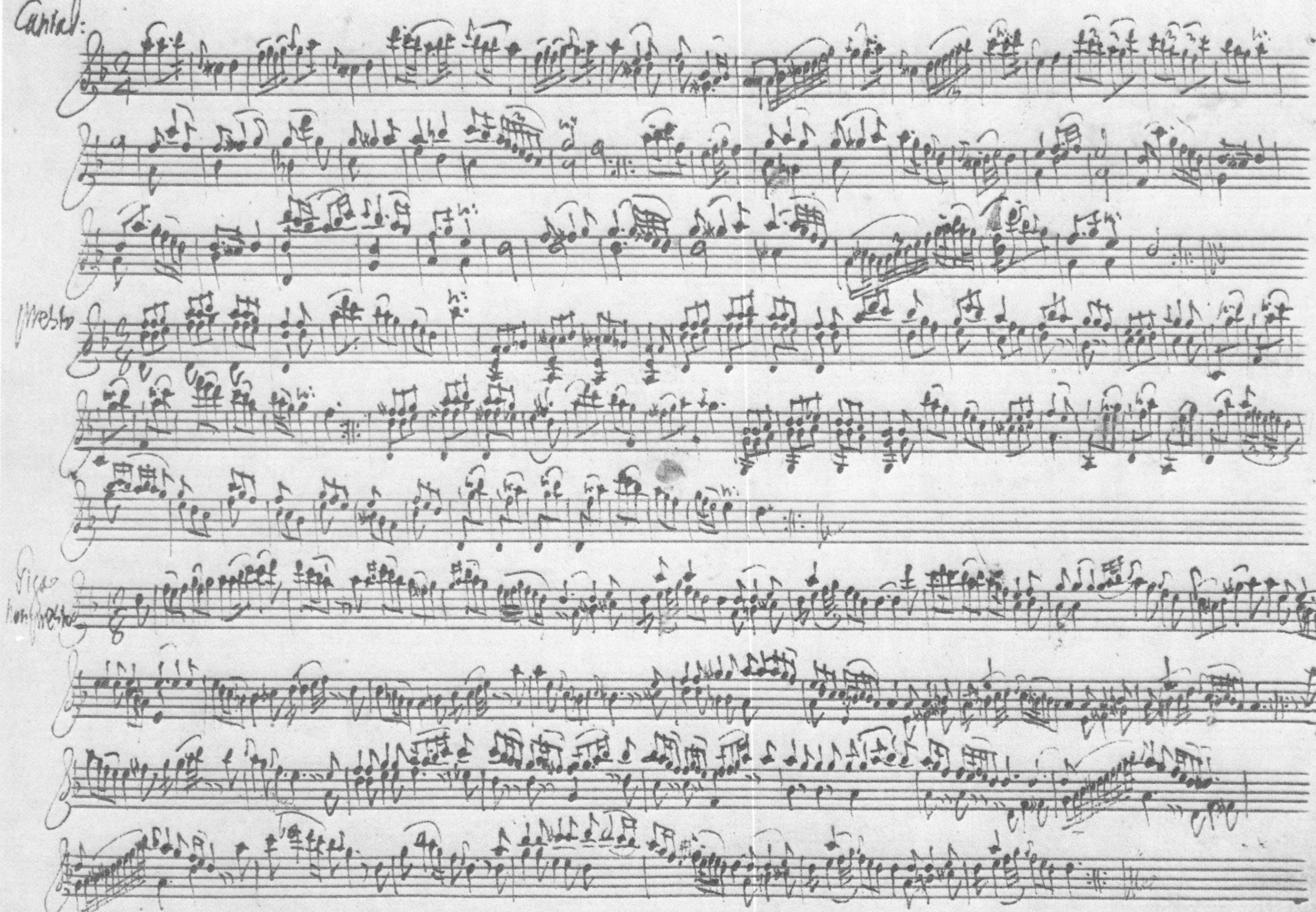
Presto
Giga

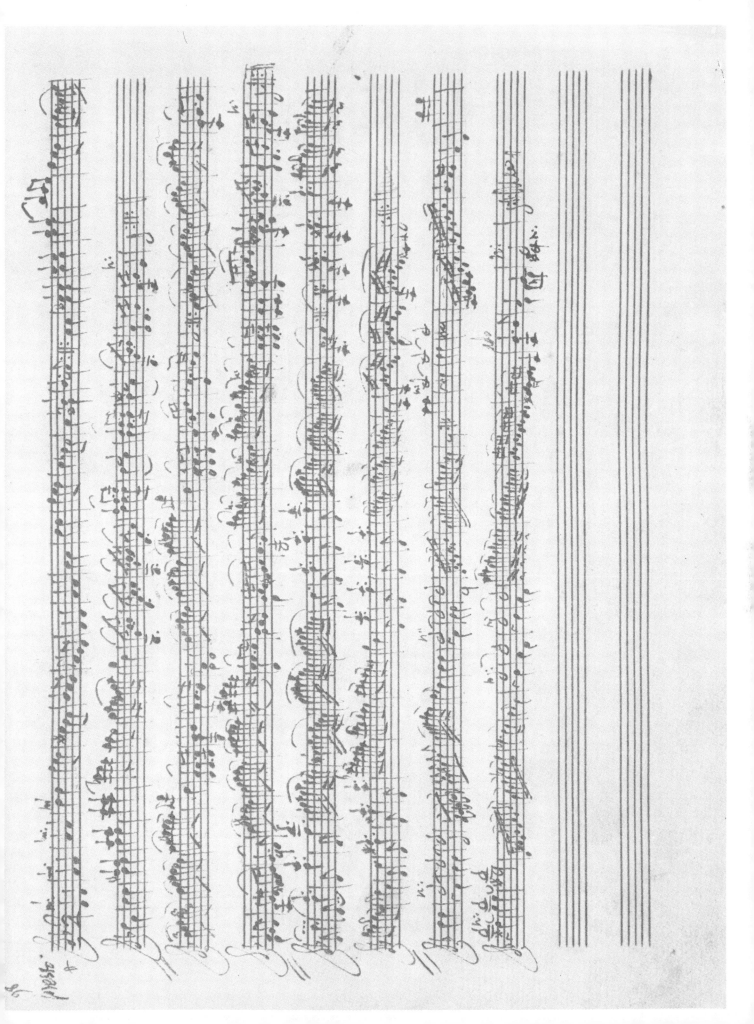

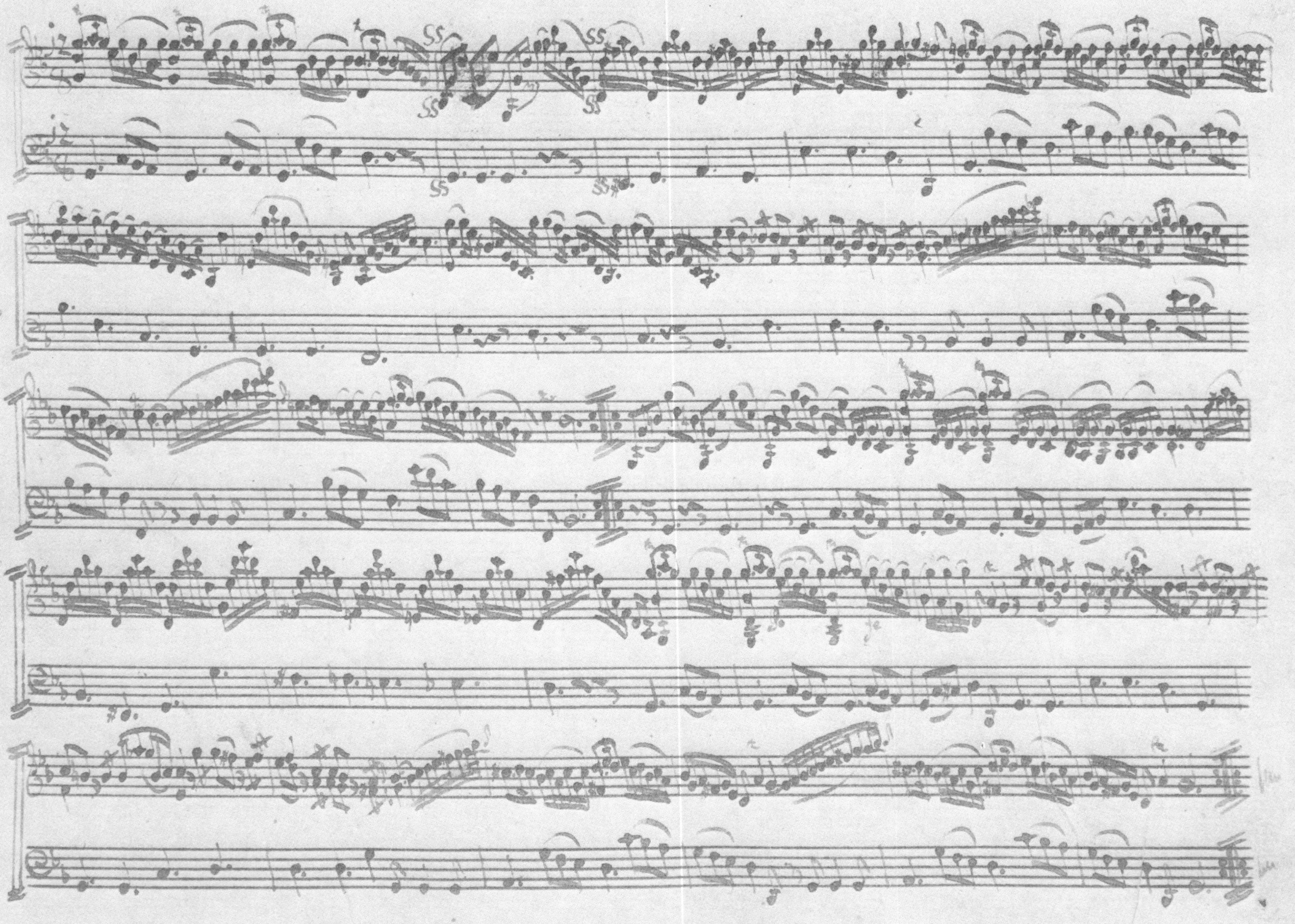

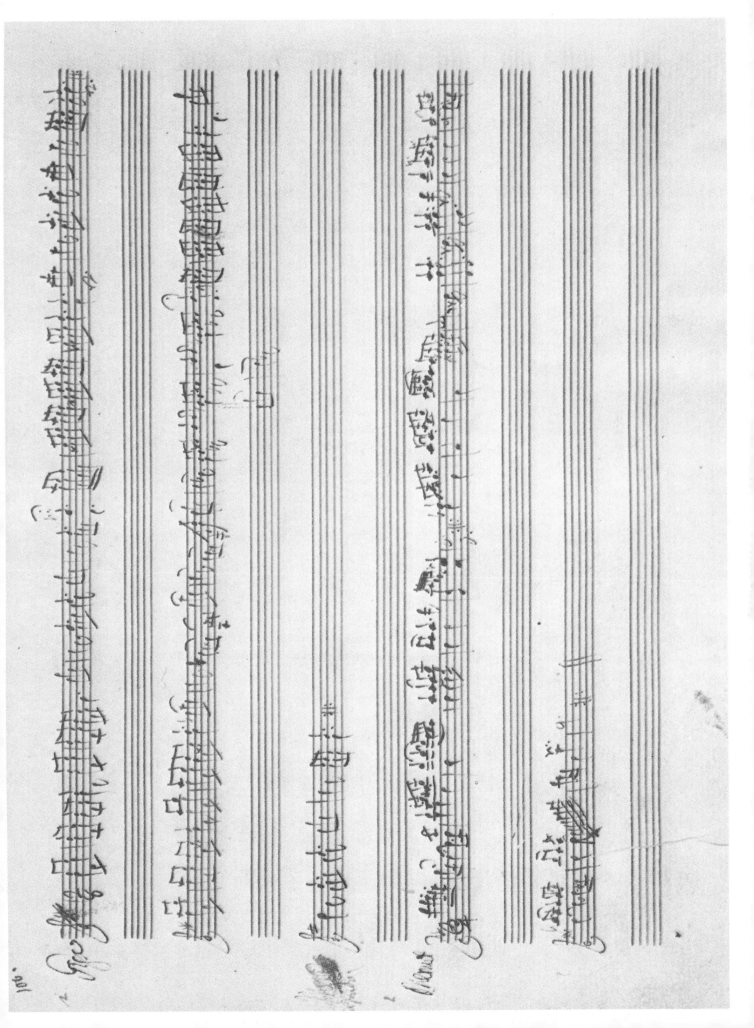

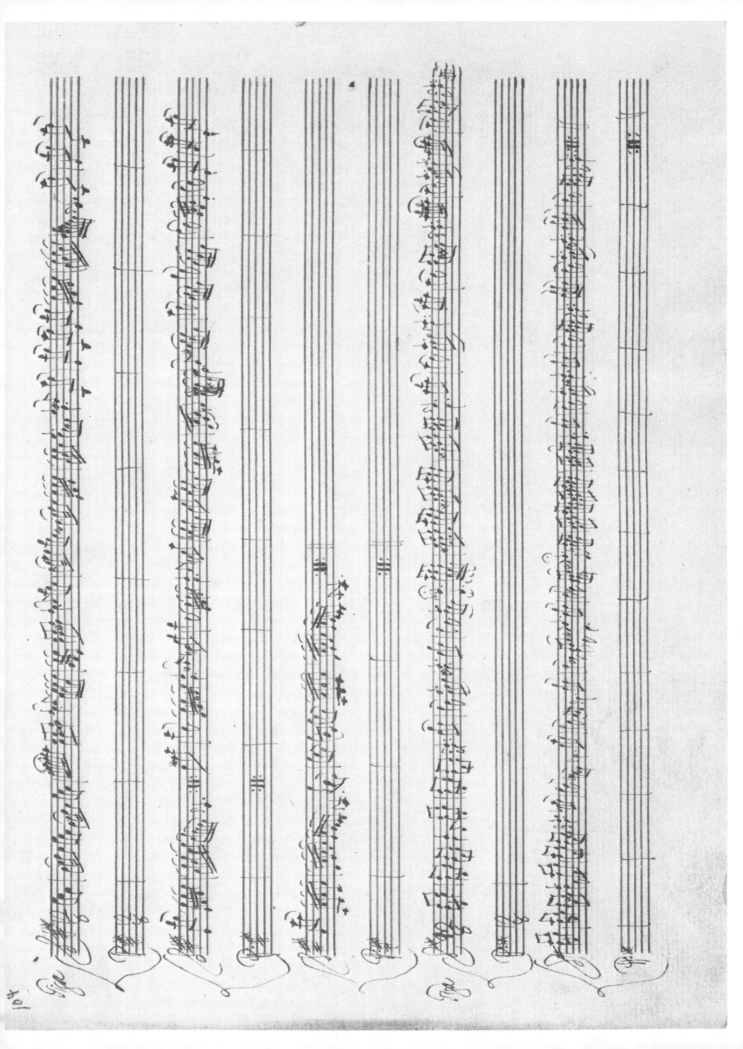

105

L'art de l'archet.
Die Kunst der Bogenführung.
50
VARIATIONEN
über eine Gavotte
für die Violine
par
J. TARTINI.

Zum Gebrauch am Conservatorium der Musik
in Leipzig mit obligater Pianofortebegleitung,
Bogenstrich, Fingersatz und Vortragszeichen
versehen von Ferd. David.

Verlag &
Eigenthum für alle Länder von
(Propriété pour tous pays.)
JOHANN ANDRÉ
OFFENBACH a/m. & LEIPZIG.

London, Ent. Sta. Hall.   Firenze, Reg. tratt. intern.

L'art de l'archet.

VIOLINO.

J. Tartini.

8

VIOLINO.

VAR. 31.

VAR. 32.

VAR. 33.

Andante.

Basso continuo.

VAR. 37.

VAR. 38.

Andante.

Basso continuo.

VIOLINO.

LITERATURE ABOUT GIUSEPPE TARTINI
AND HIS WORK

Abbado, Michelangelo e Petrobelli, Pierluigi, "Giuseppe Tartini," *Enciclopedia della Musica*, Volume Quarto, Milano, 1964, pp. 353-358.

Abbado, M., "Presenza di Tartini nel nostro secolo," *Nuora rirista musicule italiana*, 1970.

Anonymous (G. Gennari), "Elogio del defunto Sig. Tartini," *L' Europa Letteraria,"* IV/I, 1770.

Anonymous, "Saggio sopra la scienza del Sig. Tartini," *L' Europa Letteraria*, II/I, 1771.

Auer, Leopold, *Violin Master Works and their Interpretation*, New York, 1925, pp. 1-6.

_____, *Moya shkola igry na skripke, Interpretatsia proizvedenii skripichnoi klassiki (Violin Playing as I Teach It, Violin Master Works and their Interpretation)*. Editor: I. Yampolsky, Moscow, 1965, pp. 93-94, 131-136.

_____, *Violin Playing as I Teach It*, London, 1921, pp. 140-142.

Bachmann, Alberto, *Les grands violinistes du passé*, Paris, 1913, pp. 312-365.

_____, *An Encyclopedia of the Violin*, New York, 1966, pp. 221-223.

Bezekirsky, V.V., *Kratkii Istoricheskii obzor muzykal-no-skripichnovo iskusstva s XVII po XX v (A Short Historical Survey of Violin Art from the 17th to the 20th Centuries)*, Kiev-Warsaw, 1913, p. 4.

Beyschlag, Adolf, *Die Ornamentik der Musik*, 2. Auflage, Leipzig, 1953, pp. 1 4 5 - 1 4 7 .

Benedetti, Giorgio, *Giuseppe Tartini*, Trieste, 1896.

Bouvet, Charles, *Une Lecon de Giuseppe Tartini et une Femme Violiniste au XVIII-e Siècle*, Nouvelle Edition. Paris, 1918.

Boyden, David D, "The Missing Italian Manuscript of Tartini's Traité des Agremens," *The Musical Quarterly*, July 1960, pp. 315-328.

Brainard, Paul, *Die Violinsonaten Giuseppe Tartinis*, Dissertation, Göttingen, 1959.

_____, "Giuseppe Tartini." *Die Musik in Geschichte und Gegenwart*. Lieferung 120/121, pp. 130-137.

_____, "Tartini and the Sonata for Unaccompanied Violin," *Journal of the American Musicological Society*, 1961, No. 3, pp. 383-393.

_____, *Le sonate per violino di Giuseppe Tartini*, Catalogo tematico, Milano, 1975.

Brückner, Karl, *Giuseppe Tartini (1692-1770)*, "Der fortschrittliche Geigenlehrer," 1932, Nos. 3-5.

Capri, Antonio, *Giuseppe Tartini*, Milano, 1945.

Dounias, Minos, *Die Violinkonzerte Giuseppe Tartinis, als Ausdruck einer Küstlerpersölichkeit und einer Kulturepoche*, Wolfenbüttel—Berlin, 1935. (Neudruck, Wolfenbüttel-Zürich, 1966).

Duckles, Vincent and Elmer, Minnie, with the assistance of Pierluigi Petrobelli, *Thematic Catalogue of a Manuscript Collection of Eighteenth-Century Italian Instrumental Music In the University of California, Berkeley Music Library*, Foreword by David D. Boyden, Berkeley and Los Angeles, 1963, pp. 296-355.

Ehrlich, A., *Berühmte Geiger der Vergangenheit und Gegenwart*, Leipzig, 1893, pp. 269-358.

Eitner, R., "Tartini, Giuseppe," *Biographisch-Bibliographisches Quellen-Lexikon der Musiker und Musikgelehrten*, 9 Band. Leipzig, 1903, pp. 355-358.

Elmer, M., *Tartini's Improvised Ornamentation*, Dissertation, Berkeley, 1962.

Engel, Hans, *Das Solokonzert*, Köln, 1964, pp. 10-12, 99-103.

Fanzago, Fr., *Elogi di Giuseppe Tartini, primo Violonista nella Capella del Santo di Padova*, Padova, 1792.

Fanzago, Francesco, *Orazione delle lodi di Giuseppe Tartini*, Padova, 1770.

Farina, E., *Giuseppe Tartini nel bicentario della morte*, Padova, 1970.

Fayolle, F.J.M., *Notices sur Corelli, Tartini, Gaviniès, Pugnani et Viotti*, Paris, 1810, pp. 11-23.

Fellowes, Edmund H., "Tartini, Giuseppe," *Grove's Dictionary of Music and Musicians*, Fifth edition, Volume VIII, London, 1954, pp. 312-315.

Fétis, F., "Tartini," *Biographie universelle des musiciens*, Tome huitième. Bruxelles, 1844, pp. 328-333.

Forno, Agostino, "Elogio del Celebre Guiseppe Tartini," *Elogi Italiani*, Napoli, 1792.

Ftasson, P.L., "Giuseppe Tartini primo violino e capo di concerto nella basilica del Santo," *Il Santo*, Padova, 1972.

Gerber, Ernst L., "Tartini, Giuseppe," *Historisch-Biographisches Lexicon der Tonkünstler*, Leipzig, 1790, pp. 617-624. Also: *Neues Historisch-Biographisches Lexicon der Tonkünstler*, Leipzig, 1812-1814, pp. 322-323.

Ginsburg, L.S., "Tartini, Giuseppe," *Muzykalnaya Entsiklopedia (Music Encyclopaedia)*, Vol. V, Moscow, 1981, pp. 445-448.

———, *"Giuseppe Tartini v russkoi muzykalnoi zhizni." "Slavyane i zapad, sbornik statyei k 70-letiu I.F. Belza" ("Giuseppe Tartini in Russian musical life." "The Slavs and the West.") A collection of articles in honour of the 70th birthday of I.F. Belza*, Moscow, 1975, pp. 170-178.

Goldin, M., *The Violinistic Innovations of Giuseppe Tartini*, Dissertation. New York University, 1955.

Grünberg, Max, *Meister der Violine*, Stuttgart-Berlin, 1925, pp. 22-30.

Hawkins, Sir John, *A General History of the Science and Practice of Music*, Volume the Fifth, London, 1776, pp. 375-379.

Hiller, Johann Adam, *Lebensbeschreibung berühmter Musikgelehrter und Tonkünstler neuerer Zeit*, Teil I. Leipzig, 1784, pp. 267-285.

Hortis, Attilio, "Lettere famigliari di Giuseppe Tartini," *Archeografo Triestino*, vol. X, Trieste, 1884.

Huet, Félix, *Tartini. Étude sur les différentes Ecoles de Violon depuis Corelli jusqu'à Baillot*, Chalons-sur-Marne, 1880, pp. 54-65.

Jacobi, E.R., "A.F. Nikolai's MS of Tartini's Regole per ben suonare il Violino," *The Musical Quarterly*, 1961, Aprila, pp. 207-223.

Kirilov, Nikolai, *Skripachi XVII, XVIII i XIX stoletii (Violinists of the 17th, 18th and 19th Centuries)*, St. Petersburg, 1874, pp. 13-19.

Kohlmorgen, Walter, *Das Buch der Violine*, Zürich, 1972, pp. 340-343.

Kuhac, Franz Xaver, "Josip Tartini i hrvatska pucka glazba," *Prosvjeta*, 1898.

Laurencie, Lionel de la, "Traité des agréments de la musique de Tartini (1771)," "L'école française de violon de Lully à Viotti," *Etudes d'histoire et d'esthétique*, Tome III, Paris, 1924, pp. 64-74.

Leonie, Sergio, Segati, Giovanni, Pierobon, Rocco, Manara, Filippo, Colasanti, Arduino, *Discorsi per le onoranze a Giuseppe Tartini*, Padova, 1924.

Mendel, Hermann, Reissmann, August, "Tartini, Giuseppe," *Musikalisches Conversations-Lexicon*, Neue wohlfeile Stereotyp-Ausgabe. Leipzig (s.a.), pp. 111-114.

Morossi, Francesco-Antonio, "Elogio di Giuseppe Tartini," *Elogi di Italiani*, tomo VIII, Venezia, 1782.

Moser, Andreas, *Geschichte des Violinspeils*, Berlin, 1923, pp. 250-269.

———, *Geschichte des Violinspiels. Zweite verbesserte und ergänzte Auflage von Hans-Joachim Nösselt*, Erster Band. Das Violinspiel bis 1800 (Italien). Tutzing, 1966, pp. 225-240.

Nel giorno della inaugurazione del monumento a Giuseppe Tartini in Pirano. Trieste, 1896. Giuseppe Tartini, La vita (M. Tamaro). L'opera musicale (G. Wisselberger).

Newman, William S, *The Sonata in the Baroque Era*, Chapel Hill, 1989, pp. 189-192.

Nordio, Mario, *Giuseppe Tartini. Il XXV anniversario della fondazione del Conservatorio di musica Giuseppe Tartini 1903-1928*, Trieste, 1929, pp. 11-28.

Pasini, Ferdinanado, "Il Tartini a Giuseppe Valeriano Vanetti. 12 lettere inedite, *Pagine Istriane,* Capodistria, 1906.

Petrobelli, Pierluigi, "Giuseppe Tartini," *La Musica,* Vol. IV, parte prima. Torino, 1966, pp. 573-584.

_____, *Giuseppe Tartini. Le Fonti biografiche,* Venezia, 1968.

_____, "Per l'edizione critica di un concerto tartiniano (D. 21)," *Musiche italiane rare e vive,* Siena, 1962, pp. 97-128.

_____, "Giuseppe Tartini," *Enciclopedia della musica,* VI, Milano, 1972.

_____, *Tartini, le sue idee e il suo tempo,* Roma, 1967.

Pincherle, Marc, *Les violinistes,* Paris, 1922, pp. 62-66.

Planchart, A.E., "A Study of the Theories of Giuseppe Tartini," *Journal of Music Theory,* April 1960.

Pougin, Arthur, *Le Violon, les Violinistes et la Musique de Violon du XVI-e au XVIII-e siècle,* Paris, 1934, pp. 100-115.

Pulver, Jeffrey, "The Literary Works of Tartini," *Monthly Musical Record,* LII., London, 1922, p. 215.

Raaben, L., *Zhizn zamechatelnyx skripachei. Biograficheskie ocherki (Lives of Outstanding Violinists. Biographical Essays),* Moscow-Leningrad, 1967, pp. 27-36.

Riccati, G., "Esame del sistema musico del Sig. Tartini," *Continuazione del Nuovo Giornale dei Letterari d'Italia,* 1781.

Rosenschild, K., *Istoria zarubezhnoi muzyki do serediny XVIII veka. Vypusk pervyi (History of Music till the Middle of the 18th Century. Issue 1),* Moscow, 1963, pp. 191-196.

Rubelli, Alfred, *Das Musiktheoretische System Giuseppe Tartinis,* Winthertur, 1958.

Schering, A., *Geschichte des Instrumentalkonzerts bis auf die Gegenwart,* 2 Auflage, Leipzig, 1927.

Stoeving, Paul, *Von der Violine,* Berlin, 1906, pp. 198-206.

Straeten, E. van der, *The History of the Violin,* London, 1933, Vol. II, pp. 5-11.

Straznicky, Stanislav, *G. Tartini und der kroatische Volksgesang* (H. Riemanns Festschrift), 1919.

Tartini, Giuseppe, *De'Principi dell'Armonia musicale contenuta nel diatonico genere,* Dissertazione, Padova, 1767 (Facsimile editions, New York, 1967 and Milano, 1975).

_____, "Lettera alla Signora Maddalena Lombardini, inserviente ad una importante Lezione per i Suonatori di Violino," *L'Europa Letteraria,* Venezia, 1770, V/II, pp. 74-79. Facsimile London edition of 1779 in Italian and English (translated by Dr. Burney), New York-London, 1967.

_____, *Traité des agrements de la Musique,* Paris, 1771. Mit dem Faksimile des italienischen Original-textes herausgegeben von Erwin R. Jacobi. Celle – New York, 1961. (In the Italian original there is a chapter called "Regole per le arcate" added). There is a supplement to this edition giving a letter from Tartini to a pupil, containing important instruction for those playing the violin. (See Bouvet, Charles).

_____, *Trattato di Musica secondo la vera scienza dell' armonia,* Padova, 1754. (Facsimile edition, New York, 1966; the German translation was edited by A. Rubelli, has a commentary by him, and was published in Düsseldorf in 1966).

_____, *Treatise on the Ornaments in Music,* Translated and edited by Sol Babitz. Early Music Laboratory. Los Angeles.

Tebaldini, Giovanni, "Giuseppe Tartini," *Gazetta musicale di Milano,* 1896, Augusto, p. 568.

Themelis, Dimitris, *Étude ou Caprice: Die Entstehungsgeschichte der Violinetüde,* München, 1967, pp. 42-50, 59-66.

Ugoni, Camille, *Giuseppe Tartini, sua vita. Della Letteratura Italiana nella seconda metà del secolo XVIII.,* Brescia, 1820, I, pp. 1-28.

Untersteiner, Alfredo, *Storia del Violino, dei Violinisti e della Musica per Violino,* Milano, 1906, pp. 93-100.

375

Wasilewski, Wilh. Jos. v., *Die Violine und ihre Meister. Fünfte wesentlich veränderte und vermehrte Auflage von Waldemar Wasielewski,* Leipzig. 1910, pp. 125-145.

Winn, E.L., "Tartini's Devi's Trill Sonata as taught, revised and interpreted by L. Auer," *The Musical Observer,* New York, 1920.

Zilioto, Baccio, "Gianrinaldo Carli e Giuseppe Tartini," *Pagine Istriane,* Capodistria, 1904.

LIST OF THE RECORDINGS
OF THE WORKS OF TARTINI

Violin Concertos[1]

Concerto in D major
  M. Abbado, Mailander String Orchestra

Concerto in D major and G major
  E. Melkus, Vienna Academic Band, A. Wenzinger

Concerto in D major, E major, F. major, G major and A major
  A. Gertler, Zurich Orchestra, E. de Stoutz

Concerto in D minor
  P. Rubar, Winterthur Symphony Orchestra, H. Scherchen

Concerto in D minor
  J. Szigeti, String Orchestra, W. Goehr

Concerto in D minor
  J. Szigeti, Columbia Symphony Orchestra, G. Szell
  J. Tomasow, Chamber Orchestra of Vienna Folk Opera
  Z. Francescatti, Zurich Chamber Orchestra, E. de Stoutz
  W. Schneiderhahn, Lucerne Festival Strings, R. Baumgartner

Concerto in D minor
  R. Principe, Quartet I.C.B.S.

Concerto in E major
  A. de Ribopierre, Winterthur Symphony Orchestra, H. Scherchen

Concerto in E major and F major
  L. Weiner , Chamber Orchestra

Concerto in E major, F major and B major
  L. Ferro, Virtuosi di Roma
  W. Schneiderhahn, Vienna Symphony, K.H. Adler

Concerto in G minor
  M. Rostal, Winterthur Symphony Orchestra, W. Goehr

Concerto in A major
  J. Szigeti and N. Magalow (Kl.)

Concerto in A minor
  W. Schneiderhahn, Vienna Symphony, K.H. Adler

Six Concertos
  R. Biffoli and ?

Concerto in D
  Toso, I Solisti Veneti, Scimone

Concerto in E major
  Amoyal, I Solisti Veneti, Scimone

Concerto in E minor
  Amoyal, I Solisti Veneti, Scimone

Concerto in G major
  Amoyal, I Solisti Veneti, Scimone

3 Violin Concerti (in A, in D, in G)
  Gertler, Zurich Chamber Orchestra, Stoutz

6 Violin Concerti (in A, in A minor, in B minor, in C, in D, in F)
  Toso, I Solisti Veneti, Scimone

Concerto in A, in B flat, in G
  Accardo, I Musici
  Sobol, Rome Chamber Orchestra, Flagello

---

[1]After the name of the orchestra is given the name of the conductor

Violin Sonatas

Sonata in A (Pastorale), in G minor, in D minor, Sonata a quatro in G, a tre in D, a tre in D minor
   Toso, I Solisti Veneti, Scimone
Sonata in G minor
   Somach, violin; Jahoda, piano
Sonata in G; *Devils Trill*
   Luca, violin; Richman, Bogatin
   Oistrakh; Bauer
Sonata a quatro in D
   Lugano Soloists, Soc. Cameristica

Miscellaneous

Concerto a cinque in G for Flute and Orchestra
   Rampal, Saar Radio Chamber Orchestra, Ristenpart
Concerto in D for Flute
   Rampal, I Solisti Veneti, Scimone
Concerto in D for Trumpet
   André, Academy of St. Martin-in-The-Fields, Marriner
   André, Paillard Chamber Orchestra, Paillard
Concerto No. 2 in G for Flute and Orchestra
   Rampal, I Solisti Veneti, Scimone
Concerto No. 3 in G for Flute and Orchestra
   Rampal, I Solisti Veneti, Scimone
Concerto No. 4 in G for Flute and Orchestra
   Rampal, I Solisti Veneti, Scimone
Concerto in F for Flute and Orchestra
   Rampal, I Solisti Veneti, Scimone
The Art of Bowing
   Melkus; Scheit, Schulz, Planyavsky, Salter
Concerto in A for Cello and Strings
   Blees, Stuttgart Ensemble
   Rostropovich, Zurich Collegium Musicum, Sucher
Concert in G for Flute and Orchestra
   Gazzelloni, I Musici
   Marion, Prat. Ens.
Concerto in D for Trumpet and Orchestra
   Bernard, Ens. Instr. de France, Wallez
Sonata for Violin and Cello, *Didone Abbandonata*
   Oistrakh, violin; Bauer, cello

INDEX

Back endpapers:
An eighteenth century
engraving of Padua.

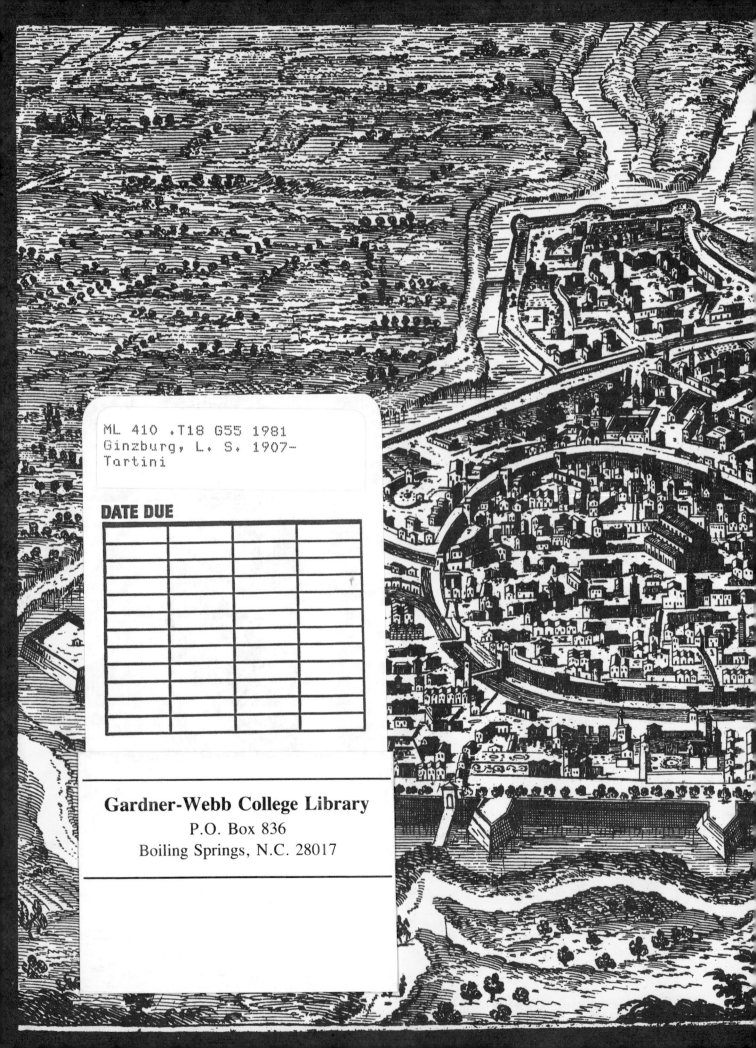